STRANGE THREADS

An Odyssey Through Community Theatre

STRANGE THREADS

An Odyssey Through Community Theatre

Jack Blackburn

Jack Blackburn

KERPLINK BOOKS

© Jack Blackburn, 2013

Published by Kerplink Books
www.strangethreads.co.uk

A CIP catalogue record for this book is available from the British Library.

ISBN 978-0-9575915-0-9

Book layout and Cover design by Clare Brayshaw

Prepared and printed by:

York Publishing Services Ltd
64 Hallfield Road
Layerthorpe
York YO31 7ZQ

Tel: 01904 431213

Website: www.yps-publishing.co.uk

CONTENTS

POSTLUDE

PRELUDE

The way we are living
Timorous or bold
Will have been our life.

SEAMUS HEANEY

What the painter adds to the canvas
are the days of his life. The
adventure of living, hurtling
towards death.

JEAN-PAUL SARTRE

Seldom, very seldom, does
complete truth belong to any human
disclosure; seldom can it happen
that something is not a little disguised,
or a little mistaken.

JANE AUSTEN

Tell all the truth but tell it slant.

EMILY DICKINSON

**BEGINNER
(1972)**

**ENDING
(1991)**

MACBETH

BLUE

Prostate Biopsy Conversation

ABOUT THE WORK

My bare arse sticks out over the bedside. Cold gel. Mr James finger presses my swollen prostate.

"Not to worry, duck", says the nurse whose role it is to pat my hand, and distract me with conversation. "But you've been here before, haven't you? Yes, of course, but you missed your last appointment, didn't you?"

"I was working in Germany."

"Oh, that's nice." Mr James probes. "Was it a holiday?"

"No. work."

"Really, and what do you do over there?"

"Theatre. I work in theatre."

"You'll hear the usual sound", says Mr James, "and this time I'll take extra samples. Just to make doubly sure."

I know they can never be doubly sure when it comes to prostate biopsies.

I'm worried. The nurse sits, wide-eyed, impressed.

"That's very special", she says........and then it dawns on me: she thinks I cut open prone anaesthetised bodies in an operating theatre, feel the bits, cut more, remove rot, clamp, fit prosthetics, re-build, clean up, stitch up, and thus with witty televisual type banter, save lives. German lives in my case.

"No" I explain, "I do the real *(kerplink)* thing."

"That's the sound, just to remind you", says Mr James.

"In my theatre I work with the whole of human life."

"Everything?" lightly holding my hand.

"Oh yes, the real serious stuff. There's been:

Terrorism – Fallen

Media Exploitation – City Sugar

Injustice and Pain – The Possibilities

Sexual Politics – Lysistrata *(kerplink)*

Nuclear Apocalypse – Riddley Walker

Suicide – Tira Tells Everything

Apartheid – Africa

Mutilation – King Lear *(kerplink)*

Edgy Gangsters – The Dumb Waiter

Cannibalism – John Dollar

Family Values – The Stone Book

Rape – Welcome to Hard Times *(kerplink)*

Murder – Macbeth

Lost Love – Krapp's Last Tape

Pollution – Mr Noah and the 2nd Flood

Women's Suffrage – The Hard Way Up *(kerplink)*

I wince. "You're doing very well Mr Blackburn. Just relax a little." And she pats the hand she holds, smiles reassuringly. "That's better mi Duck. It all sounds very nice. Very interesting."

Abortion – Touched

Ethnic Cleansing – Indians

Foot Fucking – Nana

Unemployment – Man Oh Man

Flogging – Female Transport *(kerplink)*

Mining Disasters – Pommie

The Rise of Nazism – Arturo Ui

Capitalist Obsolescence – Trummi Kaputt

Education – Our Day Out

Wife Beating – Punch and Judy *(kerplink)*

Utter Despair – Not I

and **Anarchy, Utter Anarchy** – School for Clowns

and others.

I ran a theatre company when I was young called ACT (Arts Centre Theatre). 82 productions in all. *(kerplink)*

At every kerplink I wince, slightly, at that itch of discomfort which each tearing pull brings, and I gently squeeze the nurse's hand.

"Don't worry, duck, just two more to go."

"AND", I continue, "all the pleasures, joy, *(kerplink)* laughter, sharing, love, complexity and wonder of life. That was my work."

"You should write a book, Mr Blackburn", she says as Mr James squeezes *(kerplink)* the last sample, withdraws the probe, and asks me not to move. I'm nipped and bloody. He wipes me clean with soft tissue, and the nurse hands me the nappy.

"Wear it for 3 days, just in case. and sit in the next room now, and don't leave before you've passed water. You've done very well, my dear."

I thank them and sit beside an older man in the waiting room. It's his first visit, he's shaking:

"I'm scared stiff of this, you know, don't want to be here."

"Oh, it's my 4th time," is my blasé response, "You'll barely feel it."

"When I were a lad, I joined up, I were in the Parachute Regiment," he says, "I'd rather jump out of a plane any day than this."

Yes, I thought. Bold and timorous, no parachutes here.

Ten days later I return. Mr James smiles: "You're clear, I don't think we'll need to do this again."

A Director's Dozen - He gives notes

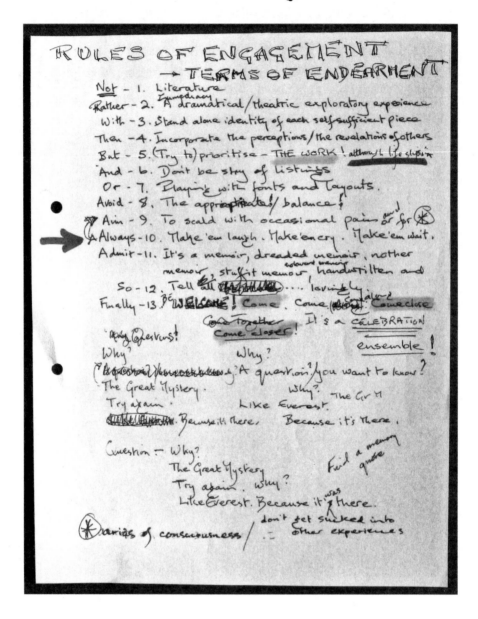

RULES OF ENGAGEMENT
→ TERMS OF ENDEARMENT

Not - 1. Literature

Rather - 2. A dramatical/theatric exploratory experience *Immediacy*

With - 3. Stand alone identity of each self-sufficient piece

Then - 4. Incorporate the perceptions/the revelations of others

But - 5. (Try to) prioritise - THE WORK! *although life slips in*

And - 6. Don't be shy of listings

Or - 7. Playing with fonts and layouts.

Avoid - 8. The appropriate/ balance!

Aim - 9. To scald with occasional pains or for ✶

Always - 10. Make 'em laugh. Make 'em cry. Make 'em wait.

Admit - 11. It's a memoir, dreaded memoir, nother memoir, stuffit memoir, handwritten and

So - 12. Tell all .... lovingly

Finally - 13. WELCOME! Come. Come. Come close
Come Together   Come closer!   It's a CELEBRATION
ensemble!

Why?   Why?
A question you want to know?
The Great Mystery.   Why?   The Gr M
Try again.   Like Everest.
Because it there.   Because it's there.

Question = Why?
The Great Mystery   Find a memory quote
Try again. why?
Like Everest. Because it was there.

✶ arias of consciousness /   don't get sucked into
other experiences

He settles to the task - meeting the crazy old woman

MOSTLY MEMORY

But, when I settled to think, I realised that whatever I wrote would depend on memory, and that, of the words, phrases, sentences I wrote, many had been appropriated, stolen even, into my wordhoard from elsewhere. I had to be serious about memory, and read a number of essays from which patterns of influence emerged.

Memory is, in fact, a creative, fallible process, highly prone to suggestion and other distorting influences. (Christian Jarrett)

which is certainly the case in this process.

And then:

Two forces go head to head in remembering. The force of correspondence tries to keep memory true to what actually happened, while the force of coherence ensures that the emerging story fits in with the needs of the self, which often involves portraying the ego in the best possible light. (Charles Fernyhough)

in the light of which, and in the cause of a certain balance, I decided to invite contributions from some of those who worked with me.

An alert came from John Walsh's memoir *Are You Talking To Me?*, which is conceived around a number of signal films which have punctuated his life:

At its best memoir vigorously examines and questions the memory, a second imperfect medium through which to perceive; immediate perception being the first. People read memoirs because of the quality of the writing and the value of the insights.

I had read and admired Dominic Dromgoole's *Will and Me* some years earlier and it sowed a thoughtful book-seed in my mind. However I chose to avoid theatre-based memoirs when I began to write, but did read a number of books in which creators describe their working procedures and the consequent interactions with their personal lives. These included the film director John Boorman's *Adventures of a Suburban Boy*, the illustrator and Children's Laureate, Anthony Browne's *Playing the Shape Game* and Martin Gayford's wonderful account of Lucian Freud's working practice in *Man with a Blue Scarf*!

Then in a totally different key Tony Judt's *The Memory Chalet,* which made me aspire to a beautifully perceptive gentle lucidity of style which I know will always elude me.

We do what we can. Mine is another way; our memories are a story to suit our self. Memory makes storytellers of us all. I will tell you stories in the hope that they may make you seek out and love theatre.

A Listing - An Acknowledgement

THE COMPANY

"Everything is biographical", Lucian Freud says. What we make, why it is made, how we draw a dog, who it is we are drawn to, why we cannot forget.

Everything is collage, even genetics. There is the hidden presence of others in us, even those we have known briefly. We contain them for the rest of our lives, at every border that we cross. (Michael Ondaatje)

John Baraldi
Elizabeth Boston
Ian Bryson
Lilian Hobbes
Liza Kerr-Bonner
Michael Heathfield
John Hargreaves
Michael Twelves
Tim Anger
Pippa Deegan
Sally Fairhead

Anne Hargreaves
Trevor Oswald
Joyce Bryson
Graham Robinson
Ian Rochard
Janet Shaw
Ann Taylor
Chris Taylor
Margaret Taylor
Don Wilkinson
Judy Hopkinson

Steve Mann
David Naylor
Mary Nichols
John Colthorpe
Ian Falconer
Peter Milnes
Barbara Jackson
Angela Stevenson
Susan Dove
Peter Williamson
Joanna Newman
Hilary Ellis
Leah Hargreaves
Keith Forman
Michelle Smith
Graham Corps
Michael Simmonds
Stuart Vickers
Susan Coxhead

Bet Heathfield
Ollie Wilmost
David Andrews
Jonette Bown
Sue Bradford
Lorna Dexter
Jo Taylor

Bernadine Turner
Andrea Peat
Anthea Benton
June Blackburn
Chris Hodkinson
Allan Kealey
Gary Benson

Hilary Buckley
Surriya Qazi
Alison Rothwell
Kim Barklett
Sandra Blackhead
John Ellis
Betsy Rayner
Miranda Cook

Dave Brierley
Timothy Husband
Robert Eagle
Kevin Sheldon
Gary Fern
Alison Harrow
Andy Portman
Andrew Mitchell
Marcia Ley
Steven Davies
Gary Birtles
Nick Burkinshaw
John Needham
Martin Taylor
Simon Barber
Steve Shaw
Neil Richards
Bob Eagle
Kev Stone
Bill McDonnell
Ian Brackenbury
Beverley Saunders
Paul Valentine
Audrey Pigeon
Charles Monkhouse
Paul Garrod
Michael Williamson
Ros Price
Stephen Cox
Warren Greaveson
Anne Cottam
Gerry Turvey
Margot Bartlett
Nigel Rudd
Sylvia Key

Paula Banner
Reg Shore
Corinne Shore
John Connolly
Susanna Blackburn
Nigel Corbett
Irene Dyrda
Paul Longden
Helen Owen
Guy Richardson

Charlie Wheatman
Paul Mulargyk
Roddy Powell
Ken Richardson
Ian Smith
Phil Tomlinson
Joel Turner
Tina Wilton
Brian Sargent
Alan Williamson
Timothy Storer
Sarah Cooper
Richard Brunton

Sheila Nix
Jackie Williamson
Martin Wiltshire
Nigel Jardine
Sharon Burns
Tim Biller
Ivan Brentnall
Chris Cameron
Jill Jones
Ray Jones
Ashok Ranchod
Betty Whitaker
John Scattergood
Richard Burns
Ruth Linacre
Richard Moore
Simon Bell
Lynette Collis
Philip Gadsby
Lynsey Gregory
Philip Handley
Adrian Hardy
Sahra Overton
Julie Snell
David Staves
Donna Strange
Tracey Strange
Rosemary Till
Cathy Crawley
Mandy Atherton
Zoe Bruce
Julie Hetherington
Nadine Wall
Sarah Gadsby
Simon Harrison

Marie Hewitt
Amanda Hubbard
Karen Hollis
Catherine James
Kyren Limb
Joanne Mc Dowell
Melvin Broadhurst
Nigel Turner
Pete Marsden
Daniel Harvey
Catherine Carnes
Nigel Jardine
David Turner
Claire Brewer
Lyndon Fletcher
Judith Green
Philippa Handley
Adrian Heathfield
Pete Lawton
Richard Moore
Malcolm Nix
Eric Popplewell
Tim Riley
Paul Sansom
Andy Stacey
Jane Washing
Thelma Wood
Emily Rutledge
Thelma Rowley
Robert Nimmo
Julia Tindall
Andrew Leigton
Angela Thomlinson
Inca Winson
Mary Bartlett

Mike Francis
Alastair Scrivener
Shaun Snow
Gordon Pearson
Liz Towne
Chris Truman
Charlie Watson

Bridget Ardley
Ros Francis
Jerry King
Michael Plant
Pat Plant
Emma Plant
Helen Taylor
John Taylor
Louise Wain
Anne Billinge
Tessa Brough
Pat Cleaver
Mary Lievesley
Jane Ardley
Charlotte Caudwell
Elizabeth Ede
Justine Frost

James Goodall
Laura Knowles
Anne Pickworth
Ben Tabbenor
Sally Wragg
Gary Bidmead
Richard Taylor

Peter Knowles
John Bishop
Bob Bache
Bernard Charlesworth
Russ Hubber
Bill Darley
Andrew Bidmead
Alan Brownlee
Martin Hill
Kevin Parker
Martin Parker
Julian Sanderson
Roger Green
Graham Goodall
John Youatt
John McCaul
Gloria McCaul

Irene Truman
Helen Dimond
Peter Hill
Charlotte Caudwell
Anne Osborne
Maggie Edge
Anne Knowles
Marjorie Shimwell
Pat Waterfall
Jean Youatt
Geoff Hopkinson
Ian Gill
Bernard Charlesworth
Barbara Hopkinson
Sarah Edge
Nicola Bishop
Rebecca Figg

Helena Wardle
Frances McCaul
Louisa Hoyes
Rachel Wachlarz

Ellen Rhodes
Natalie Etches
Jessica Bristow
Nicola Mather
Richard Edge
Daniel Bacon
Phillip Gosling
Jenny Osborne
Hannah Shimwell
Jim Carney
Mary Lomas
Jill Carney
Bill Darley
Sonia Thorpe
Duncan White
James Bacon
Maxine Bennett
Ian Weatherley
Neil Ardley
Mike Hoyes
Liz Lomas
Peter Knowles
Teresa Oldfield
Helen Taylor
John Taylor
Louise Wain
Liz Lomas
Martin Hill
Martin Parker
Alan Brownlee
Julian Sanderson
Peter Hill
Ida Brown
Ian Gill
Geoff Hopkinson

Jan Wilson
Sarah Dorsett
Baljit Saini
Tamsin Gregory
Karl Wilson
Jamie McPhie
Mathew Peberley
John Gibson
Carl Mathewman
Phil Wright
Tim Stone
Cathy Saxton
Mark Veevers
Mandy Wilson
Richard Gentle
Simon Clarke
Cath Acons
Roger Moore
Debbie Jackson
Maureen Leighfield
Nina Dyson
Deborah Carrol
Trudie Barber
Ian Harrison
Richard Mason
Rob Crump
Alex Key
Sandy Hodgson
Siobhan Taylor
Peter Collis
Paul Ttereve
Ben Hunt
Lisa Fenton
Mark Bosson
Hazel Collis

Andrew Cook

Fiona Wass

Claire Dakin

Sonia Wiser

Anthony Wheeldon

Joanne Smith

Martin Aistrope

Michelle Greene

Nadia Wall

Dale Swain

David Kearey

Adrian Squires

Rebecca Mahon

Dawn Dickenson

Derek Pykett

Claire Thornstone

Vivian Ellis

Ian Smith

Phil Coggins

Marcus Pickering

Karen Woods

Damian Asher

Julia Walker

Mark Berry

Louisa McPhie

Sonia Standell

Helen Hagman

Caroline HIl

Julie Munkley

John Ryan

Linda Lee Welch

Simon Hilton

Rebecca Thompson

Kathy Cooke

Heather Boardman

Tony Baker

Robin Oldroyd

Sally Anne Atkinson

Beverley Ison

Paul Burton

Isabel Franzen

Sarah Hartley

Chris Smith

Mike Haigh

Ben Knott

James Venner

Sara Wan

Cath Acons

Samantha Hoskin

Pola Livesey

Jo Hoyle

Diane Heron

Nick White

Lavinia Dean

Annabel Mitchell

Jo Smith

Emma Benson

Phil Coggins

Dick Coggins

Barbara Scrivener

Kay Elliot

Sheila Harding

Andy Stuart

Karen Hollis

Jane McDonald

These people define a part of my identity. Some I can no longer recall, some few are dead, some I still know well. They represent a shared purpose and a joie de vivre, people whose company is tonic because of the verve of their approach to life, their preparedness to engage with varied versions of the sense of life, and so often the passion, the thought, the observant wit they focus on it. Over the years they brought a whole load of skills, knowledge, talent, commitment and imagination; then, together, we told stories, we made theatre.

ACT 1

Needs Must Theatre

MACBETH FOR BEGINNERS

The United Kingdom was in crisis, a three day working week imposed, public premises closed at 5pm, daylight lighting forbidden, unemployment threatened a country utterly changed after the energy and optimism, and breaking from past traditions that had marked the sixties. There would be no purpose-built Studio Theatre as had been promised. The building programme was axed. No money, no staff, no actors, no budget, no dream – just time and a space.

There were three of us full time. John Baraldi, my assistant with particular responsibility for Youth Theatre development and Tim Anger, stage manager and technician, and myself. Ian Bryson was allocated part-time and prepared to be flexible, while John Hargreaves was able and willing, to give whatever support was needed for Design, Costumes and practicalities.

We hold a meeting in the pub, lunch at the Chesterfield Arms. I buy the beer, not often, but this time.

- We have a space, a PHASE ONE HALL, open, high, ridiculously two storeys high, a ludicrously tight box stage at one end without access, with a minimal fixed lighting system fixed to illuminate only the unusable stage.
- What to do?
- We've got to begin somewhere, and soon.
- Macbeth! What else?
- We have the space, The Empty Space, and the play.
- Words! We have no money but we have the best play ever. Brilliant. It's "a triumph of concentrated lyricism", "a great poem of death and darkness... hallucinatory from one end to the other, a compact mass of words, images, sounds... everywhere there is uncertainty, ambiguity, indecision, the promise of evil, all the menace hidden in the poisoned air of a sick and accursed country."

- Convinced?... I'll buy another round of drinks. We'll involve the audience.

My naivety troubled John Baraldi, an American with Stateside theatre training, who, in stark contrast to any rough theatre readiness, had a more purist perfection-seeking penchant.

- We have three male actors. We share the parts, the men's parts. We share everything. We're all in this together. Needs must.
- THE SET. No set, a couple of screens and five rostra blocks.
- BLACK PAINT Jet Matte
- COSTUMES Black clothes, no problem.
- 3 WITCHES. I'll get them. Preferences – beautiful and sexy or haggard and old.
- A CROWN Crude raw iron brutal and rusted. Hargreaves will make it, he can weld.
- A DAGGER Ditto as above. Big. Vicious. Death dealing deadly!
- ARMOUR That shredded matted coir stuff that's used by upholsterers, chunked up and tied with rope. We'll be big, wild, threatening.
- LADY MACBETH Lizzie. Irish firebrand, she's it, she'll do it, she frightens me.

"You frighten me", says John, and nods, snuffles, doubts. "Another beer?" I ask, "with crisps?"

and FOOD for the banquet, we'll play to small audiences, 48, 52, seated at tables, banqueting during the interval.

"I'll buy it," says Hargreaves, "love it, roast chickens to rip apart, a big ham for slicing, big bread, flagons, baked tatties, red apples, short bread, punch, finger bowls, sacking on the tables."

"Liver, tripe, sweetbread?" asks Ian. I can tell he's warming to the idea. "Spittoons?"

BIRNAM WOOD? The audience, if they drink enough, they join in. Create SOUNDS and feel the rotten heart of Scotland.

John drops his head to the table, rocking back and forth. "It's a tragedy for Christ's sake, it's fucking Shakespeare." He was not a man to swear lightly.

"I agree, if we don't curdle them with the pain we put in that tragedy it will fail. It's MACBETH FOR BEGINNERS: they sit up close, we act in among them, imagine a small space for us on the blocks, massive shadows on the tall wall. We'll be there, they'll feel the horror."

THE SCRIPT Just the best bits, the whole thing would be too long and we need to get something soon, there'll be less rehearsal, less people, less problems.

Ian remains quiet, but is of accord. Hargeaves, I've nailed him. Baraldi –
Long Pause:

"Do I get to wear the crown?"

"Yes! But I'm the one who'll get to die."

TO BEGIN, I have another great idea, we'll con the audience.

We finish our beers, and go our separate ways. Baraldi calls after me, "The
con? We make them think it's pantomime?" He waves, blows me a kiss.

The casting is quickly completed. Three mature students negotiate free
time schedules to play the three witches, they are neither haggard nor old.
With a death delivering scornful grimace Lizzie agrees to play Lady Macbeth,
but then smiles a little,nearly. Baraldi throws his hat in, warily, the M--- word
has never passed his lips, he is from proper theatre.

We rehearse quickly, the production comes together, the national crisis
eases, the lights go back on.

In 1952 I was the beginner, twelve years old and a scholarship boy, having
passed the exam to go to Rothwell Grammar, a largely working class school
serving the kids of the Rhubarb Triangle and the Yorkshire coalfield. At the
end of the summer term of my first year there was to be a school camp and
my mam said I could go but only if I saved up my pocket money of a shilling
a week. She made me a sleeping bag by sewing up the side and along the
bottom of a folded grey army blanket that my dad brought home from the
war.

This marked the beginning of a series of firsts. The first time I'd been out of
Yorkshire apart from one short holiday in Morecambe when I was seven. The
first time I had been camping and the first time anywhere without my parents.
The trip was to Stratford upon Avon and I knew that Shakespeare had lived
there. We camped a mile out of town in a farmer's field by the riverside, eight
boys sleeping with their feet pointing inwards to the central pole of an army
surplus bell tent.

The town was very nice, posh to my eyes, being so different to the
industrial towns of the West Riding of Yorkshire that I knew. After we visited
Shakespeare's Birthplace and Ann Hathaway's Cottage, I bought tiny painted
plaster cast models of the two houses with their names in tiny print on the
bottom, one for my mam and the other for my Aunty Fan, short for Fanny
which no one called her. This was another special beginning, the first time I
had had enough money to buy presents.

We played cricket and rounders with the girls on the campfield and went
for nature walks along the river meadows in a landscape so much more
benign and soft and a different green to our Up North where we lived with

coal slag heaps, bombed out industrial wasteland and acres of commercial rhubarb fields.

There was an Ice Cream Parlour in Stratford where you could sit outside at little round tables. I didn't know such places existed although my Grandma did have a front room, which was never used, called a parlour. At the end of our street the kids would wait for the arrival of Ice Cream Tony with his pony and trap – he sold cornets; here at the parlour you could get a Knickerbocker Glory for one shilling and three pence, a good bit of my saved up spending money. But I looked forward to the last day, when, having not spent a penny more, I would buy one. I was that kind of lad, the extravagance was scary. Knickerbocker Glory! Flippin' heck! I loved those two words, 'Knicker' slightly naughty, 'bocker' totally mysterious and 'Glory' – just sort of like it sounded glorious. This was another beginning, a fascination with words, their sounds and hidden meanings, a fascination with words which was to become the very essence of my work.

And then there was the Shakespeare Memorial Theatre. I knew the Grand and Empire Theatres in Leeds from visits to pantomimes, but this was a modern building, overlooking the river and fields. Again, I didn't know such things existed, but looked forward to the day, two days before Knickerbocker Glory day, when we would go there for an afternoon matinee to see a play called Macbeth.

I knew Shakespeare was special and a great writer at the time of Queen Elizabeth the First and we now had just got Queen Elizabeth the Second. But I had no idea how or why he was important. On the day, we had to be smart, wear school ties and polish our shoes, a gang of short-trousered Tykes, Leeds Loiners, on our best behaviour off to see the play. As we entered the theatre it was dauntingly big, awesome, my chest tightened. It was nothing like the theatres where I'd seen the pantos. We went up flights of stairs. And flights and flights of stairs – "up in the gods" our teacher Leachy told us. We sat here at this side, the girls were over there. I was beginning to wheeze, struggling to breathe. Asthma recurrently wrecked my life.

The play began, I was unable to concentrate: strange amazing words spoken out loud and artificially on a gloomy stage, men acting with long strides and big gestures and clattering soldiers, men killed, witches in smoke. I was fascinated but couldn't understand any of it. My breathlessness was aggravated by the airlessness, the summer heat, the sheer perched upness of our position; the inability to breathe could be frightening, would a next breath ever come?

Two nice, kind ladies offered me a mint. Our teachers were downstairs somewhere with the older pupils. The mint didn't help. I knew nothing could. One of the ladies, the taller one, she dressed pre-war, offered to take me outside on the balcony, and she talked with me for a few minutes and then she suggested it would be better if I stopped outside and I said yes.

I spent nearly two hours on the balcony watching the swans glide by on the sweetly flowing Avon, wishing I could go back inside, but, knowing no respite, lungs tightening, I stayed on the balcony, heard applause when the play ended, and descended the flights of stairs with our gang of mates. As we returned along the river my chest cleared. I was the second fastest runner as we raced along the towpath. Only Stephen Ward could beat me and he always did.

So it goes.

Barely two years later we read Shakespeare round the class, scenes from Henry IV with Falstaff and his gang. It struck a chord with me, especially Pistol his sharpness, and that name. I'd never be a Falstaff and had no kingly ambition, but Pistol appealed to my maverick boy's temperament.

Our newspaper was The Daily Herald, the working class socialist paper, and it had certain special offers that caught my attention. The Charles Atlas Body Building Programme offered a free introductory booklet, it promoted itself with two small drawings, one of a very thin man on a beach having sand kicked in his face, the other of a muscled hulk walking off with the girl in a bikini swim suit. This seemed a great idea, I was very thin my dad called me Spratty after Jack in the nursery rhyme. The booklet cost only the price of two return postage stamps. I practised the exercises assiduously for years but never developed into a hulk, just wiry strong. However, I never got sand kicked in my face, and as for girls in bikinis...

A second offer was for Odhams Book Club, in special editions for Herald readers: an English Dictionary, a Home Management Handbook, a World Atlas, a Medical Dictionary, a book of Photographs of Animals of the World and The Complete Works of William Shakespeare, this last either cloth-bound in red, or the de luxe version, buckram-bound in black with embossed image of Shakespeare's head on the front cover. I saved birthday and pocket money until I had enough, bought a Postal Order in Rothwell post office and waited. The de-luxe edition duly arrived. I had never dreamt I would own such a magnificent volume, printed on india fine paper, with a frontispiece picture of him, and an introduction, and a short explanatory essay to each play, and an index of characters at the back – Pistol was there. I started to read, the first in the book was The Tempest, I started there. My mam and dad shook their heads, bewildered.

The doctor advised that fresh country air would help my asthma. Within months we moved to a remote smallholding on the moorland top of Otley Chevin in the Yorkshire Dales. At my new school, an old established middle class establishment, Prince Henry's Otley, I was not considered suitable to study English literature for my ordinary level examinations. This was largely a class issue, how were they to know I was avidly reading Shakespeare every evening. Some members of staff performed scenes from Twelfth Night when I was in the fifth form. One part was played by Kenneth Senior, a pupil younger than me, a tall, gawky lad, who spoke with a silly voice and acted out an awkward gormless embarrassment up there on the stage with teachers. From reading the play I knew Andrew Aguecheek. What I didn't know, couldn't have imagined, was that ordinary lads could act proper! Why had they asked him? Why not me?

I continued reading, discovered Jaques and his dog, the twins in Comedy of Errors, Crookback Richard III, the lost girl in Pericles, Lady Macbeth who talked about smashing her baby's head in and I loved Macbeth's last stand, it seemed valiant to me no matter what he had done, and I learnt by heart the speech:

Tomorrow and tomorrow and tomorrow creeps in this petty pace

to shout to the wind on the Pancake rock

told by an idiot signifying nothing

at the Chevintop late on winter's nights.

Seventeen years later my first production in Derbyshire was "Macbeth for Beginners". It was my first public production. I was a beginner.

Promises fall away.

An actor stands at a lectern, soberly dull, and reads the account by Doctor Simon Dee of his attendance at the first ever performance of Macbeth. This text has great historical and documentary significance but is very formal, the reading is monotonous and "BORING" shouts a voice at the edge of the audience, to be quickly accompanied by slow handclaps, hissing and almost silent boos from three young women sitting at a table at the other side. The tempo of their clapping, and volume of their noises increases and transforms into the Witches' chant as they await the arrival of Macbeth and Banquo to whom their destinies are foretold.

Cut to Lady Macbeth reading the letter from her husband that makes a promise of kingship, and her calling on the spirits that tend on mortal thoughts to unsex me here. Here and fill her from the crown to the toe top-full of direst cruelty. Macbeth returns, "My dearest love" are his opening words and she kisses in succession his hand, his eye, his tongue as she persuades and prepares him for the murder.

The King arrives. The King is killed. The tension of the bloody hands and the knocking on the gate. The Porter's drunken speech releases all tension.

The King arrives and retires to sleep.

Is this a dagger that I see before me? Macbeth asks. The dagger is held by a witch, big, upright, erect, in front of his eyes, she kisses its tip, turns it horizontally and with ghastly elegance the witches pass it floating through their hands.

The King is killed, a bloody murder, followed by the tension of the bloody hands scene and the knocking at the gate.

The Porter's drunk rigmaroling speech releases all tension.

Narration from the lectern explains the flight of Macduff and Duncan's sons when the new king is crowned, but unsettled.

The murderers, one actor and one witch: "moiderers, my liege, whom the vile blows and buffets of this woild have so incensed they care not what they do" [TRY IT] leave to murder Banquo, and return, the deed is done/not quite done.

Macbeth wears his crown with pride, the new sovereigns are safe, ensconced, and host a banquet to celebrate their accession. The banquet is revealed, the audience invited, join the celebration, eat, drink and be merry for tomorrow... The King chats with his subjects promising better things for Scotland, more sunshine, more haggis, fewer midges and kilts for all. The Porter sings a comic song and the audience join the chorus, Lizzie reads a love poem, and the three witches sing the Andrew's Sister's hit: "Sisters, Sisters, there were never such devoted sisters" – and the audience applauds, and Macbeth sees Banquo's Ghost sitting on his throne and Macbeth panics and his Queen keeps control and the Ghost disappears and quick reappears and the sad sick scene plays out to its end.

All is quiet. Narration leads us into the second half. Macbeth revisits the witches. We forego the apparitions.

A witch plays the part of Lady Macduff joking with her off-stage son, a scene that's gentle and touching. The moiderers appear and murder her in an ugly and disgusting manner, the dagger shoved up her cunt.

The approach of the English Army is announced.

Lizzie sleepwalks. I ask her to play the scene in bewilderment as if she dearly loved her husband. At the end she takes the doctor's hand imagining he is her one love, suggesting softly:

"Come, come, come, come, come. To bed. To bed."

The battle is announced. Macbeth calls for his armour.

There is a shriek of women, a three witch yelling bounce of an echoey scream that stops him sharp.

"The Queen my Lord is dead."

Macbeth moves to the body, lifts it, cradles it, kisses gently, holds it close; they become a bundling, a croppled blother of man, mass of armour and dead fresh flesh. He puts his face to hers and begins:

Tomorrow, and tomorrow, and tomorrow,

Creeps in this petty pace from day to day,

To the last syllable of recorded time;

And all our yesterdays have lighted fools

The way to dusky death. Out, out, brief candle!

He closes her eyes, with love, then looks away

Life's but a walking shadow, a poor player

That struts and frets his hour upon the stage,

And then is heard no more;

He carelessly casts her aside without a glance, he stands

it is a tale

Told by an idiot, full of sound and fury

Signifying nothing.

He turns to face the audience, the cruel iron rusted crown now held as a fearsome weapon and he challenges, dares anyone, anyone not of woman born, to take it from him. The audience stand as one, leave their tables and move toward him. Birnam Wood. He is killed with the dagger. The crown is taken from his dead hand.

We were all Beginners. We were very serious about the work. In the acted scenes we determined to achieve a genuine deep tragic involvement. We knew we gripped our audiences, but often wondered what would stick in their minds, the tragedy or the food.

T.S.Eliot has written:

"About anyone so great as Shakespeare it is probable that we can never be right; and if we can never be right, it is better that we should from time to time change our way of being wrong."

Ian Rochard who will work with me throughout ACT's history has written:

In the very early days of ACT I took some students to a workshop presentation of Macbeth. I wasn't particularly impressed by the acted sequences, but the (mostly very physical) participatory elements thrilled. me. As the workshop progressed I found myself losing my inhibitions and becoming increasingly immersed in the world we were creating. I was back in my childhood, playing at The Cisco Kid and The Lone Ranger. It was the first time I had glimpsed Macbeth (a play I had studied as a literary text and seen several times in performance) from the inside – and I wanted more!

The First Western

WIND IN THE BRANCHES OF THE SASSAFRAS TREES, René de Obaldia

There are strange threads that stitch a life together.

1973 – CHESTERFIELD, DERBYSHIRE. "That's my Daddy!" a five-year-old child cries out as LYNX-EYE, Chief of the Comanches, very very bad, leaps into the log cabin with a fear-inspiring yell and stands, muscles rippling, minimum loin clothed, stripped war-painted body flexed, ripe for bodice ripping and violation of Sue, who plays Pamela, 17, a provocative beauty, slightly untamed joint product of homesteaders John Emery Rockefeller and Caroline his stalwart wife.

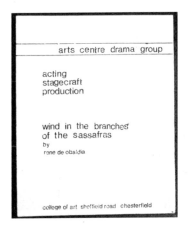

The child weeps, loud, tearful; she has never seen her Daddy like this.

In Act One the same actor had, as specified by the playwright, played PARTRIDGE-EYE, Chief of the Apaches and a traitor to them, a friend of Palefaces, kind and trustworthy, and the child had shown no concern.

But now . . .

Her mother carries the poor, sobbing, troubled infant out of the Theatre. This was good as two minutes later Carlos, proud, handsome, the strong silent hero with a will of iron and a star of tin, shoots nasty Lynx-eye, her Daddy, dead.

Which could have resulted in serious trauma.

I was the actor.

I was the Daddy.

The child was my daughter Susanna.

1944 – VICHY FRANCE. The German forces have taken control of Southern France. In the Provençal market town of Apt on the Calavon river at the foot of the Luberon mountain the pharmacist is collaborating, supplying and supporting the Nazi occupiers. The local Resistance network decides it must act. The traitor is sent a message informing him that a consignment of drugs is due to arrive for collection at the Railway Station on a certain train. He arrives at the station in good time to await the arrival of the train. A Resistance gunman shoots him dead.

Later that day an exhausted blood-stained cyclist arrives in the medieval village of Cereste, situated below Le Grand Luberon some twenty-five kilometres further up the Calavon valley in the remote Basse Alpes department. The cyclist is rushed to a safe house. Capitaine Alexandre, regional leader of certain Resistance operations, is based in Cereste. He is in fact René Char, one of the most important French poets of the twentieth century, a close friend of Picasso and Braque and previously an important contributor to the Surrealist movement and the intellectual life of Paris. He was born in Provence, and has returned here to the land he loves to fight the invaders, vowing not to publish anything until France has been Liberated.

1947 – PROVENCE. René Char suggests to a young theatre director, Jean Vilar, that he starts a Festival of Theatre in Avignon in order to revive a popular theatrical culture in Provence. This was one of the key arts initiatives of the second half of the twentieth century. It sowed a seed for the wider ranging adventurous approaches to the creation of theatre which so transformed and extended production practice, and contributed to the total revitalisation of live performance.

1956 – PARIS. Jean Vilar is invited to open the TNP, Théâtre Nationale Populaire, a newly built open stage modern theatre dedicated to the production of contemporary work, and to challenge the rigid traditions of the Comédie Française.

1960 – PARIS. I was a student at the Sorbonne, preparing, as I thought, to be a French teacher, when I became aware of the true, the vast, potential of theatre. The TNP production which most fixed itself in my mind was *La Résistible Ascension d'Arturo Ui* by some German playwright called Bertolt Brecht of whom I had never heard, with Jean Vilar playing the leading role of Arturo Ui, a Chicago gangster version of Adolf Hitler. This production, bold, graphic, brash, yet with a dry 'Brechtian' core, set my mind imagining. Pointing towards a path that . . .

1972 – CHESTERFIELD. I was offered a wonderful opportunity. A job whose terms of reference were: to develop film-making and theatre at all levels throughout the County of Derbyshire. The first full production of a script that I did in my new role was *The Wind in the Branches of the Sassafras*, by a French playwright, René de Obaldia.

2001 – PROVENCE. Loving France and speaking the language, I continued visiting the country throughout my working life. With Margot, mon amour, I bought a small Provençal house in the medieval village of Cereste, not far from the Rue du Nid d'Amour and the house where René Char had made his base during the war. In 2005 Georges Roux, a local poet and writer, who had been a young adolescent but close to Char during the war years, published a memoir, *La Nuit d'Alexandre* about life in the village during those Dark Years. In this book I read for the first time the story of the killing of the Apt pharmacist. The name of the blood-stained cyclist, the assassin, was René de Obaldia.

1964 – PARIS. *Wind in the Branches of the Sassafras* is acclaimed in Paris, runs for five hundred performances and is widely performed in Europe and South America. It takes all the ingredients of the traditional western and sends them up hilariously. It has a wonderful up and at 'em knock-about quality and suited our purposes admirably, whilst at its core there is a kernel of serious comment – Indians are killed, the family are called the Rockefellers and at the end of the piece they have a vision of :

> a black river! A black river right under out feet . . . A river of black blood . . . It's OIL! One well, two wells, three wells . . . Four hundred wells, five hundred wells . . . Two thousand wells . . .

and the enumeration continues into the tens of thousands as the curtain falls.

1973 – CHESTERFIELD, DERBYSHIRE. We had to make a really good impression with this, the first production by ACT (Arts Centre Theatre), a name John Baraldi had come up with. John and Ian Bryson worked with me on the preparation of the play. The plan was to create something we could use with secondary schools as an introduction to live theatre which would also serve as a straight full-blown good night out for the general public. We had just finished *Macbeth for Beginners* and most of the same cast were available. We expected this, a comedy western, to have broader appeal and thus fulfil the 'at all levels' criterion.

I persuaded John Hargreaves, my designer, to act for the very first time, he was perfect for John Emery the frontier homesteader. Baraldi was ideal for the drunken Doc Butler, Big Lil would play Mamma, too good-looking really, but make-up would age her. Gypsy Sue, packed with sex, was a ready-made man-hungry Pamela. Sally, posh and damaged virgin was an unlikely but pathetically convincing, sharp-shooting whore. Michael Heathfield (who later became a major player and director of Lancaster Theatre) was prepared to bunk off school and play the son Tom, a rather colourless no-good. Bryson, a shoo-in for the super cool gunslinger sheriff.

The programme for schools was ingeniously worked out. We would invite groups of forty 14-16-year-olds for the day. On their arrival they entered our larger playing space to find the elements of the set stacked in its separate parts, walls, doors, windows, floor. Costumes were displayed on mannequins. Furniture and properties were laid out for inspection as an exhibition – there were pots and utensils, tools, an axe and logs, six guns and rifles and whisky bottles, clay pipes and tobacco, hair pins and ribbons, a cross and a Bible. The star of tin. A bow and arrow.

This exhibition became the basis of what the play might be about. They were not to be told in advance.

We discussed westerns and got to work improvising scenes, sometimes using short extracts from the script, played the hunting escaping game, worked out gunfights and ways of dying, practised accents, walked tall.

We asked what they knew about oil, this in the days before it became the major environmental and political issue it is today. We asked their opinions of the fate of the Red Indians/the Native Americans. And finally asked for suggestions as to how we could, in the theatre, shoot a bow and arrow across the audience from a galloping horse through the window of the log cabin.

All serious stuff, no mention that the play was a comedy.

We then all together built the set, positioned the props, took the costumes backstage, put out the seating and demonstrated the lighting and how it was changed. Played some sound effects, the "old fashioned, handle turning, wind machine" and war drums. A bow and arrow were placed behind the back row of seats, and we admitted we didn't have a horse in the place.

The group left for lunch and returned as the audience for an afternoon performance.

This was a first effort. A learning experiment. It worked: they much preferred it to another day in class, but the mornings proved jerky and ill-focused. We realised our ideas were too ambitious to hold and engage groups of forty teenagers. Our expectations of what they might achieve in the improvised scenes were misjudged, and it was difficult to decide what, or indeed whether they had learnt anything. In the end we accepted that the experience of being in a new environment and meeting different people on different terms was justification enough. The performance was too long to meet school bus schedules and pupils' expectations so we judicously shortened the play and 'tamed' its content. All in all we were satisfied with this first effort, but left unsettled.

However, the evening public performances were a total success: the comedy worked better, subtleties of text were appreciated, the implied meaning of body language and behavioural traits were recognised and enjoyed, as were all the tropes of stock cinema westerns, every character stereotype, every verbal cliché.

We felt surprise and pleasure when the response was so positive, basked in the laughter, played more raunchily, enjoyed a proper interval, and thrilled at the shocked surprise that our AMAZING coup de théâtre engendered. That was the moment when . . . NOT the moment when Lynx-Eye pounced with evil intent on Pamela, ripping away her bodice, only to be shot through the heart by Carlos the heroic sheriff, who with the coolest dignity takes off his stetson and at arm's length covers her bared and beautiful breast whilst gazing steadfastly into the distant horizon. NOT the amazing, barely understood, fact of millions of gallons of crude oil gushing out of the ground at the end. NO! – the truly astonishing moment came when an arrow flew across the auditorium twanged thud quivering into the cabin's wall, and the mouth gawping cast, eyes askance, filled with fear, looked outside and realised that Lynx-Eye's marauding Comanches were about to attack.

How did we do it?

Magic! – one of my great ideas.

2011 – PROVENCE – Another thread. It is spring in Cereste. Aline my neighbour, an archeologist, who loves theatre, loans me the book of her 'cousin' Claud Confortès, an important metteur en scene and actor. He took a role in Jean Vilar's *Arturo Ui* which so inspired me in Paris in 1961.

The American Calls

NEDYPT – North East Derbyshire Young People's Theatre

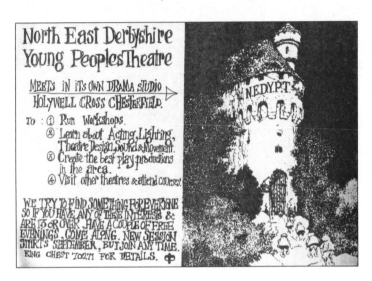

North East Derbyshire Young Peoples Theatre

MEETS IN ITS OWN DRAMA STUDIO
HOLYWELL CROSS CHESTERFIELD.

To : ① Run Workshops.
② Learn about Acting, Lighting, Theatre Design, Sound & Movement.
③ Create the best play productions in the area.
④ Visit other theatres & attend courses.

WE TRY TO FIND SOMETHING FOR EVERYONE SO IF YOU HAVE ANY OF THESE INTERESTS & ARE 13 OR OVER, HAVE A COUPLE OF FREE EVENINGS, COME ALONG. NEW SESSION STARTS SEPTEMBER, BUT JOIN ANY TIME. RING CHEST 70271 FOR DETAILS.

I had been at work in Chesterfield for nine months when the American called to see me. John Baraldi was Assistant Director at the Civic Theatre in Chesterfield. Tall, wispy bearded, and quietly snuffly spoken perhaps because of his flattened nose, he had come for two reasons, the first, would I let him present his production of a short play by Edward Albee at the Arts Centre, and the second, could I offer him some working space. He had run an Easter Holiday Project for young people, and now wanted to run a Summer School. We discussed his plans, which chimed with my intention to create a Youth Theatre. I talked to the Principal the same day and secured John employment as my assistant with responsibility for Youth Theatre and a shared contribution to Theatre in Education (T.I.E.) projects.

Youth Theatre was an exciting late-sixties movement built on the understanding that teenagers would be passionate and committed to theatre work if challenged with suitable material approached through active workshopping, and with the responsibility for the whole process of preparing and presenting live performance. This was radical, in stark contrast to traditional Amateur Dramatic practice which operates from an age-based hierarchy, the same leading actors getting lead roles, and young ones starting with roles which often involved little more than leading the Elderly Vicar on stage and announcing with a neat curtsey and very polite voice, "The Vicar, ma'am". Youth Theatre challenged the new generation of young people to be creative and responsible.

After a successful summer project in 1972 NEDYPT was established, and John began to work with his group in some abandoned schoolrooms. These were barely suitable, and remained redolent of proper education; a more real theatre space was required. There was a much under-used Victorian chapel in the town centre which had devolved into the care orbit of the local YMCA. After tentative negotiations we managed to acquire use of the premises for a reasonable rent. The pews were ripped out, the windows boarded, a lighting rig installed with control room on the gallery, the floor was sanded and the walls painted black, much of this work being undertaken by NEDYPT members. It proved to be a more congenial place than my supposedly dedicated theatre space.

For three years John did some astonishing work. Summer projects, annual Christmas shows taken to the hospitals, introductory workshops and main productions. He raised money from Granada Television to make a short film, and took a small group production to perform in Stockholm. He received total allegiance, perhaps too much, from the fifteen to nineteen year-old youngsters who worked with him. This work peaked with an astonishingly powerful production of Peter Weiss' very contemporary Marat-Sade play, largely directed by Dawn, a member of the group.

However, there were constant problems: issues about the lease of the building, fund-raising disappointments, and the failure of the College of Art to offer John a permanent contract. He contributed to my work. I even managed to persuade him to perform for ACT on two or three occasions. Acting was anathema to John. Eventually he took the opportunity to move to a more secure position and was appointed to set up a Youth Theatre in Paisley, Scotland. Members of his group were selected for roles in the popular film *Gregory's Girl*. He brought them down to Chesterfield for a weekend of performance, workshop and camping in the Peak District, which was really rewarding, and good fun, as the two groups of theatre mad youngsters mixed and met.

From there John moved to Greenwich, which had promised great things but did not deliver, and he wrote asking if he could return to Chesterfield. This would have suited me, but the Principal, in theory a great supporter of our work, was very much against re-appointing someone who had chosen to move on. I wrote to John to this effect. In the long run this was probably the best outcome for him. He had a glittering career becoming Director of Riverside Studios in London and latterly Principal of E15 Theatre School.

John Baraldi was one of the very crucial early influences on my personal engagement with theatre.

After John's departure we employed a promising young woman, but I think the work did not suit her. I had presumed she would develop a programme of independent projects but she needed support I was unable to give. Her boyfriend was desperate to get back to London and after about three months they returned there.

For the next twelve months I ran NEDYPT with support from Pippa Deegan. This was a new generation, and her presence was great for their morale. We did two main productions, *Mooncusser's Daughter* and *Indians*, but there was neither summer project nor Christmas show.

When Pippa left suddenly, to be with her boyfriend, money was available to advertise again, and we appointed another young woman, the theory being this gave a better balance to what we might undertake in the T.I.E. area. She assured us she was starting a new life after the break-up of her engagement to an Italian who had returned to Rome. Within a matter of weeks she was flying to Rome for weekends, and shortly after left, with apologies; they were to be married.

Three misses. NEDYPT wasn't in crisis, quite, but it began to look as if we should have reappointed John B. In an act of hope, and some desperation, I turned to John H./Hargreaves and Jill Jones to share the running of the group just for a season whilst I tried to hammer out better contractual terms for a new appointment. John, who was my main man at the time, jumped at the opportunity; he could use it as work experience for the teacher training course he had started, and get paid for it. Jill had been a drama teacher and was a valued supporter of NEDYPT. She had been the chaperone on the Stockholm trip. Unfortunately, I had failed to measure the temperamental gulf between the two of them. They were incapable of working together and I spent too much time keeping them at arm's length from one another. But they did manage to forge another group of talented and committed young performers. A small party accompanied John in a mini-bus to the Avignon Festival where they performed street theatre to try and recover their costs. They returned destitute, but thrilled, eyes wide opened.

Then Bill McDonnell turned up, who was the next person to become crucial to my involvement. Barely five feet tall, already balding in his late twenties, with a left eye looking east by north north east heavenwards, he was a tense bundle of muscular mental energy. He had recently returned from touring in the Communist Bloc of Eastern Europe with Steven Rumbelow's Triple Act Theatre production of *King Lear*.

Steven and I had been in contact some years earlier when I arranged for him to film his script of *Joan of Arc* at the College's Hasland Road site whilst we tried to arrange some way for him to make the Arts Centre his home base. He found a better option at Newark. A roamer and over-reacher at heart, the last I heard of him he was in the Peruvian Andes developing a piece based on traditional Inca practices. This mutual contact gave Bill and I an initial if ethereal common ground with some basis for mutual co-operation and understanding. Bill was a committed socialist whose work always had a serious social and often political dimension. Brecht was his touchstone, theatre for the people, thinking entertainment. He established a new and differently oriented regime for NEDYPT, less show, more real business. We won an award from East Midlands Arts to employ a writer in residence who worked with Bill for four months, and were able to re-establish the full programme of Youth Theatre activity.

There was a strong impetus behind the Youth Theatre movement at this time, the late 70s, and a National Association of Youth Theatres was founded, of which Bill and I became executive members together with representatives from Leicester and Newcastle, two authorities heavily involved in the Youth Theatre movement.

When a National Youth Theatre Festival was established Bill attended with NEDYPT productions for three successive years, but then decided that the event was becoming too much of a showcase rather than a collective meeting of like-minded workers and young people, and decided to concentrate on locally based development work.

We worked together on varied and various T.I.E. Projects, and Bill was the lynchpin in two important ACT productions. However, the contract still remained notionally temporary, and eventually Bill decided to leave to start his own company in Sheffield. Again I was without an assistant.

At my suggestion the new, newly appointed Director of the Arts Centre called a NEDYPT committee meeting to discuss its future. The following morning she called me into her office and explained with stern emphasis that I was not to put forward alternative proposals, nor disagree with her proposals at such a meeting. She was very severe. Nor was I to suggest any independent direct action by the committee. Since John Baraldi and I founded the Youth Theatre it had always had its own independent identity and freedom of action, the idea being that the young people should retain a sense of ownership, and involvement in the ongoing work. Within weeks a full-time Arts Centre facilitator was appointed on a permanent contract. This was the way things were done in the 1980s. The world had turned, management and administration ruled supreme. I had time for neither fawning, nor facilitators who have no creative skills. I chose not to attend meetings, nor did the NEDYPT committee ever reconvene.

The Youth Theatre did continue under the leadership of John Connolly, but on a more limited contract. John, a talented artist and teacher, had worked with ACT on several productions and I felt he would he a good candidate to take on the Youth Theatre Leader's mantle. It would be impossible for him to take on the scale of activities that had previously been possible, but John committed himself to a series of productions of challenging twentieth-century scripts, including such modern classics as *Woyzeck* and *Christie in Love*, as well as annual summer projects. John has acknowledged how invaluable this experience was in giving him the opportunity

> to cut my teeth as a director with hundreds of young people, before setting up Compact Theatre, a successful professional small scale touring company.

With changing priorities, and pressure on funding in the late 1980s, NEDYPT eventually ceased to exist. In 2007, thirty-five years after its beginnings, a group of original members used social networking to arrange a celebratory reunion. About fifty turned up, all of them edging towards fifty years of age, to meet in what had been our Chapel Studio, now a night club. Each of them attested to the liberating and rewarding thrill that had been their membership of NEDYPT. A man approached me, who I eventually recognised as Buffalo Bill. He now ran five businesses, two in England, the others in Europe, and insisted that he learnt about teamwork and adventure from his time with the Youth Theatre. I recalled him as a young lad, confident but rough edged. Baraldi came, wondering if, how, they might integrate a community theatre oriented element into the theatre degree course at E15. It was an evening of smiles and reminiscence; everyone who came, many now with teenage children themselves, was so appreciative of their youthful involvement. I lost my virginity in this place, said Mandy. I tried to look askance.

The Youth Theatre was so important. It did exist for eighteen years. It was invaluable – not for making actors, but for strengthening communal bonds and enriching youthful experience. For so many years NEDYPT had a strong individual, worthwhile identity – then it was no more. So it goes. In theatre the process of generation and regeneration needs to be forever ongoing.

"Bean Sprouts"

TIRA TELLS EVERYTHING THERE IS TO KNOW ABOUT HERSELF, Michael Weller,
THE DUMB WAITER, Harold Pinter.

(Learning about acting – Part 1)

Whilst Baraldi concentrated on establishing the Youth Theatre, Ian Bryson and I worked on two Theatre in Education projects for primary school pupils. *The Magician who lost his Magic* was a thrill-packed show, with magic, that stressed the need for sharing and co-operation when the going got tough. *Mr Noah and the Second Flood*, a simple comic piece which we toured, was about caring for the environment, the second flood being plastic and other waste materials.

We were still beginners and I needed to learn more.

Acting fascinated me, my work depended on it, but I never had the ambition to be an Actor, although I very much wanted to learn about acting and enjoyed the challenges of performance. I read standard texts by the great theoreticians and a whole gamut of systems mongers as well as actors' memoirs. I attended a variety of short courses to meet and mix with a range of practitioners, all of which provided food for thought and working practice to explore. In the twelve years I was a regional assessor for the Arts Council of Great Britain I watched many, many performances in midland and northern main houses, the likes of Sheffield's Crucible, Nottingham's Playhouse, Bolton's Octagon and Stoke's Victoria, as well as a very varied range of small-scale touring productions and Theatre in Education. I absorbed influence, sometimes stole ideas, determined never to copy and judged performance. However, at this, an observer's remove, I learnt about staging and production values, and especially about effective engagement with audiences, but little about the actual experience of acting, how it happens, how best to make it happen.

Over the years I played a number of parts, mostly in T.I.E. Projects or small supporting roles in ACT productions, but never worked under any other's direction. Always stressing the ensemble identity of our working process, I relied on support and advice from members of the group. Eventually, during the twenty-,six years of work I did experience, really experience and understand, those things about acting which I had always intuited, believed, known in my gut, were possible and achievable. Primarily how not to **act**, but rather how to do it, be there. How to be real. How not to **act**.

Four projects have primary significance in my process of learning about acting. These included three major roles, Arturo Ui, Professor Molereasons and Blue together with the two short plays I address here. These two, dating from early in my career, were embarked upon specifically to learn about acting as much as anything else.

There had to be other justifications of course. *Tira* was a short play for two actors, needing only a chaise longue as its set, and few props. The production plan was to take it into people's houses, perform in a domestic context for the owners, their family, friends, neighbours, pets, whoever (but not children!). This approach validated my brief – to develop theatre at all levels. Could anything be more community oriented than playing in people's houses? Of course, it limited us to people with quite large houses, and to those particular people who, for whatever reasons, wished to invite us into their homes.

Another reason for the project, and in all honesty, perhaps a main one, was that it gave the opportunity to work with Pippa, and to kiss her five times as five different characters. She played Tira, the young woman whose fantasies come to life showing how much the capacity for romantic self-perception persists.

Michael Weller writes :

"All five male roles are played by a single actor [that is the test I set myself]. The style of each scene is exaggerated . . . each of the men is a grotesque. Each should have one very marked mannerism – Edward has a Samurai War Dance, Poof has his Clint Eastwood, Brute has a fart or a belch and Tira is a flower.

Edward's dance is clumsy, awkward and funny to watch – but fierce. He means it. Poof's Clint walks like Clint, looks like Clint, has a western accent but Poof's voice. Brute's fart is elaborate and disgusting. Tira's flower is beautiful."

I just loved working up these ridiculous caricatures. It was a totally uncomplicated process, I was barely self-critical, just let rip. I fear it was a vanity project, purely for my indulgence. But I had acted very little at the time.

As Edward I'm a blimpish, awfully, awkwardly English middle class office worker with a wife: *"Yes, she's sitting home, poor wretched thing that she is"*.

with a Samurai War Dance which challenges David Brent's on the embarassment scale, and a totally inadequate seduction technique.

As Poof I'm the cool Clint cowboy poof, who after asking Tira what her name means, explains:

"Oh, but it has to mean something. Names always mean something. Take mine. Poof. Self-evident. Or Po Ling Chien which means:

Mountain Stream.

Trees bend.

Frog Jump. Gronk. That's a haiku. Just Tira?"

I found this a tricky one. I felt more like Andy Warhol than Clint Eastwood, just couldn't make the connection.

As Lucio I getta to playa da Italiano, an den I saya my favorite line: *"Da body, she shimmer forever in da cinemascope of memory, but da face she is forgot."*

Shallow and cheap.

As Brute I get to slap her, she hits back, we grapple rolling on the ground. I spit a mouthful of sandwich in her face. Tira picks off a piece and examines it: *"Ham and cheese!" (she eats it) "With mustard."*

They said I was typecast – the bastards! Weller recommends a mime sandwich.

As Tib I get to play broody, shy, sitting with my head between my legs, never smiling, pausing for a long, long time before allowing Tira to kiss me. He is a cruel disappointment to her. Again they said I was typecast – the bastards!

I had learnt I could do this kind of hyper showboating performance, pull focus, convince the audience, make them laugh, or hate me when I slapped her around. It was good training, but not a way to learn what I needed to know. There was an empty core, perhaps a necessary one? or am I deceiving myself? at the heart of every thing I had done. I sort of gobbled up the characters in learning the lines, finding a walk and the talk to go with it, then flicked a switch and spewed them out in performance.

Audiences really enjoyed the play, partly I suppose because of the circumstances in which they watched it. But mostly because of the counterpoint which Pippa made to my characters. I did learn from working so closely with her. I learnt about emotion. Quite naturally, by temperament, Pippa was a past master of subtlety, meeting and matching my dextrous extremes without losing the core of her essential being. Hers was a more difficult task than mine; she had to be the real thing.

Michael Weller writes:

"In her monologues Tira is herself. In her encounters she gradually acquires qualities complementary to those of her suitors. She plays roles. But her roles aren't rigid, aren't fixed. For brief moments when the line or the moment feels that way she lapses into Tira. These moments are blinks."

Sometimes audiences would be sitting inches away and she always remained true. She would address them, sigh, smile to herself, pause on a question, pause again. They rode with her wherever she took them, even as she took them to the end, where Tira, having told everything there is to know about herself,

now commits suicide,

    (a drum roll starts off stage)

        by holding her breath

           until she is dead.

Tira is a flower, Tira's flower is beautiful.

Concurrently with performances of *Tira* I began to prepare Harold Pinter's *The Dumb Waiter* with Ian Bryson, a strong, clenched, closed, more overtly inexpressive actor, diametrically opposite to my flamboyant up-and-at 'em style.

Two men, who may be gangsters, await instructions in a basement. The instructions come via a dumb waiter, which with each successive rackety rumbling slam- dunk arrival becomes a potentially more ominous and increasingly threatening third character. Casting myself as the obviously uncertain, more insecure of the two characters I would have to play down; the script demanded it and so would our partnership.

Another short play, for a tight space. I was influenced in setting it by having seen the famous productions of Ionesco's *La Leçon* and *La Cantatrice Chauve* at the tiny Théâtre de la Huchette in Paris twelve years earlier, in which a stunningly precise naturalism serves the bizarre demands of theatre of the absurd. The productions still play after more than fifty years.

Hargreaves boxed in the ridiculously impractical proscenium platform we had inherited to create a dank, unkempt and bleak basement. There was a torn soiled mattress, an orange box, one short scratched graffito on the wall and the tattered remnants of a busty pin-up photograph – pinned up. Tim Anger, stage manager par excellence, was hidden behind the dumb waiter built into one corner. He mastered its trundling noisy arrival with cool precision – so much depended on him. An audience of twenty-four was squeezed into the basement with us (four rows of six, in tiers). It was claustrophobic and unpleasant, the idea being that they should feel as trapped as we were, and react to the dumb waiter with the same initial suspicion and then worrying expectancy as we did.

We worked on lines, plotted moves, tested interactions and honoured pauses. We developed a mutually suspicious relationship and thoroughly enjoyed our immersion in the troubling world of Mr Pinter. It seemed fine. I was working in a more quietly natural way than ever before. Unsettled in the part, as I should be perhaps; after all he was that kind of character. Was I learning about acting?

More work was needed, reacting to the dumb waiter's descents. Those seconds of anticipation as we awaited its trundling down to a clattering halt needed work to command a trajectory – a balance of sameness and variety through time.

Again, with audiences so close every millimetre of our being had to be right. The held breath, the quick glance, the lip bit, the fingers crossed, the weight shifted, the damp palm wiped, the subtle signal, the worried sniff, the querying eyes, the muscle tensed, the sub-conscious shuffle, the self-conscious grimace, all timed, held just so, until the one or the other of us went to open the dumb waiter's doors to find a cryptic message or a restaurant order on the shelf.

I take out an order for a Chinese meal, which includes – "Bean sprouts".

In a late rehearsal the words came out of my mouth in a new way – a kind of tenuous questioning edge of a lisp, nothing like the way I had previously spoken, and my body spoke it, not just my voice. From that moment on my playing of the script changed. I had found the character, I realised I knew who I should be, found myself fully invested in the part, not acting but being.

The play fulfils the demands of Aristotle's classical Unities: one suite of action, in one place, during one period of time. From the banal situation we found ourselves in at the beginning to the gunshot that rings out at the end I knew how to live the real- time process we were experiencing. I was learning about acting. Subsequently I learnt other things, but never again repeated the actual real-time immediacy of this role. I had transcended the limits of pretence; I now knew what it meant to be utterly, truly, in character.

Baraldi Whistles That Phrase

THE DAUGHTER-IN-LAW, D. H. Lawrence

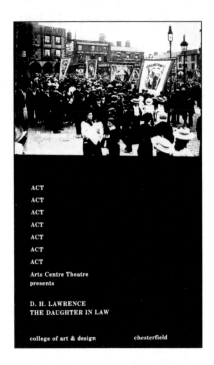

ACT
ACT
ACT
ACT
ACT
ACT
ACT

Arts Centre Theatre
presents

D. H. LAWRENCE
THE DAUGHTER IN LAW

college of art & design   chesterfield

D. H. Lawrence is for me the great English writer of the twentieth century. His novels, short stories, travel writing, poems, criticism, essays and letters are a formidable body of work. In 1968 his three collier plays written between 1909 and 1911, which had never been successfully produced or appreciated, were rediscovered and presented with great success at the Royal Court Theatre. Richard Eyre has described *The Daughter-in-Law* as "a blinding masterpiece".

In 1974 I bought the Penguin edition of these plays and immediately realised how appropriate they were to my wish to use material that originated in the North Derbyshire area, and chose *The Daughter-in-Law* for our next production. Written wholly in the Notts-Derbys dialect and being a kind of savage commentary on the mother and sons theme of *Sons and Lovers*, Lawrence called the play "neither a comedy nor a tragedy – just ordinary". It tells the story of how, during a period of industrial strikes, a couple married only seven weeks, he a miner, she an aspirational woman, have to face the fact of discovering that a neighbour's daughter is pregnant by the miner. The play is a sustained look at the interaction of family relationships in a mining crisis. The play had local resonance and I knew I wanted to do it.

Tha' mun do as tha' will, Sidney lad, but tha's noan goin darn t'pit.

I was born and spent the first fourteen years of my life in Rothwell, a pit village on the Yorkshire coalfield. My great-grandfather was a miner. And so was my grandfather, a man of the same generation as D. H. Lawrence. The above were the words of advice he gave to my father when he left school at the age of fourteen. As he was a miner my grandfather missed being conscripted for the 1914-18 war; however, some twenty-six years later an injury to his right hand ended his employment at the pit. He had been proud to be a member of the miners' culture. A black-stained jagged scar on his bald head fascinated me as a child, and I knew that he worked at Lemon Royd, but no one would explain to me what or where this was. Later I learned it was the sewage works – his last job gave him neither shared pride, nor satisfaction, nor much money.

He was a talented musician and founder member of Rothwell Temperance Silver Band, the members of which had to take the pledge never to touch alcohol. In the front parlour was an upright pipe organ, in the kitchen a piano and cases with trumpet and euphonium. As a consequence of his finger injury he never played any of these. My father took his advice and became a driver, a rare skill in the 1920s. Until she died in the 1980s by which time everyone drove, my mother would proudly proclaim that, "Our Sid is a driver."

The winding wheel head of the mine was visible from the end of our street, and I knew the times when the pit's steam locomotive tanker came along the single-track line to collect the day's coal or slag and would run down the street to watch its smoky chugging progress. However, Roddil Pit as it was known was virtually worked out and most of the locals were bussed out to neighbouring pits in the bus driven by Cliff Lunn, my dad's best mate, who got rich and well-to-do, as he was prepared to drive the night shift miners to and from work. I'd get up early to watch the night shift return, or, more dramatically, go down the street to meet the day shift coming home after dark on winter evenings. The men wore blackened clothes with leather knee pads, eyes extra bright shining through their coal dusted faces with the occasional strangely startling glimpse of a stark white bare skin neckline or chest if a shirt button were open. They wore their helmets and clattering hobnailed boots and each one carried his snap bag and Davy lamp. (My great-grandfather left me his pocket watch and fob, and my grandfather's Davy lamp came to me when he died. We used both of these to dress the set of *The Daughter-in-Law*.)

Many of the miners were lads, Bevin Boys, down from Geordie land in the north-east, dragooned into the mines to support the war effort, and a decent alternative to conscription in the Armed Forces. When I was young, during the war and into the early 1950s, the miners were very positive, having done 'their bit to beat Jerry', and were pleased to be nationalised when the Labour party came to power in 1945. There was none of the industrial strife, implicit in each of Lawrence's collier plays, which returned in the 1980s when an extended strike against the policies of the Thatcher government was broken and the coal industry effectively dismantled.

I feel very privileged to have my origins in this culture even though the trajectory of my life has been totally divorced from it. It's difficult to explain; a birthright I suppose.

I really wanted to do it.

I knew we could do it because I could cast it perfectly. Philippa Deegan would handle the cruelly harsh confrontations and be devastatingly moving throughout as Minnie, the daughter-in-law. John Hargreaves as her sensitive/coarse-natured husband Luther Gascoigne was born to the part both physically and temperamentally. Betty Heathfield, wife of the General Secretary of the National Union of Mineworkers, would play his dominating, interfering mother, and Ollie Gilmour, the living embodiment of an early twentieth-century working class elderly wife and mother was real in voice, demeanour and attitude, speaking the dialect so naturally she found it difficult to read and learn that same dialect in the artificial context of a playscript. I would play Joe, the younger son, a bit of a lad, laid off after breaking his arm down the mine.

It was that 'just ordinary' which challenged and appealed to me. Lawrence wanted to write a new kind of play about working class life outside the modes of contemporary theatre of which he wrote:

> I am sure we are sick of the rather bony bloodless drama we get
> nowadays – it is time for a reaction against the rule and measure
> mathematical folk . . . We have to hate our immediate predecessors
> to get free from their authority.

He saw Tchekhov as the new thing in drama, but feared that his own work would not find the producer to "whip-in" the audience which he felt sure existed for his plays. He rejected the idea of over-theatrical shaping language:

> I cannot bear art that you can walk around and admire.

The following is an example of the register of the dialogue he created :

Minnie: You nearly made me drop that saucepan. Why are you so
         late?

Luther: I'm non late, am I?

M: You're twenty minutes later than yesterday.

L: Oh, ah I stopped finishin a stint, an' com up wi' a'most
         last batch. (he goes to sit at table)

M: No!

L: Tha art throng!

M: Yes and everything's reddy and will be spoiled.

L: Then we'd better eat it afore a wash me.

M: No, no – it's not nice -

L:	Just as ter's a mind – but there's scarce a collier in a thousand washes hissen afore he has his dinner. We niver did a-whoam.
M:	But it doesn't look nice.
L:	Eh wench, th'lt soon get used ter th'looks on me. A bit o' dirt's like a veil on mi face – I shine through th'andsomer. What hast got?
M:	You're not to look.
L:	It smells gud.
M:	Are you going to have your dinner like that?
L:	Ay, lass – just for once.
	(she sets a soup tureen on the table, and lights a lamp. He watches her face in the glow)
L:	Th'art non bad 'luikin' when ter's a mind.
M:	When have I a mind?
L:	Tha's allers a mind – but when ter lights th' lamp tha'rt in luck's way.

Read the extract again. Catch the tone the guarded banter of a man struggling in a fracturing relationship. There is scope for actors here.

Raymond Williams wrote:

> He brought to the drama a capacity for the rhythms of speech, most notably in *The Daughter-in-Law* – which in the end he developed to change not only the dialogue but the narrative and analytic tones of the English novel.

For research we read Lawrence's early stories to set the background, and his essay *Return to Bestwood* written in 1926 during the General Strike, which describes a trip to Chesterfield, the town with the twisted spire, where the heroine of *Lady Chatterley's Lover* goes to do her shopping, as well as the conditions and faces of mining communities whose men were defeated in attempts to improve their lives. This essay was included in the programme brochure we prepared for the production as was a selection of extracts from the Headmaster's daily records of life and work in the North Derbyshire Primary School in the mining village of Unstone. These, covering the period from 1874 when Lawrence was born to 1909 when he wrote *The Daughter-in-Law*, are so vivid, so individual, so piercing:

1883, Oct 29 – Attendance Officer says Scarlet Fever is becoming prevalent and that many children are likely to be absent in consequence. Four of the scholars have already died from fever.

1884, Mar 22 – The difficulty of getting in the children's pence is increased by a strike at one of the pits, no work at another, and the prospect of the largest pit closing.

1884, Mar 29 – Another pit has stopped work. I am instructed not to press unduly those who fail to bring their pence.

1885, Oct 11 – One mother has been buried during week dying of Typhoid Fever. Two children are ill of the same disease, and fever and Scarlatina are in the village . . . Boy hurt on train line. Taken to Chesterfield Hospital.

The casting was perfect, but that's no guarantee of a perfect end product. The rehearsal process was very rewarding, each actor fitting naturally with the character they played. The opening scene is long and proved too much for Ollie's throaty voice and rather elderly memory, so we shortened it discreetly, not, I think, to anyone's disadvantage as Ollie was so right for the play. The Chesterfield Hospital made a full plaster cast for my broken arm, and when the supervising Sister began to doubt whether this was an appropriate use of National Health Service resources, I promised to make a donation to the nurses' Christmas fund and returned the following day with a box of chocolates. I arrived in full broken-armed costume, in character as jumped-up cocky whistler Joe, and winked at one pretty young nurse. There was blushing, me, I blushed, lost my character.

John Baraldi, recently arrived in England from his native USA helped with the scenes that involved me, veering between amazed bewilderment and bewildered amazement at the barely comprehensible broad north Midland dialect whose richness of rhythms and vocabulary were totally alien to him. I offered him the part of the cabman. He jumped at the opportunity to carry on Minnie's suitcase and say his two lines: "He'af a crown" and "Thank yer. Gud arternoon". The entire working process was a delight, no ructions, no differences, no stormy weather.

We decided to perform in the newly converted Chapel Studio. The place had personality and a certain fitting atmosphere, above all we were the keyholders and could decide if and when to use it. It felt period perfect for the Lawrence play, and I knew exactly how I wanted to stage it. A small raised kitchen space with table, two chairs, a range and shelving; the whole action to be played out on this very cramped space backed by enlarged period photographs to set the mood. The audience to be seated very close. I wanted it to be a 'fly on the wall' type experience for them.

My ideas seemed to work against the nature of the play. You'd expect an 'ordinary' script about 'ordinary' lives to have ordinary staging, naturalistic, down-to-earth, simple. My instinct, however, called for something different, period but not plain. Baraldi argued that my proposal was arty, inclined to sentimentality, and in bare-bone honesty he was right, but there was something, a something perhaps about the joint leads, their essential characters and charisma, which made me want their honest ordinariness to be explored in a special context. I can explain it no better.

A stroke of magical serendipity supported my cause: we were given access to a hoard of early twentieth-century glass plate negatives of Chesterfield life. We selected ten: views of the town, a tram, children playing, shops, workers, a miners' rally with banners abundant, the park in spring blossom, snow blocked streets and a full-length portrait of a local police constable, proud, robust, rotund in his uniform. ("Ah, he cuffed me lug when ar were a young 'un," said Sid, our caretaker, with a grin and a sniff.) These were enlarged each one to ten feet by four, and pasted to panels, which were offset and overlapped to create a close background to the black-painted kitchen and furniture. We needed little in the way of props to dress the set – I suggested a couple of pots, a panchion for bread making and

"I'm off," was Hargreaves immediate response, "to Pearsons, Seconds."

Pearsons was the local pottery, famed for its range of traditional salt-glazed pots. Within two hours he returned with about a hundred different pots, all types and sizes, tureens and bottles, vinegar jars, salvers, pitchers and brine pots and bottles, stockpots and roasters, pie dishes and ramekins, loaf pots, preservers, bung jars, porringers and a panchion, all seconds, scrounged for free.

"It's a small kitchen, John, what's the idea?"

"We'll paint 'em black, all of them."

"What on earth? . . ."

"Coal Black!" and we did and he built them up as a massed black pot background an irregular balanced display linking the kitchen with the photographs, and by some strange chemistry it did become a home with its own meaningful identity. It was this production which confirmed my commitment to sets that allowed the audience to share the performance rather than simply watch it. And for that to be effective the spatial context is of supreme importance. I still regard this as our best ever set. It was not naturalistic, but offered a real, lived characterful individuality – no photographs of it exist. Step up, be there, and the actors loved working on the set, with the impact of so many particular moments of interpersonal drama being heightened by the space in which they were played out. There was:

- The awful dawning on Minnie of Luther's situation as he awkwardly blurts it out.
- Broken-armed Joe driving Minnie to distraction by smashing, accidentally on purpose, two best white plates.
- Raging Luther ripping up the artist's prints that Minnie had bought with her own money.
- Minnie flirtatiously preferring Joe to her husband.
- Her confrontations with the mother, so brutally raw.
- And above all the end, as they realise their mutual love and need of one another, when Luther returns, injured head bleeding from a confrontation with blacklegs.

I put music to this ending. Again Baraldi demurred, again quite rightly, in correct Lawrentian terms. So much depended on Pippa throughout the performance, such a range of challenging emotional response, and then those last goose-pimpling heart-aching moments. Not overtly, but fierce emotion must be wrenched from these words and the moments between them.

Minnie: My love – my love!

Luther: Minnie – I want thee ter ma'e what tha can o' me.

M (crying):   My love – my love.

L: I know what tha' says is true.

M: No, my love – it isn't – it isn't.

L: But if ter'lt ma'e what ter can o' me – an' then if ter has a child – tha'lt happen ha'e enow.

M: No – no – it's you I want. It's you.

L: But tha's allus had me.

M: No, never – and it hurt so.

L: I thowt tha despised me.

M: Ah – my love!

L: Dunn say I'm mean, ter me – an got no go.

M: I only said because you wouldn't let me love you.

L: Tha' didna love me.

M: Ha! – it was you.

L: Yi . . . (he looks away) I'll tae me boots off.

M:	Let me do them.
L:	It's started bleeding. I'll do 'em i' aef a minute.
M:	No – trust me – trust yourself to me. Let me have you now for my own.
L:	Dost want me?
M:	(She takes his hands) Oh! My love. (She takes him in her arms – He suddenly begins to cry.)

And the play ends.

The music was a salve to this encounter, softened the exchange, made it extraordinary. My heart turned as I watched them. It brought tears to the eyes of the audience. Pippa pulled it off.

> stuff happens
>> silly things happen
>>> I fell in love with her.

On occasions one faces the impossibility of not loving.

This production meant a great deal to me; it was early in my career, and was as good as anyone could hope for, fully realised. I would not have wished to do it in any other context nor with any other group of actors. I had learned a great deal, it gave me confidence. For personal reasons the historical context, related to a culture now lost, that I had grown up in as a child, a culture that spoke the language of my childhood was so resonant, bringing so many memories to the surface. In addition, the portrayal of a couple struggling to come to terms with a very personal issue echoed a situation that I had faced when – when the need to be a couple and continue to love had endured.

This was the last time I worked with John Baraldi. We didn't meet until thirty-five years later in 2008. As we reminisced he whistled a few phrases of a lost haunting tune. I paused listening, familiarity dawning. He whistled again, softly, with a twinkle in his eye. It was the music I had insisted we use for *The Daughter-in-Law*, a theme from the Truffaut film *Jules et Jim*, and it was lodged still in his memory.

Then, some moments of quiet, some moments of quiet.

Together: the rituals, pleasure and politics of co-operation

MOONCUSSER'S DAUGHTER, Joan Aiken

The title is a steal adopted from the title of a book by Richard Sennett which is concerned with those aspects of human relations which have most interested me in personal terms, and most influenced my working practice.

When Baraldi left I appointed a replacement with responsibility for developing the programme of the Youth Theatre. This young woman left after a few months and I decided to work with NEDYPT during the interim, offering Pippa a part-time contract to support the T.I.E. and Youth Theatre work. A new generation of young people turned up for the new season and I chose to direct *Mooncusser's Daughter* with them. The script resonated with me as it is built on themes from *The Tempest* and *The Winter's Tale*.

The play is set on a remote lighthouse island. A father has banished his daughter years earlier; she unexpectedly returns to her island home shortly after the arrival of four very bad types who have come to search for a very special book, The Book with all the secrets of the world. It is locked away in a deep cave inhabited by Caliban.

The script is magically serious, with some comical silliness, it is movingly poignant, with some scope for sensitive character development. There are nine human characters and a talking bird, the Macawmak, and nine songs which punctuate the action.

These last offered me a new opportunity, to work with live musicians, and a specific challenge, the decision to commit myself to the full complement of twenty-five young people who wished to work together. Now, forty years after the event, my memory mis-serves me. I know that at best memory is a creative, fallible process, highly prone to suggestion and other distorting influences, and am aware, as readers must beware, that this fact determines and affects the way I write, the experience I recount. I vividly recall moments in the production, but have no genuine memory of how I managed to integrate everyone in the piece and make them equally value our work together. This even after re-reading the script.

I do, however, recall what I learnt.

During my ten years as a schoolteacher in Cambridge I had used drama and presented short bits and pieces of performance, and made some short movies with the secondary modern lads who were my charges. It was the 1960s, a wonderfully unrestricted time to be a schoolteacher. The team of teachers I led were imaginative and creative, and we enjoyed the freedom to explore progressive approaches to education. Our group work in the combined arts and humanities was balanced with more traditional class teaching of the sciences, mathematics and technical/practical subjects. I believe these boys were very well educated within the bounds of our resources and the culture of schooling. The whole process happened in the context of formal education. My role was that of Sir, the teacher, responsible for discipline, for standards, for control, as well as for learning. In the early 60s there was still a strict formality – pupils were addressed by surname. I had a cane, which I had used. At the end of each summer term we would be asked to go through the Educational Suppliers Catalogue and submit an order for pencils, exercise books, blotting paper (ball-point pens were frowned on), rulers, chalk (for throwing at recalcitrant pupils), blackboard dusters, waste-paper baskets, drawing pins and a cane (standard, extra swishy, or special de luxe). By the end of the 60s the cane was no longer available, but Sir remained Sir.

Now, with NEDYPT, I found myself one of a group with whom I could mix on my own terms, be my natural self, relate without formality, admit and accept weaknesses and bewilderment, push them really hard. Above all, I could shout and admit to vulnerability without it being identified as weakness. It wasn't to be Us and Them, but rather us together. When we met in the Chapel Studio, which some of them had helped to convert, we were able to be together in a truly enriched mode, the give and take togetherness of rehearsal and performance becoming the touchstones and templates for creative social action. I found this quite difficult sometimes, more difficult than the kids, who adapted more readily than I. After all I was the director and the ultimate success of the project depended on me. However, I can think of no better source than drama for this kind of learning, this rich conversation. Doing, rather than simply studying, accustoms us to the everyday practice of co-peration, and in the creation of a drama successful interaction enlists the body as well as the mind. Social relations are experienced in the gut.

I learnt much from musicians; they work with a more precise discipline which totally depends on performers in rehearsal having to grasp others' viewpoints but stand their own ground, a practice which in fact underlies any joint exercise which deserves success. With *Mooncusser's* I was particularly well served when some of the group recommended Michael Simmonds to me. He was sixteen, perceptive and a brilliant young pianist who had yet to learn the advantages and rigours of co-operation, as he had to work with two beginner guitarists, a complexly apologetic ukulele player and a percussionist. But Mick provided a wonderful base talent on which to build the musical and song elements of the script. Mick subsequently worked with me on several shows, I employed him as pianist to the Arts Centre modern dance group and he quickly moved on to become rehearsal pianist for Ballet Rambert and keyboard player on Joan Armatrading's first world tour.

I am totally unmusical in any technical sense, I can't sing in tune, and the way those amazing sounds are coaxed out of musical instruments remains a magical mystery. But I know what I like, and used live music and pre-recorded tracks in many productions. My initial problem with Mick revolved around the fact that there were a number of things he couldn't do, or so he said – one of them included playing fewer notes. We often came to loggerheads over this issue alone. Whenever I suggested a tremor of atmosphere or a hint of support, Mick would understand, but still throw the whole piano at the moment. I should have got him to listen to Bill Evans' contribution to Miles Davis', *Kind of Blue*. Mick served us so well, but was impatient in the role of servant, not appreciating the time inexperienced actors need to master a song.

It fascinated me to observe the similarities and stark differences in the ways musicians and actors approach their performance. It was thrilling to watch the increasing sentiment, the confident potency of the songs, a number of ingenious, Shakespearian song influenced lyrics offered with a natural unassuming warmth which refined whilst enriching the dramatic atmosphere. By the time we reached an assured level of competence, we were a team, no contest for priorities; we worked together.

I learnt from the care with which the work with the main characters had to be approached, as they represent such a range of types and stereotypes.

Lord Boss, a King of Crime, and his cronies are a gang of duplicitous knockabout pantomime villains in search of The Book; Caliban is a monster, monstrously sad and malevolent; Macawmak is a ridiculously inconsequent talking bird; and Fred is a benign ghost. These strange beings are countered by three very real human beings: Saul Bilkanchor, the Mooncusser, is a misanthrope, guilt-ridden by the deaths of a child and his brother Fred. His wife, Ruth, is a good woman; she has become blind. Sympathy, their daughter, has been banished from the family by her father, and has trained as a ballet dancer.

Each of these roles is a considerable challenge in its own right, and the balance between this rich disparate ragbag of characters must be subtly orchestrated. The daughter is the lynchpin for the action. I cast Alison Rothwell in the role; she was physically attractive, confident and open in workshops, and settled into moments of calm, self-contained rest. I gambled on my instinct, so aware of the role Pippa had played in *The Tempest*. I asked Alison to be natural. At her entrance she comes running through the audience, she slings her bag onto a chair, pauses a moment noticing her mother's dark glasses, then dashes to hug her with joyous warm spontaneity – then – then – the gradual dawning realisation that her mother is blind. The running was her choice, the throwing the bag her choice, that pause her instinct; out of these was born the tremulous pained sympathy of their conversation. When I asked her how she came to it she said with simple pride, "I hug my mum". I never hugged my mum, never.

It is from that moment in *Mooncusser's* when mother and daughter are reunited that the scenario is developed and a tragically conflicted family history unfolds. The challenge of this play is marking that tragedy whilst sustaining its magically unreal, thoroughly theatrical essence which leads, after encounters and attempts at reconciliation, to final scenes where there are complex transitions. The baddies, with the exception of young Gritty who has become a friend of Sympathy, become ghosts. Saul, his bitterness unrelenting, is transmuted into Caliban. So many strange interlocking strands are brought together. Caliban grabs The Book and claims to have them all at his mercy. He vows he will now go back into the world and wreak vengeance; he will mow down forests like mustard and cress; he will trample the cities like carpets; he will drink up the oceans like – . . . lemon squash! He realises he hasn't got the key to The Book, and Sympathy reminds him that he can't read anyway.

Ruth accepts, with contented resignation, that she will henceforth live with the several ghosts (she can see them and enjoys their eccentric company). Gritty offers to stay at the lighthouse and will look after her. Sympathy leaves the island with her mother's blessing.

I often wonder why I seek any adequacy in words to communicate the real life emotional charge of passages such as these in performance.

Is there a message? What is the learning? Learning from both this script and my developing dramatic practice. Is any attempt at justification needed?

In real life it seems we have to work at making and re-making bonds with friends, family, colleagues and fellow citizens, which is what is best in theatre practice. We are different from each other as we are divided in ourselves – let's talk, and pay attention to the whole person and their local habitation.

Together, with co-operative engagement, we, a bunch of kids and me, we had created this world and its strange music. It was never a contest, always a shared collaboration. I had learnt the beginnings of a modus operandi. We had enjoyed the sheer good cheer of making this show.

And memory?

Two forces go head to head in remembering. The force of correspondence tries to keep memory true to what actually happened, while the force of coherence ensures that the emerging story fits in with the needs of the self, which often involves portraying the ego in the best possible light. (Charles Fernyhough)

Ah! Marcello – Beware.

And memory?

A crazy old woman who hoards coloured rags and throws away food.

Run Pippa Run

THE TEMPEST, William Shakespeare

inch-meal	sea-swallow	mid-season	over-topping
red-hot	demi-devil	many-coloured	rye-straw
nettle-seed	wave-worn	lass-lorn	dear-beloved

ACT PRESENTS THE TEMPEST

It's stolen Admin Time. I'm writing at my desk. I'm making lists. I'm thinking of my clapped out car. Trivia is clouding my mind and my will. I should be in Nottingham. I need a poster design. I've booked a mime group and can't fix the fee. I know I'll lose the Chapel Studio. I'm trying to make my next move, but can't move. And I really should be in Nottingham within the hour. A Mad World, mad world, mad world, My Masters. I'm, I'm . . .

"Jack."

I look up. It's Pippa, who left six years ago. I clench my heart to arrest the flood of emotion. I know I will be graceless, cold, in a bewilderment of racing heart-aching tremors. Does she know how much I loved her?

fresh-brook	high-day	up-staring	honey-drops
	virgin-knot	strong based.	

"Jack?" with a raised eyebrow, and shyly shimmering hint of that smile.

Yes, I had loved her dearly. Pippa was my muse, and she left. I can barely hold her gaze. She has returned, unannounced, seemingly unchanged, returned to me, and all I manage are awkward fractured phrases, holding back, helpless, making myself helpless, in the company of one of the loveliest human beings I have ever known. I cannot let myself come out, be here with her. Graceless. Utterly. I leave for Nottingham.

rock-hard	sour-eyed	skill-less	urchin-shy
	brine-pits	pole-clipt	spell-skipped

A few days later a small parcel is delivered. Inside a slip of paper: "I hadn't realised", no address, no phone number.

> Dost thou attend me? Thou attendst not.

> I pray thee, mark me. Dost thou hear?

This sense of the blood pulse drumming through and obscuring the rational process.

> Miranda has all the open-mindedness, the willingness to be
> impressed, the capacity for wonder, that a story-teller could desire.
> She is all sympathy and eagerness to believe the best.

How does one write seriously of something so evanescent as a muse? So overwhelming. Something that could be a mere vanity prop. Or some kind of prosthetic to keep the wheels of the creative machine turning. Or, could be a source of pure inspiration.

> Miranda is alive and individual from the breathless anxiety of her
> opening speech. She is never afraid, for all her delicacy of mind,
> of expressing her feelings, and this candour of soul reaches an
> exquisite climax with her famous:

> O, wonder!

> How many goodly creatures are there here!

> How beauteous mankind is!

> O brave new world

> That has such people in't.

Pippa played Miranda. Miranda **was** Pippa in *The Tempest*.

Lorna Dexter had approached me suggesting we work on a Shakespeare production together. I think she may have seen the *Macbeth for Beginners* that I had done a couple of years earlier. We both agreed on *The Tempest*. Lorna would work with the actors on the script, the language and their individual characterisations. I would create the vision, the dynamic, the context of sweet sound and movement that would fill the magical island. And the Chapel Studio would become the island, and the audience would be on the island with us, in the thick of it, all around, and Hargreaves would work with me to design that enchanted place where such bitter-sweet real-time action is played out.

Philippa Deegan, small, stockily graceful with deep bright eyes and ready laughter was a nineteen-year-old beauty therapy student, of all things, who wanted more, and had come to work with us when we needed a young woman to play a small but important part in a Theatre in Education project. A project that considered beliefs and responsibility, honesty, courage and loyalty. Her character, had allegedly, betrayed a cause. She stood against a high, long, drab wall, grey painted, lit by a harsh tight cold spot, alone to face interrogation.

Soft-questions   Hard-questions   Mean-suppositions

Insidious-hints   Whiskering-violence

Lingering-threats   Possible-violation and Malice   Cruel-Malice.

the adolescent audiences looked away, or bowed their heads, held their breath, and some few wept and . . .

Pippa broke into the "Quality of mercy is not strained" speech from *The Merchant of Venice*, pleading on her own behalf, and the room was stilled and filled with such emotion as could barely be contained. And I knew we could work together, and make a fabulous *Tempest*, because Pippa was Miranda born.

But the rehearsal process proved slow; inexperienced players struggled with the language, came with pre-conceived notions of how to be Shakespearian. Others found it problematic, as two totally different temperaments were building the piece; and yet others were scared, not happy at all at the prospect of sharing space with the audience. And in addition I had chosen the once in a lifetime chance to explore the vocal, physical, magical possibilities of playing Ariel myself.

But -

But But But

we were bogged down,

and I became anxious, taut and fraught about the production.

It was dry and febrile.

We needed a tipping point.

And suddenly I saw it. There it was!

But Pippa said, "No! I can't, that's silly, can't possibly! How can I?"

And Lorna agreed.

"You can Pip," I insisted.

She was wearing a long loose-flowing affair made of the cheapest mutton cloth, that was fitting and right, and she loved it, as it shaped her body, but modestly.

"How can I in this dress?"

"You have to. Hitch it up."

"Look at my feet Jack, horrible horrible feet."

"He's lusting for you. He's tried to rape you Pippa. Damn you Deegan, he wants to **breed – YOU**, to fill the island with his kind. Listen to me again."

I'd persuaded Hargreaves to play Caliban. Hargreaves, who was fierce and filled with proud passion, Calibanesque in his very being, stood louring beside her, amused and wondering.

"You've got to do it, girl! Child! You've both got the words. Listen, Feel. You do feel them. I can tell. I know," and she looked at me and I melted. Sharing. Begin John, slip the coin in your mouth.

Caliban: This island's mine by Sycorax my mother,

Which thou tak'st from me. When thou cam'st first,

Thou strok'st me and made much of me, would give me

Water with berries in't, and teach me how

To name the bigger light, and how the less,

That burn by day and night; and then I loved thee,

And showed thee all the qualities o' th' isle,

The fresh springs, brine-pits, barren place and fertile.

Curs'd be I that did so! All the charms

Of Sycorax, toads, beetles, bats, light on you!

For I am all the subjects that you have,

Which first was mine own king; and here you sty me

In this hard rock, whiles you do keep from me

The rest o' th' island.

Prospero: Thou most lying slave,

Whom stripes may move, not kindness! I have us'd thee,

Filth as thou art, with human care and lodg'd thee

In mine own cell, till thou didst seek to violate

The honour of my child.

Caliban: O ho, O ho! Would't had been done.

Thou didst prevent me; I had peopl'd else

This isle with Calibans.

Miranda: Abhorred slave

Which any print of goodness will not take,

Being capable of all ill! I pitied thee,

Took pains to make thee speak, taught thee each hour

One thing or other. When thou didst not, savage,

Know thine own meaning, but would'st gabble like

A thing most brutish, I endow'd thy purposes

With words that made them known. But thy vile race,

Though thou didst learn, had that in't which good natures

Could not abide to be with; therefore wast thou

Deservedly confin'd into this rock, who hadst

Deserv'd more than a prison.

"There, you're in it Pippa. Good. Don't scold. Keep helping him, don't be harsh, feel for him. And you, yes, you must use his harsh-felt, wretchedly-eloquent heart-felt Caliban response that is coming at you."

Caliban :   You taught me language, and my profit on't

Is, I know how to curse. The red plague rid you

For learning me your language!

And then, as he comes for you

hag-born   utter-out   man-monster   still-vexed   fleshy-fly

ever-angry   fly-blowing   bed-fellows   horse-piss

RUN – PIPPA – RUN!

"I've told him, Pip, I've told him if he catches you he can rip off that frock. And he will, Deegan, he will, of course he will because he's Hargreaves, and a bastard, and he wants you."

All this in front of the cast, then, softly, to Pippa alone, "But please – don't let him catch you, don't let him catch you please."

There is a photograph that came into my possession some months ago which captures that run, that moment. The sense of danger must not disappear. That hare-skinned run of barely a dozen-strides became an electric-trigger for the cast. Those few running seconds moved the whole rehearsal process onward and upward several gears. We went back to the opening-tempest scene and decided to frighten the audience with the wind and the shouts and the battering clattering chaos of ropes swinging and bodies careering as the sails tumble collapsing down and are fixed fast to create the mysterious magical island within which the audience is seated.

Ultimately I was very proud of the show. It was tense and funny and colourful and energised, filled with emotion and struggles.

Ian Rochard describes his first experience of working with ACT:

When Jack invited me to be in a production of THE TEMPEST, although I was apprehensive, having no idea whether or not I could act, I was ready to say yes.

I remember the rehearsal period as a mixture of fear and excitement. The show was directed by Lorna Dexter with Jack's assistance. For several weeks we improvised around scenarios drawn from themes and situations in the play. I was greatly in awe of the talent shown by the more experienced members of the group, whose endless free inventiveness contrasted sharply with my clumsily self-conscious efforts. I was particularly impressed by John Hargreaves, playing Caliban with a speech impediment (which he practised by keeping a coin in his mouth) and Jonette Bown who played Trinculo to my Stephano and Gonzalo to my Sebastian. However, something was keeping me going, although I wasn't sure what it was. I did have huge faith in Lorna and Jack to pull it all together. They seemed to have real clarity of purpose even though they weren't happy with the limited progress being made by some of the cast.

When we started to use the text I began to feel a little more comfortable. I now had something to hide behind and could speak the verse in a way that made sense, despite my inability, at that stage, to create two different and credible characters. Sebastian, I found fairly straightforward – a clever (though not as clever as he thinks he is) manipulative villain, seemed to come quite naturally and during rehearsals for the 'Royal' scenes most of the attention was on the actors who played Alonso (the king) and Antonio (my fellow plotter). They both struggled to deliver what the director wanted. However, when it came to those scenes featuring the low-life villains (Caliban, Trinculo and Stephano) I seemed to be very much under the cosh. I could feel how constrained my attempts at Stephano were, despite all the help and advice I was receiving.

Towards the end of the rehearsal period I became convinced I had made a big mistake. I could not act. There was no doubt about that. Stephano, instead of being a comic highlight, was the weakest element in the show. I wanted to pull out. I decided to give it one last go and during the journey to Hipper Street (our rehearsal venue) I remember suddenly realising how I might move forward.

When Stephano first appears he believes himself to be alone. I needed to do the same. I needed to free myself from the sense (which had so dogged me up to that point) of being observed and judged. When later in the evening, I made my entrance as Stephano I somehow managed to persuade myself that I really was alone on the island and was able, for the first time, to deliver the opening lines (a song and its commentary) with disinhibited conviction. It was a pivotal moment for me.

From then on things improved. The audience was so close as to be almost part of the playing space and as I grew more confident in my performance I discovered how to relate to them, particularly in my role as Stephano. I took heart from the comments of a colleague, a lecturer in English Literature, who described the production as the best TEMPEST he had seen. The only mishap – a massive collision of heads (with Jack), when being chased by the spirits of the island. I thought I was going to pass out, but just about held it together to the end of the show. Jack didn't seem at all affected – perhaps he was deeper into role (as Ariel), than I.

There is a second photograph of Pippa as Miranda. It has a concentrated-stillness, focused and wondering, as her father explains the circumstances that brought them to the island when she was an infant. I can sense her. Charged. Emotion here counterpointing any sense of danger. She was born Miranda.

Pippa worked with me for three years, played in five productions and assisted with three others. Our association encouraged, enabled, allowed me to seek out undreamed-of realms of theatre and ways to work with it. She was a joy to be with, all enquiring and fun.

One day, when I knew she would leave, I watched her pinning posters on a notice-board. Without forethought I came close behind her, and gently held her breasts, quickly, lightly, and stepped away surprised. She turned, abrupt, sharp – saw me – a look, a pause, that soft knowing smile played in her eyes. I blushed. A pause:

"They're mine, Jack, small and nice."

"Would you believe me if I said I never, ever, ever, ever do that kind of thing?"

"More than a handful is too much. That's what my brother says."

sight-outrunning sea-marge still-closing never-surfeited

   sea-sorrow   drowning-mark

     sea-change

     rich

     and

     strange.

Rilke: To love is good, for love is hard, Love between one
     person and another that is perhaps the hardest thing it is
     laid on us to do, the utmost, the ultimate trial and test,
     the work for which all other work is preparation.

Failed.   Fail again.   Fail better.

Proud – The Second Western

INDIANS, Arthur Kopit

- I'm here, and so is Pippa.
- I know Tim. You realise what we're after is . . .
- Yes, we do.
- There's a lot of them, Tim, and we're all just standing around . . .
- You wanted a lot. *The Mooncusser's* gang invited their mates.
- Yes, but we're all milling around in the Chapel and I didn't expect so many.
- You're not glad?
- Suppose so. It's okay. Count them Pippa.
- I have done, there's thirty-six.
- There, Tim, that's what I call a lot.
- You said you wanted a cast of thousands.
- Not literally.
- Jack, get on with it. There's thirty-six, twenty-three of them boys – that's great. They are all keen. Then there's Hargreaves and Tim and me, and Jill Jones will be around to fuss and comment and encourage and chaperone and **praise**! – so you can concentrate on what you're good at.
- Meaning what, Pip?

- Meaning you won't need to praise!
- She means we'll all help. They won't all act, some want to be techies, stage manage, operate lights, they'll work with me.
- She means I'm uptight.
- You are. And Mick Simmonds will do the music.
- Thanks Pip – sweet and trouble What about the movement? The War Dance? The floozies in the Saloon Scene?
- Joyce Bryson will come.
- Mm . . .
- You know most of them. They know you. I'll just keep them laughing.
- At me probably – that's the name of the game, isn't it?
- It helps. We'll always, Jack, have – the four elephants!
- Tell her, Tim.
- She's right.
- This is the second Western. It's important to me. You just don't realise. Neither of you realises it's the biggest thing I've done.
- It's not done – you're avoiding starting.
- Pippa, sometimes I wobble. *Indians*. They do know it's Red Indians?
- Yes, but we call them Native Americans.
- Not in the play we don't.
- O.K. Red Indians, *Indians*, but that's all they know. Stop pacing around. You're wearing **The** tie and your two shirts so you're supposed to be feeling good. We're all waiting, chatting, teetering. Be prepared. You always say that to me.
- I am really . . . I do need them. It's as the title implies, *Indians* depends on a large company of Indians, ever present, hovering, haunting, dying. Call them together, Tim.
- Don't Tim. You do it, Jack.
- Thanks Pip. I do love you so much. Remember . . . we'll always have… Call them up, Tim.
- Dearly Beloved, Brethren, and Sisters, we are gathered here today in this most hallowed place.
- Don't be silly Jack!
- We've got to start somewhere! O.K. kids, we're going to learn what happens to truth when anyone tries to find it through illusion. We're taking on a big play, but it's brilliant, somebody said it's one of the necessary American plays of the Sixties, and the R.S.C premièred it in 1968 just six years ago. It's by Arthur Kopit. Look at this listing.

Pippa, my lovely and beautiful assistant, will now hold up her chart. Higher dearie. The writer calls it A Chronology for a Dreamer. That's our starting point.

CHRONOLOGY FOR A DREAMER

1846   William F. Cody born in Le Claire, Iowa, on February 26.

1866   Geronimo surrenders.

1868   William Cody accepts employment to provide food for railroad workers, kills 4,250 buffaloes. Receives nickname 'Buffalo Bill'.

1869   *Buffalo Bill, the King of the Border Men*, a dime novel by Ned Buntline, makes Buffalo Bill a national hero.

1872   Expedition west in honour of Grand Duke Alexis of Russia, Buffalo Bill as guide.

1876   Battle at the Little Big Horn; Custer killed.

1877   Chief Joseph surrenders.

1878   Buffalo Bill plays himself in *Scouts of the Plains*, a play by Ned Buntline.

1879   Wild Bill Hickok joins Buffalo Bill on the stage.

1882   Sitting Bull surrenders, is sent to Standing Rock Reservation.

1883   Buffalo Bill's Wild West Show gives first performance, is great success.

1885   Sitting Bull allowed to join Wild West Show, tours with the company for a year.

1886   Standing Rock Reservation visited by United States Commission to investigate Indian grievances.

1890   Sitting Bull assassinated December 15.

1890   Wounded Knee Massacre, December 25.

–   That's all real history, not fiction. We've got to make it true, true as theatre.

The play is constructed from a succession of comic and serious, stark and lyrical scenes, punctuated by a recurrent trial scene in which the Indians state their case against the Whites to a commission of senators. The Great White

Father (the President) has refused to meet them. Kopit wants to convey a feeling of simultaneous time and non-chronological sequence to disorient the audience. It all takes place in the context of Buffalo Bill's Wild West Show. He sees his script as a dream, with nightmare dimensions, and wants people to feel the play rather than think it. I'll read a bit of what he says:

> This was what I had always wanted. To create an impression. Not something didactic, but something musically amorphous.

- I can't do amorphous music.
- You will, Mick.
- And viscerally disturbing, like a bad dream to be thought about after it's all over. Pieced together again – like a puzzle.
- Jack!
- Pip, don't interrupt, you're stopping my flow.
- You said you'd work from the off. You're talking too much.
- What's visceral?
- It's about guts, Alison, meaty, raw, intensely felt sensation, so you have to give your all. I love the scale and scheme of this play, and think we can.
- Jack!
- Yes, Pip! Yes Pip yes, you're not my keeper.
- You're not keepable, nor capable sometimes.
- Tim, gag her! O.K. It's Hunters and Hunted. Half here, the rest there. Bare feet.
- Bare feet?
- Yes! Alison, **bare** feet. Half here, half there.
- So, game on, I start.

I wonder whether it will work with such a large group, but feel that enough know me and my ways to make it worthwhile. The idea is to make them bond, lose inhibitions, and use their bodies and voices expressively. I will move amongst them, work with them. I'll watch them close, their faces, their concentration, their moves, their stillness. Individually they take a space anywhere on the floor, then they walk anywhere, anonymously, they choose their speed of walk, their inner attitude, but must ignore everyone around them, then on my signal, stop, frozen, no scratching, no twitching, stilled and waiting. On NOW half tense with fear, the remainder, hunters, take up the hunt, crawling, stalking, pausing, seeking, sniffing, dashing, searching, poised, alert. At CHANGE the hunters freeze, and the hunted seek to escape, to hide, to flee, to cower, to creep, to rush, to listen, to hope, to fear. They use the bodies of the stock-still hunters as landscape, as hiding places, as fearsome objects or poles of security as they seek invisibility. At CHANGE they freeze and the hunters recommence. I ask for more imaginative use of the space, freer interaction with the bodies – use them, touch them, clamber over, in, around them. We continue the game alternating roles, hunters get to play hunted, and I vary the rhythm of the hunt with rapid staccato changes some of barely a few seconds in length.

At a pause, I suggest they create a soundscape – the stilled will make sounds – jungle noises, or wind; Alison raises an eyebrow; or grating, whistles, squawks, clicks, yells – but it mustn't become a continuous cacophony, they must listen and create the sounds with a degree of harmony and use silence, be aware of its power. Visceral, I say, be visceral; Alison raised a mocking eyebrow; I'll get my own back later. We re-mix the two groups and start again. It's exciting to realise the developing confidence as I move amongst them, watch, feel their strength, look deep into their eyes as they begin to show more body awareness, stretch further, gesture expressively, vary their strategies, become bold, quick and slow, and are careful of their nature. At the signal DIE the hunted die, choosing their own mode of dying, quick, or slow, spectacular or simple, with dignity or ugliness. And Mick, you make amorphous music on the keyboard. He tinkles a phrase of chopsticks; I'll get my own back later; and the hunters, from their stillness begin to beat a rhythm on their bodies, and there's stamping feet, and the keyboard's notes must be shapeless, counter to the rhythm. It has to be a group thing, celebratory but mourning.

It works. They are fifteen, sixteen, seventeen years old and show neither embarrassment nor awkwardness. They created and held the atmosphere. Their bodies changed. I don't want the tobacco-shop Indian. I want strange, strong, physical animals with a natural native grace. The success of the play depends on the Indians. They must create an authentic dreaming. The Indians will wear loin cloths and little else. We'll cross that bridge later.

But there is more. It all happens in the more dominant context of the Wild West Show, much of the rest of the play includes the ebullient rowdy razzmatazz of circus, the real Buffalo Bill's Wild West Show billed as An Absolutely Original and Heroic Enterprise of Inimitable Lustre. So this play, a telling of real historical events, uses a show which itself is offering a version of historical truth, the foundation of a myth that sustains a whole society.

The challenge, the question that Kopit faces us with in this script, is what happens to truth when one tries to find it through illusion. Kopit has created, with full conscious artistry, a non-illusion (i.e. a real life show) that allows the audience to sense the truth of events in a non-empathic form. He achieves a Brechtian effect. *Indians* distils the truth of real events, working over real historical material that is fundamental to the myth of the West.

That strange process, moving from actual experiential truth to its representation as 'truth' in a work of fiction, a drama, fascinated me as a director.

Now, many years after the production, the nature of the piece fascinates more than ever. I face the dilemma of how to communicate the excitement, the fun, the discoveries of working with the group and how to balance that with a fuller description of the script, the former depending so much on the latter.

The play is a complex sprawling epic which travels from Buffalo Bill's Wild West Show to the real prairie, from the White House to the Massacre at Wounded Knee. Many scenes are inherently cinematic, and the playwright handles these with astute ingenuity, making exciting visual theatre and metaphor. For example, the decimation of the Great Buffalo Herd which spelt the end of the Plains Indian's way of life, and makes a terminal clash with the Whites even more inevitable, is acted out by Indians wearing buffalo skins.

With similar metaphorical ingenuity the White Man's 'civilising of the Savage', is presented as a 'fictional dream' in which Buffalo Bill, with a rawhide whip, enters a lion's cage in which the naked, half-demented (is this real, or performance?) Geronimo ("Most Ferocious Indian Alive, Scourge of the South West") is imprisoned, strides up to the Indian, then gallantly, defiantly turns his back on the impotent Geronimo. This moment has been established with all the oompah razzle dazzle of show biz scene setting by

... two cowboy roustabouts with prods. They are enormous men, much larger than life-size. Their muscles bulge against their gaudy clothes. Their faces seem frozen in a sneer. Even their gunbelts are oversized. They prod Geronimo along, raise the gate to the centre stage and coax him in.

The scene is immediately followed by another of realistic, yet frustrated absurd debate in which John Grass, the Indian's spokesman, and the Senators are at loggerheads over the meaning and values of successive Treaties. The scene ends:

John Grass – We were also . . . promised a steamboat.

Senator Morgan – A steamboat?

Senator Dawes – What on earth were you supposed to do with a steamboat in the middle of the plains? (He laughs.)

John Grass – I don't know.

(He turns and looks in confusion at Buffalo Bill: who turns helplessly to the senators. As – Lights begin to fade.)

Sitting Bull – Where is the Great Father, Cody? The one you said would help us. The one you said you knew so well.

(As the lights go to black, a Mozart minuet is heard.)

And, cut to The White House, where Ned Buntline, author of *Scouts of the Plains* will affirm the true legend of Buffalo Bill, Indian Scout, and Kopit's version with simultaneously expose the illusory veracity of that legend. The Ol' Time President is identified as a crafty folk-wise politician. Cody despises his lack of knowledge of the real West. The Ol' Time President subscribes to the legend totally; he wears imitation six-shooters, rides a mechanical horse and saying he can't do magic never leaves The White House.

Being a good President is like being a great eagle . . . you've got to know when to stay put.

These are scenes we have to create. I prepare the actors and Pippa monitors them, whilst I prepare another group. I don't want just acting but a full deep understanding of the import of their actions. We work well together.

Indians is a splendid challenge for a director, for an ensemble. Each scene is both thought-provoking and moving; many have a pained lyrical beauty which I found to be barely matched in modern playwriting. It suited me enormously. It is a humanising work whose relevance goes beyond the actual fate of the Native Americans, while its portrayal of a William F. Cody struggling to find the truth and understand the import of the consequences of his past actions is intriguing and difficult. At the heart of the play is Cody's growing, despairing realisation of himself as victim of his own legend, a legend which renders him quite impotent to be other than the tool of the civilisation which needed Buffalo Bill and the whole mythology of the West to justify and sustain its expansionist and genocidal policy. That particular myth, Buffalo Bill, Scout of the Plains, that illusion does reflect historical fact, the true fate of the Indians. Kopit refuses to print the legend; he renders his drama so much more powerful by establishing his protagonist, not as a Star of a Show, but as CODY, a man with a kind of tragic stature whose personal flaws and misjudgements haunt him as he struggles to change in response to the events he has somehow unwittingly engineered.

Ned Buntline, a key figure with some charlatan attributes, is intrinsic to the action of the play, vigorously promoting the legend which Cody abhors. Annie Oakley performs her sharpshooting act with an immaculate, faultless panache, which attests to the sanitised legend. This illusory context is counterpointed by the famous real speech of Chief Joseph. Wild Bill Hickok is the realist who sees through the claptrap of the legend making. He wanted to play Bat Masterson in Buntline's novelettish drama *Scouts of the Plains*, but Buntline insists they see how he makes out as Hickok: "Fer Chrissakes, I am

Hickok," he says, and playing himself for real wrecks the drama. However, finally, he succumbs to the legend with a vengeance, and proposes the world-wide marketing of cloned Buffalo Bills. There is so much more – the saloon scene with Dancing Girls; the Hunting Party of Grand Duke Alexis; Teskanjavila the Indian princess played by an Italian Opera singer "bosomy and half naked throughout the scene"; Sitting Bull speaking at length as he demonstrates his great chief authority by leaving the stage and taking the Indians with him. Sitting Bull is as good as dead; we never see him alive again. After the Massacre at Wounded Knee Cody meets Sitting Bull's ghost; they discuss the past. The Indian affirms that they had been friends. When Cody tries to say a few words in defence of his country's Indian policy, the ghosts of more dead Indians rise up, stating:

> I am Sitting Bull and I am dying . . . Crazy Horse I am dying . . .
> Geronimo is dying . . . Lone Wolf is dying . . . etc. . . . etc. . . . .

There is a final nightmare reprise of the Wild West Show. Chief Joseph repeats his great speech of surrender, they are the final words of the play:

> Tell General Howard I know his heart. I am tired of fighting. Our
> chiefs have been killed. Looking Glass is dead. The old men are all
> dead. It is cold and we have no blankets. The children are freezing.
> My people, some of them, have fled to the hills and have no food
> or warm clothing. No one knows where they are – perhaps frozen.
> I want to have time to look for my children and see how many of
> them I can find. Maybe I shall find them among the dead.
> Hear me, my chiefs. I am tired. My heart is sick and sad. From
> where the sun now stands, I will fight no more.

Rough Riders of the World tour the ring in silent triumph. Buffalo Bill enters, alone, on a white stallion, a hobby horse. He waves his white stetson to the unseen crowd. Indians appear from the shadows. Lights fade.

The sustained dignity of Chief Joseph's speech, its steady, clear-sighted statement of fact, has devastating impact at the end of the sequence of events the play has re-created. It is, in a play with many, the final coup de théâtre. A wonderful moment for the boy who spoke it.

One day Hargreaves turned up with a heap of dull red dyed coarse cloth, tore it into strips and handed them out with pieces of rope. He gave each girl a triangular-shaped piece with ties. Tell them John – but gently, be gentle – "You lot, get your clobber off", he says with a wide broad grin and cheeky eyes, "then put this piece between your legs and pass it front and back over the rope tied round your waist". Some look wary, some puzzled, a few wide eyes shocked. "The triangles are for you lasses to cover your top." They love

John, he's big, and positive and cuddly – with kids. Can't we keep our pants on? "Get 'em off!" No pants, no bras. Sheer shock now, rebellion – some amusement and lots of whys from the girls, why? BUT WHY? We'll show our bits. We'll show our bits. Do we have to? You don't have to, I tell them. Jill in chaperone mode told me I was asking too much. I agreed, but said we should try it, they could but try it. I stand back. Hargreaves can take the flak, he's the cuddly one.

Alison is looking at me with questions in her eyes. She played the pivotal role of Sympathy with a real nice delicacy and authority in *Mooncusser's*, and she knows I appreciate her work but offer no favours. Does this count as a great idea? she asks. Do it, I say. Some of the lads have already started. You'll look great, I tell her. She did. They all did. Nervous, but inhibitions soon disappeared; they had gained physical confidence and a sense of presence from the workshopping.

And now? Alison asked, eyes crossed, pigeon toed, trembling vigorously.

And Hargreaves pulled out sacks and tipped buffalo hides on the ground. They were large enveloping capes of that old-fashioned coarse curled coir upholstery filling sprayed dark brown. Mis-shapen pieces are crudely stitched together with coarse string so that their shape will hang across an arched back. You hold it across your shoulders, Hargreaves says, hump it up, bend your backs and tweak to fit. It's scratchy, itches their naked backs. We persevere. Secretly they are enjoying this. It triggers one boy's asthma. He will die, but as an Indian not a buffalo. We rehearsed in a large arena, Wild West space, with the audience on three sides. I limited the seating to allow us more space.

We create a herd of about fifteen. They move in unison, they practise a stampede, and then another, but our playing space though large constrains them. We work out a relay system, changing patterns of movement, whilst others graze or rest motionless.

A shot rings out and a buffalo falls. Then the others, shot after shot, in successive faster frequency. It is a saddening scene – visceral. They lie dead for one full minute – there's music, it's amorphous. Then cowboys arrive to rip the hides from their backs tossing them into a pile.

The bodies lie still.

With each successive rehearsal, the Indians trimmed and refined their costumes until even I wondered about their scantiness. They made beads and native decorations, let their hair grow longer and lank, practised war paint which they smeared to a mess when they lost their land. They were aware of, yet unselfconscious in, their near nakedness, proud and confident in their bodies and about the performances they had to give.

Late one evening after a performance I was up on the Gallery with Tim adjusting and re-focusing lights. Tim was a quietly sensitive young man, self-contained, the best technician I ever had. As we paused and looked down on the company clearing up and preparing to leave, Tim asked: "Aren't you proud? Of this, of what they've done?"

They could be proud! Could I?

I didn't answer his question. I shrugged.

It took me a long time to get my head round the notion.

Mick was playing a lovely generous melody which felt fitting for the here and now. We were relaxing. He glanced up and, seeing me, broke into several bars of amorphous which climaxed with a thunderous hammering of the bass keys and a clever slide back to the melody.

I called down from the Gallery: "Pip! Get it right. Always remember there are **four** important elephants." "Yes Jack " and she blew me a kiss.

Deep inside there was a flutter of a tiny butterfly of pride. Visceral. Being who I was at that time I struggled to contain it. But contain it I did. Now, forty years later, I look back and realise my insecurity. Now, I can readily acknowledge that I am very proud of what we did. The project was an adventure. There wasn't a dud in the team. We'd done it together.

No Knickers! What is a person but his reputation

FEMALE TRANSPORT, Steve Gooch

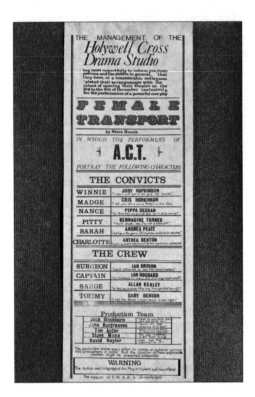

Imagine: Gently, my fingertips trace the raised raw welts of Pippa's back; it is bared and gluttered with dark clotted blood. There is bruising on the ribs and across the shoulders. The skin is broken, fresh sores seeping. Imagine: Gently, my fingertips caress the damaged flesh. A shudder, tension, as she holds herself close.

The Red Cross volunteer had driven up from Birmingham to show me how to create a freshly beaten back, a back that has been viciously flogged. I said it must look real in close-up. She said it will. An expert at disaster make-up, often working on major large-scale scenarios for police and fire service training exercises, she had readily responded to our request for advice and guidance. She approached the task with method and incredible skill, taking me through the procedures step by step. Two ways to make skin: thick or thin, and how to apply it; how to clot blood with baking powder; different shades of blue through purple to black for bruising, torn flesh, on the ribs or soft parts, fresh bruises or old bruises; fresh blood: arterial or veinous; plasma: the fluid part of blood for seepage.

The more closely I looked the more convincingly authentic the wounds seemed. **Imagine:** Gently... Pippa's back... This production was to be utterly naturalistic.

The Chapel Studio is ill-lit as the audience enter. At the far end they glimpse a cramped iron-barred cell, straw strewn, cluttered with crates and barrels, rope, tin pots, a piss bucket, some raised plank beds, a couple of lanterns.

The smell – goat's piss, chicken shit, meets them. Hens scratch and scuffle, a goat bleats, drags its chain across the floor. The cabin-boy lies prone on the deck above, he plays a penny whistle tunelessly. The audience waits, their eyes slowly attuning to the dimmed claustrophobic space. There are two crates of hens, and two goats, and six leg-shackled women. They are female criminals being transported to a convict colony in Australia. The women wear loose hessian gowns. One is knitting, another rocks restlessly, a gaunt pale pain-filled face stares with unflinching hatred, a body is sprawled motionless, possibly sleeping. The fifth stands, both hands clenched around the collar by which one goat is chained to the bars of the cell. The last is hidden in a pile of rags. The cell built by Hargreaves is real, solid, impregnable. Above the cell is the ship's deck occupied by four male characters: the ship's captain, the surgeon, the first mate, the cabin-boy. The men are rough, but clean and in uniform; they are above the women, separate, superior, they control the fate of their cargo. This is marked by the visual metaphor of the set. But in fact the men are as much victims of their situations as the women, not so persecuted, better fed, with status and power over the women, but hostages to fortune none the less. All of them are bound together in a symbiotic relationship, the crew being paid in accordance with the number of convicts who arrive at the colony, alive and in good health – hence the surgeon. Even the crew's health is not assured.

The narrative of the play tells of the events of the voyage. Most of the action involves the women, punctuated by encounters and confrontations with the crew, their various modes of survival and mutual support, as well as their differences. It is human nature raw, tempered by acts of kindness, desperation, even love. One woman has crude consensual sex with the ship's mate, they are both satisfying physical need, she gets extra food; another, reckless, rebellious, Pippa is flogged; a third breaks, fails to survive, Bernadine hangs herself; the cabin-boy falls in love, a kindly gentle boyish love, with the youngest girl convict. The last, motherly, knits, mostly silent.

The production had to be genuinely, straightforwardly naturalistic. The setting was as real as we could realise, and I wanted the same from the actors. No theatricality whatsoever, just believable behaviour, believable bodies, believable presence. I considered suggesting the convicts might spend a night in their cell; perhaps Pippa would accept a little light friendly flogging to give her first-hand knowledge of the real thing; and we could hang Bernardine, momentarily, and swing her body to replicate the rocking motion of the vessel; believable presence implied unwashed hair, unshaven legs, dirty fingernails, snotty noses, no knickers.

At such moments are reputations born.

This was the first production I had done which depended upon a concern with the portrayal of sex and violence (the flogging, with realistic sound effects, was administered off-stage, with the back make-up completed in the interval). Barely five years earlier the Lord Chamberlain's Office, which censored theatre, had been abolished. Nudity, sexual behaviour, acts of physical violence, outrageous language, even blasphemy were now possible; and this script, a very serious piece of work, was a beneficiary of these new freedoms. It was at this time that I first gained a somewhat sardonic reputation for being preoccupied with sex and violence. I've been called a misogynist, accused of harbouring a deep underlying hatred of women, and worse, much worse. It still plays out as a semi-serious, semi-mocking, slightly cruel joke. I understand it. I get it. It never goes away. It's not unfounded. Nowadays I suggest that sex and violence in the realm of theatre is rather, at a deeper level, a matter of relationships and conflict, or better still, emotion and a sense of danger, without which there is no drama. I reassure myself that sometimes prejudice can be an opinion without thinking, and opinions are often a result of emotion rather than thinking. No necessarily false emotion. Emotion is invaluable.

The ensemble playing of the women was a revelation to me. They filled that vile, cramped and horrid space with such a range of behaviour, experience and emotion. Some of it was necessarily crude and violent. Years later Bernadine mentioned to me that she had not believed a live performance could be so compelling, so involving. It changed her expectations of the possibility of drama, set a benchmark for some of the even more challenging roles she would take on with ACT.

After a performance Graham Robinson, who played the usurping Duke in *The Tempest,* came up to me, shook my hand with warm firmness, visibly moved, unsmiling. "Thank you. Thank you so much," he said, and turned and left.

A tall shamble of a young man stood nearby and approached. I barely knew him as yet. He was Charles Monkhouse, newly appointed as the contemporary Young Turk sculptor at the College of Art, a man of ideas, of sculpture conceived with reason and subtle ingenuity, constructed with great precision, not of massy carving. He explained to me that since childhood he had regularly been taken to the theatre and continued to go irregularly but it had never worked for him, on no occasion had he suspended disbelief, never found himself elsewhere. Yet that night, *Female Transport* had transported him – he had fully believed it, every moment, and he suggested we might work together. Which we did. Quite often. And climbed Munros. And lived fairly close together and still keep in contact.

Playwrights work in a complex tradition. The audience enjoys all kinds of play; they do not come to the theatre for comfort, but rather to share experience, both good and bad, that they have lived, as well as experience that they will never live.

Art exists to rattle the senses and inflame the nerves. (Ken Russell)

This was as true for the audiences of Aeschylus, the first playwright we know, as it is for contemporary theatregoers. In the introduction to her translation of the *Oresteia* Anne Carson makes comparisons between the violence in Aeschylus' plays and that in the paintings of Francis Bacon, who claimed:

> We nearly always live through screens – a screened existence. And I sometimes think, when people say my work looks violent, that I have been able to clear away one or two of the veils or screens.

This applies equally to theatre. He also says that violence will:

> ... work first upon sensation then slowly leak back into the fact... return fact onto the nervous system in a more violent way...
>
> It's nothing to do with the violence of war. It's to do with an attempt to remake the violence of reality itself.

Anne Carson comments:

> They both have an instinct 'to trap the living fact alive' in all its messy, sensational, symbolic over-abundance.

I believe the audience for *Female Transport* understood and accepted the raw immediacy of the straitened existence of the characters. This helps me feel better about the reputation, but is not the whole story. The audience does come to the theatre for all kinds of play, for pure pleasure indeed, but even that will usually be at the expense of some characterised individual or plot mechanism. Music works quite differently: "Strange how potent cheap music is." Music stirs our souls in its own different ways, but even the most profoundly moving music sears us differently than theatre. Music commandeers our emotions in spite of ourselves. It takes us. Emotion abstracted. In theatre our emotional response is manipulated in a more specific way. Theatre can generate uncontrolled laughter, or real fear, or sheer amazement at the appalling, wondrous, unfathomable nature of the human condition.

He thinks too much: such men are dangerous

THE TOOTH OF CRIME, Sam Shepard

Successful tragedy is not particularly common in the long history of theatre. This is "a play with music in two acts", a Rock Tragedy, an even less common phenomenon.

For many years Sam Shepard has been a major film actor and writer in the United States. I came across his work in the early 1970s when he was based in England; it offered the opportunity to create a work written in an emphatically stylised American-English idiom. Originally I planned to direct *Geography of a Horse Dreamer,* billed as "a mystery in two acts". The vitality of its writing linked to the quirkily ridiculous narrative struck me as particularly individual. Then, after reading *The Tooth of Crime,* published in the same volume, my excitement and my ambition knew no bounds. What bigger, better challenge could there be than to forge a marriage between rock music and tragedy? It certainly told a tale of hubris called to account, and tragedy, as they say, is in the mind of the beholder, much as beauty is in the beholder's eye. I took it on quite blindly, by instinct, my rational brain recognising a wonderful opportunity with the potential to tap into a younger audience.

But above all I needed Mick Simmonds, and met him to discuss the music, slightly doubting, as lurking heavy rock was not his style. There are only six songs in the play, but they define its nature, lift the experience into a powerful theatrical realm; this piece pays no regard to the dawning of the Age of Aquarius. The sound should raise the roof, but the words of the songs had to be understood, so the band had to back off on volume when the singing starts. I explained to Mick, the play's the thing, your music must not dominate, but it will make the play the thing. I had said 'your' music, I could tell he had jumped straight in. We could put a band together – Hargreaves played bass, Bryson was a drummer, Mick would play organ, synth, keyboard. He had lightning fast ideas, was obsessed with the originality of *Tubular Bells*, which had just been released. As he left to prepare the arrangements, I called after him: "It's not *Tubular Bells*. Sam Shepard composed the music. It's heavy and angry." He turned, grunted, beat his chest, stomped off gorilla-like. He was getting serious; lean, ghostly pale, pretty, with long black hair, he was more reminiscent of an eighteenth century Romantic poet than a Rocker. This would work.

For the lead roles, the antagonists, I asked Alan Kealey, a towering, scraggled, blond haired powerhouse Viking of a youth to play Hoss, the tragic hero; Kevin Sheldon, a skinny, grizzled, wiry weasel dynamite of a youth took on the role of his nemesis, Crow, up from the gutter, challenging the king. Both of them played guitar. Both accepted my offer.

Hoss has a woman. Bernadine would play Becky, who in her final appearance "comes on down left facing the audience. She wears a black wig and is dressed like Anna Karina in *Alphaville*," my dream vision. David Turner, Peter Milnes, Ian Bryson and myself would take four smaller roles.

Hoss is an American tribal king; he has a sexy love interest and a retinue including a doctor who keeps him in drugs and a soothsayer who uses the pop charts to foretell his future. Hoss is worried; the times they are a-changing.

> HOSS: I'm surrounded by ass holes! Can't you see what's happened to us. We ain't Markers no more. We ain't' even Rockers. We're punk chumps cowering under the Keepers and the Refs and the critics and the public eye. We ain't free no more! Goddamn it! We ain't flyin' in the eye of contempt. We've become respectable and safe. Soft, mushy chewable ass lickers. What's happened to our killer heart. What's happened to our blind fucking courage! Cheyenne, we ain't got much time, man. We were warriors once.

Then he thinks himself to his own destruction. A marauding pack of gypsies are threatening his position. A crucial battle is looming, and Hoss fights it with an insolently unassailable young gypsy, Crow, who saunters into the throne room, exudes violent arrogance and cruises the stage with true contempt. He will annihilate Hoss in a savage rock music duel.

It is impossible to adequately describe the piece, the quality of the writing. You have to be there. Bare thought-fast staccato prose, a truly challenging language, drives the narrative. The action is unremitting, restless, often brutal; there is a kind of lunatic madness pulsing through, but it is gripping and thrilling in its music.

This was a most exciting new challenge that stretched us well beyond our comfort zones, a challenge which remained exhilarating and rewarding

in spite of rough patches and recurrent wobbles. They say if you can't swim don't jump in – but I had done, regardless of whether anyone else might be floundering. We were learning, a harsh process, but learning, and after relatively few rehearsals I felt we had a grasp on the material.

We were to perform in the Chapel Studio, and I had contacted local Youth Clubs, with prior notice of bad language and some moments of nakedness, after which I had arranged a short tour of University and College venues by contacting Student Unions.

After six performances at our home base which went well we met for a song refresher before the first touring gig to Bretton Hall College near Leeds, where Lorna Dexter, who worked with me on *The Tempest,* was studying for a Master's Degree in Performing Arts. It seemed like a big deal, a breakthrough for ACT.

Alan arrived last. He said he could not would not perform any more. He offered neither apology nor explanation, seemed disinclined or unable to acknowledge or honour the work of the cast as a whole. They say there are always three sides to a story: yours, the other person's, and the truth. In this instance I never got the other person's.

I've harboured the suspicion that it was something to do with me. I was always dependent on good will and often a certain level of sacrifice. I made efforts, no promises, and people came with me. I had pushed him no harder than anyone else and he had mastered the material, performed what is a massive part with seeming confidence.

HOSS: Yeah. You win all right. All this. Body and soul. All this invisible gold. All this collection of torture. It's all yours. You're the winner and I'm the loser. That's the way it stands. But I'm losin' big, Crow Bait. I'm losin' to the big power. All the way. I couldn't take my life in my hands while I was alive but now I can take it in death. I'm a born Marker Crow Bait. That's more than you'll ever be. Now stand back and watch some true style. The mark of a lifetime. A true gesture that won't never cheat on itself 'cause it's the last of its kind. It can't be taught or copied or stolen or sold. It's mine. An original. It's my life and my death in one clean shot.

(HOSS turns his back to the audience. And puts the gun in his mouth. He raises one hand high in the air and pulls the trigger with the other. He falls in a heap. This gesture should not be in slow motion or use any jive theatrical gimmicks other than the actor's own courage on stage. To save the actor's face from powder burns an off-stage gun should be fired at the right moment. CROW stands silent for a while.)

So! – something else to learn from. It was a loss. I determined to take on board this fact and not let it happen again. We moved on. Our next project would be *City Sugar*.

Mick moved on. Thirty years later I met him; Margot was seriously ill and I couldn't talk comfortably, but it was a real pleasure to meet again. He told me, insisted, that after all these years of professional music making, the most exciting he had ever played was that in *Tooth of Crime*.

Best Intentions – Gone Awry

CITY SUGAR, Stephen Poliakoff

DON'T!
Don't,
Don't,
Don't!
John!!

But he did!

Hargreaves! damn you! and your fucking temper!

A large tin of paint, white emulsion, is hurtled across the set, the lid spinning off spewing a spurl of white, a trail splattered everywhere. Peter jumps aside, targeted, stark red flushed face, tall, yelling. Bryson sits motionless, quiet, contained, pale. Tim moves aside. Dave, sound engineer, unplugs equipment, cradles it protectively and, cautiously glancing, almost crouched, leaves the theatre. Miranda, the quiet one, quiet, sucking her thumb. Betsy Rayner, who fucks like a mule, wide-eyed, tearful, after so many hours of concentrated effort and devotion to the task. Hilary stands tense, shocked. The girls have worked so hard.

And I make, what now seems, the wrong decision.

After fulfilling short tour commitments in Derbyshire, *City Sugar* has returned to our home base, the Chapel Studio, for a final week of performances.

Stephen Poliakoff was a new young playwright, East Midlands based, and I was keen to do a contemporary piece. This script proved to be particularly interesting being a very apposite and early consideration of the possible negative consequences of the public's involvement in broadcast media. A context that now, more than thirty years later, has become an important and necessary feature of television and radio.

In *City Sugar* a local radio presenter involves, manipulates, humiliates and cheats three young women who respond to a dodgy competition offer in the early days of local radio broadcasting.

It was a great script to direct.

The lead actor (Ian Bryson) plays a brash, over-flash, egotistic and harshly cruel disc jockey. He has to master the fast, glib repartee and cynicism of the part whilst operating a twin-deck DJ console, switching mics, drinking, smoking and handling the interruptions of both an over-enthusiastic newsreader and a young over-serious studio assistant.

The three working class girls live together in shambolically cramped shared accommodation and work in a large local supermarket, this last being a particularly novel idea in the mid-1970s when supermarkets were just beginning to become the dominant source of daily shopping.

John Hargreaves – a great friend and wonderful visionary stage designer – had worked with me to devise a tightly coherent set that in a single small confined square space fixed the three distinct settings required. Along the back the grey toned radio studio was set on a long narrow raised section, tightly lit with a cooling deadening wash. Below it, side by side, was the warmly lit, colourfully shabby jumbled and cramped living room and beside that the stark bright supermarket represented by the clean, hard, white lines of an immense freezer chest and adjacent till point. The items were kindly donated by the local Co-operative store – a truly co-operative gesture.

This was their world, *City Sugar*, all of them locked together, fixed, with the audience on three sides, as close as possible, as if they were there in the studio, the supermarket, the room, flies on the wall.

We were pleased with the production; it played well and was very well received, especially by student audiences. After mastering the complications of 'live radio broadcasting' on stage, it was great to discover that the three girls, all teenagers, were perfectly cast to fit the individual roles of gauche/knowing naivety and determination the script required. So the arrival at our base the Chapel Studio with a well-bedded production was to be the icing on our cake.

On the morning of our return I was at an Arts Panel meeting in Loughborough while the technical crew were preparing for the evening performance. Early afternoon we gathered for a quick check/run. And there, centre stage, was a different freezer chest awkward, irregular, cardboard, on a wooden frame, panels sagging, lid ill-fitting, being painted with white emulsion paint . . .

What happened?

We couldn't get it in.

Couldn't get it . . . Tim?

We couldn't. It's too long.

Put it on end.

D-d-did – it's too big, won't twist, we got help, took a door off, it's heavy, weighs a ton. WOULDN'T COME IN! So we built this.

But that's emulsion Tim!

Gloss wouldn't dry in time.

What about the dry ice?

Your problem!

And the other door? Through the YMCA canteen?

Yes, we did, while you were poncing off at a meeting.

It looks awful.

We know that. We have eyes as well as you.

And they're right and I believe them and I should thank them for their efforts. But, "Ian, phone Hargreaves" I say.

And when John arrived HELL really broke loose. I know not how but within five minutes raging Hargreaves chucked the nearest thing to hand, chucked it at Peter's head . . . Peter still held the paint brush in his hand . . . A large tin of paint, white emulsion, is hurtled across the set, the lid spinning off spewing . . .

Some moments of mutual, shared, shocked silence offer, offer a pause.

And my decision was to close down the production, end it, refund ticket sales, draw a line. But Hilary argued; we could clear up, there'd never be another chance, emulsion paint washes out, she'd take stuff home to wash overnight, her mum would help, we'd find a solution, carry on in a couple of days. We can still do it. I love it, her attitude.

She had character in spades, had been wonderful to work with, in NEYPDT and now here, so ready, always forward thinking and she was, I now think, right. But at that time, that space, that little self-contained world of radio station, workplace and home that we had filled with creative action, was now so filled with rage and violence and fraught taut frustrations that the only sure thing was to call a halt. (Prove my power?) It's a measure of my unnaturally privileged position that there was no commercial imperative to continue. I did close the show.

Hargreaves wrote a letter to each of us, an identical letter, hand delivered. It was an explanation, a justification rather than an apology, in which he proposed that only the highest standards of presentation and setting, the quality of the spaces in which we played were of paramount importance and essential to the success of our work. That is a designer's position. I always told actors that if we got it right (and mostly, even from the very beginning, we did get it right) they could confidently 'be there', in an empty space, wearing string vests and Y-fronts, and still hold the audience. I truly believe this, but never put it to the test of actuality.

Hilary Ellis, who I so admired, never worked with me again. We lost it. She rode a motor bike, wore leathers, the lot, and in a collision a few months later crushed her leg. She was on crutches the last time we met, quiet, introspective, but lovely. And I was embarrassed, wanting to touch her, being nice, but not telling her she was right as I had not yet realised it.

The world is strange – filled with the most odd serendipity. I never used the men's underground lavatory in Chesterfield but once. I bolted the closet door, unhitched my trousers, sat down, and there at eye level, crudely bold graffiti – "Betsy Rayner fucks like a mule": a different note of exploitation.

Truth. Slant.

Very Hard Work with Sam, Will and Bill

IMAGINATION DEAD IMAGINE

NOT I

KRAPP'S LAST TAPE – Samuel Becket

KING LEAR - William Shakespeare

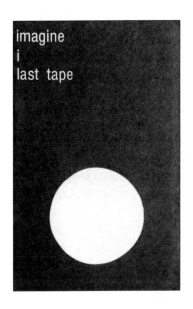

Bill Mc Donnel is a small man, balding, with a husky strong voice, his gestures strong and eloquent as were his words. He was rigorous by nature, committed to theatre and radical socialist values. He had a light-hearted but ultimately stubborn seriousness about him that frequently challenged, enriched, my more maverick exploratory approach to the creation of theatre. We worked hard together, and had worked with Bernadine to prepare *The Surangini Tales*, a selection of simply adapted morally uplifting thought provoking Indian stories for presentation to primary schools. In the process of completing a hundred and nine performances, sometimes three a day, by far the longest run of any ACT production, we were in the mood for a change. Some light relief!

I had been reading Samuel Becket for years; he remains one of my four canonical touchstones of dramatic literature alongside Homer, Shakespeare and Chekhov. Bill was similarly interested by Becket. We decided to tackle three of his pieces, to be performed as a continuous sequence in a structured environment within the black space of the Small Studio. I had never seen a live production of a Becket play, which I felt to be an advantage, making the process an even more intriguingly fascinating prospect. With limited funds and resources we could not meet every exacting standard Becket expected in productions of his work, but I felt we could certainly honour the diegesis, the nature of his writings.

Bill, who had strong ideas about the way he wished to approach the character and prepare the tapes, performed *Krapp's Last Tape*. After shared discussions he prepared all the groundwork himself, my contribution being to offer him support through the final rehearsals. Although in his early 30s Bill's appearance was ageless, and his acting dynamic suited the despairing fragility of the character as he recaptures dislocated memories of his life on an ancient tape deck. A shuffling old man who bumbles around the stage eating bananas, fussing with his belongings and glorying in the sound of the word 'spooool'. Bill's finger frantic manipulations of spools and switches, the clunk as the tape head engaged, and his wildly squint eye, created a pitch of authentically troubled engagement. *Krapp's Last Tape* is a much gentler work than Becket's earlier writing, the despair is tinged more with sadness than despair, and there is an overwhelming sense of emotion which Bill was able to evoke. Someone whose judgement I trust regarded it as an outstanding individual performance.

I suggested to Bernadine that she take the role of Mouth in *Not I*, the wonderful and very difficult monologue of an old woman spouting pieces of apparently unconnected personal information. The piece is only sixteen minutes long when played at the exhausting rapid tempo that the playwright expects. It is like running five sub four minute miles in quick succession. The original British performance was by Billie Whitelaw whose commitment to Becket's later work was total and unforgiving. She has written a description of preparing *Not I* in her autobiography *Billie Whitelaw... Who He?* which is the most interesting book by an actor I have read. Being a Yorkshire lass, spending her adolescence but a few miles from mine on Otley Chevin, Becket found her broad natural accent fitted the role, choosing that rather than the Irish brogue he had intended. So there was no contest. Bernadine was from Yorkshire, and of the many people with whom I worked is the only one I would have felt confident in facing with this task. I asked difficult things of many actors over the years but none, perhaps, more demanding than this.

As with a number of early productions I am not quite sure how we got there. *Not I* has five sequences and we worked on them successively, insisting on keeping the Mouth anonymous but real, reflecting/refracting a scrabble of inner thoughts without any overt expressive intent. Its telling of the inner life of a woman of seventy years of age who recalls a life of premature birth, mechanical survival and avoidance of herself whilst repeatedly insisting that she is sixty. The speed of it is essential – thoughts flash by like lightning. Apparently a German production contrived to make it last forty-five minutes and it simply became a boring tirade. The speed of it is what makes the audience's experience so gripping and thrilling even if puzzled. Becket said.

> "I am not unduly concerned with intelligibility. I hope the piece would work on the necessary emotions of the audience, rather than appealing to their intellect."

The strain the piece puts on the actor is increased by the fact that she cannot, must not move. All the audience should see is the Mouth tightly lit by a sharp spot. After a number of experimental attempts we found we couldn't achieve this in our space. We failed in that respect, compromising with Bernadine's barely visible, perfectly motionless black draped body on a small podium. I admired the way she worked on this text and the end result she achieved enormously.

The opening piece of the trio was *Imagination Dead Imagine*, a prose text, my favourite example of Becket's writing. I used it to inaugurate the works we were performing and the environment we inhabited. Joyce Bryson joined me to create a short movement sequence, and Charles Monkhouse created two sculptures. The first a large circular plaster cast of our two linked bodies – a crèche with two tight held, skin tight, foetally close curled bodies lying head to foot and lit in a strong beam of white light directly above. A recording of the text was played, towards its end the figures rose from their 'womb', and after a short mime/movement sequence the male left the playing area, the female climbed into the suspended net structure of the second sculpture having left one form of containment to enter another to become the Auditor of *Not I*, a figure in an attitude of intense waiting who occasionally reaches out and flaps her arms with a sense of helpless compassion.

Few people saw this production. We were unsure about how to promote it and it wouldn't tour. I'd like to think that those who did attend found it memorable even if difficult. Working on it was both revealing and rewarding, as was our next joint venture. More light relief!

We began work on *King Lear*

> Brutal, awe inspiring, blood spattered and occasionally
> unendurable, King Lear provides a sweeping landscape of world
> shaking generational conflict and miscalculation. All that remains
> at the end of this gigantic pantomime is the earth – empty and
> bleeding. (Fintan O'Toole: Shakespeare is Hard, but so is Life.)

Before joining me, Bill had toured parts of Communist Eastern Europe performing a three man and three chairs production of *King Lear* with Stephen Rumbelow's Triple Action Theatre. Stephen had filmed his version of *Joan of Arc* in the Arts Centre and there had been plans for him to be integrated into our working context, so I knew his approach to theatre – tense, bleak, harsh and unrelentingly powerful drama achieved with minimum means.

When I suggested we should produce our *Lear*, using the shortened version that Triple Action had worked with, Bill was very keen – more so when I suggested he play Lear, the role which had not been his on the previous occasion. I didn't, however, wish to replicate that production, it wasn't my style. I suggested that rather than having three chairs we should have three actresses: two would play Goneril and Regan and Edmund and Edgar and the third Cordelia. My choices were already prepared, one was an aspiring actor who had taken the young convict's role in *Female Transport*. The second was a Fashion student who had some experience of amateur acting and would work with me to design the costumes as a Course work project. The third was a Fine Art student, a talented painter who I didn't know. She was very beautiful with the most stunning long long black hair imaginable. I had this vision. The end of the play is so important. Lear, a small man, carries forward his dead youngest daughter hair trailing loose to the ground, he drops to the ground beside her, his fingers tangling in the hair, wrapping it round his anguished tear streaming face:

No. No. No life?

Why should a dog, a horse, a rat have life,

And thou no breath at all? Thou'lt come no more.

Never, never, never, never, never!

Pray you undo this button: thank you, sir.

Do you see this? Look on her, look, her lips,

Look there, look there!   HE DIES

Read that, and who wouldn't take the part of Cordelia?

I would play Gloucester and the Fool.

And the performances would be very physical, the violence telling, the madness cruel and the ending sublime. We would communicate how Lear begins in simplicity, grows into a sense of knowledge and sophistication, finds madness, is cured and transcends it. His life's journey marked by traces of the parallel plot line tracing the complementary trajectory of Gloucester and his son Edgar.

Bill was all for plainness and straight telling. I wanted shape, depth, rich visual definition. We had our differences. It was hard work. I got Hargreaves to build us an open sided box frame out of rusted scaffold poles, its dimensions corresponding to those of the Golden Mean. Set inside, another small open box form in shiny bright scaffolding, would have Golden Mean dimensions whilst maintaining that same relationship to the outer frame.

So we had the Perfect Space within which the hell, anarchy and madness could run loose. And that Perfect Space would be set just off centre in the Black Studio to allow enough room for an audience of thirty-six on three sides.

The actors, excepting Cordelia, would never leave the outer frame which became something to clamber on, swing from, smash against, whilst the smaller one became a throne, a hovel, the cliffs of Dover, a table, a bier. The space cried out for adventuring, there was no safe place within it, as a precisely manipulated lighting sequence focussed and illuminated points of action.

All this was the sum of broad ideas that would prop up our work. Bill had a brilliantly specific idea for the opening scene which became the iconic idiom that defined the look and much of the action of the production. As the play started the old King Lear would be standing central overwhelmed by the massively, extravagantly oversized cloak he wore. A cloak textured with knotting, hillocks, rips, stratification, earth bound colours. This was the land he offered to his daughters. Thirds were ripped apart for Goneril and Regan, and these thirds became their domains, to hold aloft, spread forth, drape from the scaffold, symbols of power, cuddled and cosseted.

The third that Cordelia refused to accept lay trampled underfoot, a thing to hide under for shelter, to stagger across stumbling horrendously blinded, a Blasted Heath, and the place to which you bring a dead daughter.

Bill knew the script so well he led the work on developing the performances whilst I managed the staging. There were still frequent, relatively amicable, differences, Bill believing that I was urging theatricality and visual impact at the expense of text, and he was right to a certain extent. But for me, a true and honest performance of the text remained necessarily the strong anchored base presence through which the action was played out. The performance of the words that had to be understood remained paramount.

In spite of their inexperience the actresses, nineteen/twenty year olds, proved able to make themselves fearsomely strong when necessary. They took to the space, and were helped by their costumes and make-up. We practised and encouraged them relentlessly to concentrate on speaking the meaning of their lines, finding that there was little need to worry about trying to make arbitrary differences between the male and female roles they played. As actors we encouraged them to 'be the story' without finesse of characterisation. This may sound either silly or impossible to understand! But with hard work we made it work without insisting on gruffly masculine voices or false moustaches when they played Edgar and Edmund.

And me? My heart was in it, I loved the effort! But a part of my mind was elsewhere. I was preparing The Brecht Event. I would direct and play *Arturo Ui*. The Germans were coming and would see both productions, *Lear* and *Ui*, and meanwhile Bill was preparing *The Threepenny Opera* with Nedypt. That was causing headaches and frustrations. I spent quite some time trying to pacify Charles Monkhouse who was building him a massive boat sculpture set in the Dome over which neither of them would compromise.

So, I slip in these facts to help explain, if not excuse, the fact that my Fool was rather superficial and I did rely too much on physicality, insufficiently on dredging up a true nature. I enjoyed and felt more settled in the role of Gloucester, there was a real dreadfilled excitement about the being blind. Yet, I was not totally there, not right there where I could/should have been. I was still very much in the process of learning about acting.

For Bill, his was the dream part, he played it as he chose, largely, and with his dynamic commitment carried the burden of the production with real guts and aplomb.

I wonder, would Shakespearian purists still regard us as ridiculous and sacrilegious for reducing the script to one hour and thirty minutes of continuous playing time, with two young men playing the main roles and even younger and inexperienced beginners playing dual male/female roles? I wonder?

I hope not, and recall the T. S.Eliot quotation at the end of *Macbeth for Beginners*. **The Empty Space,** the account of theatre practice by Peter Brook that I read in the 1960's was a particularly potent influence on my work. On Shakespeare he writes:

"I do not for one moment question the principle of rewriting Shakespeare – after all the texts do not get burnt... finding and conveying Shakespeare's meaning is the goal of a production, and that such meaning resides less in the text per se than in the essential living heart of the play – the poetic inner dream."

Everyone has the right to grapple with the greatest dramatic writing in the language on their own terms in the circumstances in which they find themselves and then share their discoveries in performance. We worked to the highest standards we could achieve. You only get one throw at these things and so you have to make them good. Maybe I should have waited for a clearer space, but it was a thrilling challenge, the attempt to get to the inner dream :

the thing itself, unaccommodated man,

no more but such a poor bare forked... (animal as thou art.)

Given the resources available to us and the external pressures of the Brecht Event that we were preparing we produced two unusual and challenging pieces of theatre. Our intention had been to build both pieces minute by minute and I believe we did achieve the effect we aimed for. Our audiences responded positively and generously. The Germans loved it. They were thrilled. They invited me to take my work to Darmstadt so that many more people could experience it. Which I did for twelve years.

It had been very hard work with Bill, Will and Sam, but well worth it. Well, well worth it.

A brown finger of suede

ON GREAT IDEAS! and INSECURITY

People asked?

    and I would say: Theatre Director.

        or sometimes: Director of an Arts Centre.

        (the frequently more time-consuming supporting role)

Theatre people asked?

    and I would say: I wasn't trained.

        (actors are trained like horses, greyhounds, athletes)

But how? people asked

    and I would say: I had the job so I did it, "not trying to prove I'm right, but to find out whether".

        (as Brecht would say).

And? people asked

    and I might mention: Cambridge University.

        (where many theatre directors have started.)

But deep down? people asked

    and I might say: Artistic Director.

        (but remain hopelessly self-conscious about seriously defining myself as such, except in semi-mocking exchanges with close friends and colleagues.)

    Artistic!?

And people asked?

    And I would say: Insecurity? Ah!

But why? people asked

    and I confess – my nature, the work is who I am.

        (But the real me is very wary.)

Employed by Arthur Pears, the visionary Principal of Chesterfield College of Art and Design, the very first provincial art school to be established in England, to develop Theatre at all levels throughout the county of Derbyshire, I was introduced into what for me was a wholly new context of painters, sculptors, printmakers, photographers, ceramicists, graphic, fashion and 3D designers, print technology, painting and decorating, beauty therapy and hairdressing. Each creative professional set standards which were both inspiring and challenging. The excitements of the late Sixties were still in the air, people's expectations of themselves and their art were changing. The place buzzed with an anarchic artistic but positive dynamism, enhanced by the prospect of a new purpose-built college. I was to be a part of this new initiative, and faced initial difficulties as I was introducing an entirely new area of work which, in the minds of some conservative elements, threatened to deplete their resources.

It took time.

Two years.

But ultimately I received the most wonderfully generous support from these people who defined their lives and work by the words ARTIST and ART. I realised that their environment suited me, and the work I wished to do, far better than a purely theatrically focused coterie would have done.

So? people might ask

and I would say: having neither particular talent, skill, nor god-given gift I made no claim to being an artist. So . . .

Yes? . . .

and I would say : apart from doing stuff, being there, having a good eye, and a way with words and persuasive enthusiasm I was a Nul. But a Nul who, like Brecht "was not trying to . . ." I repeat the phrase often; it covers all manner of insecurities.

And?

And I would finally admit, rather disparagingly, but that could be a clever ploy, that one way I came to modestly justify my 'artistic' credentials

was

quite simply

GREAT IDEAS!

GREAT IDEAS! were but one defining feature of my stock in trade. They brought a kind of naughty magic and delightful enrichment to dodgy moments. They never drew cheap laughter, but rather ribald gaiety, if not awed shock surprise, and contributed much to that sense of danger which must not disappear.

How to explain or understand intellectually how or where a GREAT IDEA! originates? Somewhat like the Big Bang theory of the origin of the Universe, it is suddenly, unexpectedly, but indubitably there. A recent book discusses this phenomenon arguing that those sudden blink of an eye unthought-out moments of blindingly obvious realisation will usually, perhaps always, have greater validity, be more useful, than any number of agonised over, elaborately justified solutions or decisions. Lost, stuck, blocked, my instinct was to Blink. It's like Dada.

It's the Light Bulb Factor. Whenever something quick and special might be required a light bulb flashes over Popeye's head. He downs a can of spinach and solves the problem. I would not dream of putting any of my just saved from insecurity moments on a par with Newton and his apple or Aristotle and his bath, but they were a reliable aid to resolving all manner of unforeseen problems. So often I knew, I just knew, what move was right, what gesture necessary, what image to fine tune, what communication to redefine. So frequently, venturing into a new territory, some sense of insecurity was hauntingly hovering. How far can I push them? How mad is this? Will the centre hold?

They think they understand it now. Thank God for the anterior superior temporal gyrus. We all have one; it's a small nugget on the right side of the brain just above the ear which apparently triggers Eureka moments.

The Comanche war arrow's twang! thud quivering into the log cabin wall was utterly unexpected, as was the suggestion that Caliban should rip off Miranda's frock, and these qualify as GREAT IDEAS!

Some derive from the existing pre-conditions of a narrative situation or working process. Such a one was the *Sossages for all* caper that came to be in ACT's second venture into Ken Campbell territory. The two main protagonists in *Old King Kole* engage and cope with every outrageously chaotic situation in which they find themselves by opening their enormous Paraphernalia Bag and taking out whichever bizarre object might be relevant to their getting 'out of a fix' whilst repeatedly whispering or snarling or joking or yelling "SOSSAGES!" at one another or at the audience or at me.

I blinked, and decided that every young child in our audiences, as well as young-at-heart adults, should be provided with a small replica Paraphernalia Bag programme filled with all manner of bits and bobs: a piece of string tightly knotted, a knob of plasticine, a paper clip half straightened, a secret code with a rude, naughty message 'u r a sosij ha ha', a complicated diagram, a rubber band, a printed certificate of paraphernalia competency, some used matchsticks and a cooked sausage, a small turd-like, sometimes grilled to a frazzle, sausage, hygienically wrapped in cling film of course.

At the point in the performance where every one agreed that they were very very very hungry the Paraphernalia Bag was opened and they took out large thick juicily succulent sausages and invited the audience to join THE SOSSAGE FEAST HOORAY!!

BIGGLES

Some kids gobbled with gusto, some wrinkled noses and nibbled reluctantly; sensible girls gave their sossage to their dad. An obvious zany extension to the mad caper, it was fun, unsettling and iffy. A Campbellesque tribute to the irreplaceable Ken.

Our saga, *Biggles* which invented new adventures for the renowned heroic British airman and his crew, was rich in GREAT IDEAS! We had prepared some well-plotted skeletal scripts filled with derring-do, wicked women and the highest of high drama, but they were lacking verbal richness and hooks for characterisation. Shakespeare provided these in the first two tales. Flying Officer Bigglesworth met each unlikely situation and every dastardly enemy with endless fittingly apt quotations delivered with assured aplomb to the wide-eyed amazement of both his chums and the darned attractive, but poisonous as snakes, female enemies. Occasionally Ginger tried to match the leader's quotes; whilst he, as one would expect of an officer and gentleman, remained officer class dismissive of Ginger's efforts.

In the third adventure, when Biggles and Co. are parachuted into Nazi-occupied France to make contact with the Resistance, I wanted to develop a darker, even threatening tone. On this sortie Biggles quoted, and mis-quoted, many of the sardonic film noir lines of Humphrey Bogart's Casablanca Rick including the "hill of beans" and of course "the need to do or die as time goes by". Play it, Sam. Play it again. So noble, so enduring.

The franglais the three of them spoke was a natural comic consequence of the storyline and a very effective counter to highlight the darker tone I was aiming for – the make 'em laugh, make 'em cry effect – but does not really qualify as a great idea.

However

The waterboarding sequence does.

Years before that vile practice became a major political issue regarding the ethics of torture at the time of the Second Iraq War, Squadron Leader Biggles was captured by three female Nazi double agents and suffered that very fate. The weakened, bedraggled, near broken British airman was dragged by those devilishly seductive turncoat women, with one of whom he had danced a passionate Parisian Apache dance moments earlier, to a tub of water. His head was forced under, he was held down, pushed deeper. After minutes he was wrenched out, drenched and gulping; fighting for air he was plunged back under water for further minutes after refusing to divulge the top secret contact code ("Avez-vous un crayon bien pointu"), or the name of the Resistance agent (Marcel: who wore a beret and smoked endless Gauloises). The procedure was repeated several times. Audiences paled, appalled. Strong men blanched. The kindly lady landlord of the Horsehouses pub which we frequented during our tours of the Yorkshire Dales accused me, as I ordered our after-show drinks, of "mistreating that young lad like that, you could do him harm".

"But missus, I never touched him! and I agree with your every word – after all I was the contact, I was Marcel".

Paul Sansom had a splendid pair of lungs and a splendidly positive attitude. Little did the landlord lady know, but Margot had punctured Paul's eardrum in Edinburgh whilst beating him up in the blizzardy wastes of Siberia. He continued to perform valiantly, wearing a pair of ear plugs for which he duly submitted a petty cash claim.

Some GREAT IDEAS! can be very simple but significant in their effect. In *Female Transport*, the distressingly realistic account of a convict ship transporting women to Australia, the first mate and cabin boy have an upper deck night-time conversation by candlelight whilst their cargo of female convicts sleeps restlessly and fearfully below. The scene was not working in rehearsal, it remained banal and unfocused, it was an initiation of sorts and needed a trigger to create bonding between the awkwardness of the adolescent and the grizzled knowledge of the seaman.

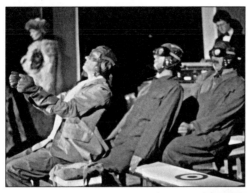

"Tattoo him! Alan! Get proddling needles, heat them in the candle flame, pots of ink, a rag and a bottle of rum. Choose an image: you're sailors, an anchor, a mermaid, a big fish or Mother. Work at the sequence with real – I mean REAL – interaction, prick his flesh, make him wince. Pace it with the words. Don't rush. They'll just sleep more. Gary – BOY! – it's down to you."

It became a quietly felt intense scene of mutual concentration and stillness that gave balance and, strangely, a sense of shared humanity to the whole cruel drama. The cabin-boy was in love with one of the convicts, the first mate had traded food for sex with another. The scene convinced and held the audience. The idea came from nowhere.

Other GREAT IDEAS! had a different, deeper importance.

Dawn joined ACT. A talented 18-year-old gymnast, physically very brave, she was hurt inside, held unhappiness inside her; she seemed damaged, her home life too difficult to express, and brought a deep-seated mix of reluctance and desire for something to give meaning to her life. She had wanted to die.

At workshops she broke through some barriers and showed promise in her acting. One night she sat beside me reluctant to leave, "I live to be here," she said, holding back tears. She took a couple of small parts and then I cast her in *Nana* as the jiminy-cricket-like dominatrix maid-servant severely disapproving of yet desiring the blatant devil-may-care sexuality of her mistress. We dressed her in an appropriately tight-fitting high-collared drab black dress with hair drawn and knotted painfully tight. Booted, wan faced, thin lipped, without make-up, scissors and keys hung from her waist, a crucifix on her bosom. She looked hateful. Perhaps it was too real, too close to the bone. In rehearsal she struggled, but could establish no connection with the character, and eventually asked in weary defeat if she could drop out of the production.

I have no idea why there was a piece of hexagonal mesh chicken wire on the Studio floor, but there it was, misshapen, in the corner. Nor have I any idea of how or why the naughty magic blessed us, but, without discussion, I fashioned a crude jagged brassiere out of it and strapped it around Dawn. It fitted, in every sense: she almost snarled, caged, as she returned to work. She knew who she was. It was her. She wore this same outside underwear contraption with self-assured pride for every performance. It bore no relation to any other costume decision, but enhanced the Egon Schiele erotic, bizarre, note I was looking for.

Sometimes, writing, I shake my head in wonder. I admired Dawn's honesty and guts, and was proud that we made it through.

A brown finger of suede is the GREAT IDEA! which was recognised and appreciated by a paltry dozen people at most. It leaves me most intrigued.

I had enjoyed, and hated, the grittily distasteful early novels of Martin Amis, and, because of that very mixed response, had considered adapting *Dead Babies*, in which the lead character at one point picks up a recently worn pair of his girlfriend's panties and notices a brown finger of suede smeared along the gusset. It is such a Jonathan Swiftian "But Celia shits" moment, leaving one tremulously balanced between embarrassingly perverse thrill at such intimate knowledge and grossed out emetic disgust.

In *Slab Boys* Hector played by Marcus Pickering, is the youngest new apprentice in the dye mixing shop of a carpet factory and is the butt of unrelenting mockery and bullying by his three young workmates. In one scene he is locked out of the workplace without his trousers and desperately tries to climb back in, arse up, through a small window. I told him he needed a brown finger of suede, clearly visible, in just that right part of his grubby baggily loose underpants. Marcus agreed. As he struggles to climb through the window, the other lads fight to keep him out or trap him in the frame. The encounter was not choreographed as would be normal practice, but I let it be played out for real, as I did for so much of this production, one of those that ran away from me.

Inevitably, only those few members of the audience sitting directly opposite the window had any chance to see both fat cheeks of his bum and the brown stain between. Amid all the chaotic wrangling it was very difficult for Marcus to get his backside into the right position.

In a book, every reader has access to every word, every listener has access to every note of a piece of music, and at a movie every watcher can see every single image. But it is a conceit unique to theatre that some of its mysteries and delights may be the reserved privilege of a lucky few members of an audience.

The lucky few? I will always remember one sublimely special moment when I watched the faces of two young women whose eyes popped, jaws dropped and mouths gaped, gawped with simultaneous oh my god shock horror before bursting into helpless giggles as Hector clambered back onto the workbench. Even the rest of the cast never knew that we shared this great idea.

People asked?

now, two decades later, I recall with mixed feelings some of my decisions.

(Overall, I am glad I made them. Overall I would have wished to be more bold.)

My work depended on instincts, emotions and feelings. Sometimes I did not trust them enough, or failed to recognise them. But all in all we achieved a standard.

I wonder.

Perhaps in years to come, when I will be really old, I will lie awake, wondering, then realising I will never know, nor need to know, whether the suede finger was real shit, his shit, or a dark coffee stain, or brown paint.

Insecurity?

So it goes.

Ah! Enough.

Simon says: Where are the Wankers?

A MAD WORLD MY MASTERS – Barry Keefe
(after Thomas Middleton)

That's not nice, Simon.

Simon says: You don't do nice, Jack!

I know that. But nor do I do wanking on stage.

Simon says : What I mean is – everything is Wonderful, brilliant casts, stunning performances, great ideas. Where's the rubbish, the Wankers?

But, I don't want to bad mouth anyone, Simon.

Simon says: There must have been some Wallys, Wastrels, Whingers, Wet blankets, Wallpaper. There always are.

What is it with you and the W's? Slow down, Simon.

Simon says: I just think you need to seek a balance. You did ask my opinion.

And I appreciate everything you say, Simon. Of course there were disappointments. Some few didn't fit. One or two hated me. Another few were uncommitted, or couldn't hack it – we worked under pressure. Others realised they couldn't act. Inexperience glared often. But as for W's, not really. A few Wannabe fame seekers, but all in all the vast vast majority gave their all, some for many years, exceeded all expectations. It was a blessed way to work.

Simon smiles, nods, understanding – perhaps.

A tiny spark switched to gleam in my head.

Simon, I says, I give you a story. You want Wankers – and I give you a whole load of them, all together, bunched, a whole cast, myself included. It's a story that wanders, but I think it's a good one. You have the time for a story?

He is dashing off to collect his younger daughter from playschool. I tell the story anyway.

It is 1977, the Centennial of Chesterfield College of Art and Design. One hundred years old, the College is proud to have been the first municipal sponsored College of Art in provincial England, and wants to celebrate in style. They have asked me to work with the Fashion Department to create a show of the period fashions of the past ten decades with ten appropriate scenes, songs, dances and narration. The costumes will be designed and created by the Fashion Department. Graphic and 3D students will do design. Beauty Therapy will provide make up and beautiful models. Painting and Decorating will paint the set. And participants will be volunteers, students who wish to play a short role, say a few words, learn to dance or march for the First World War Sequence, and they all must sing. Bet Heathfield will choreograph the dances. Dave Brierley will drill the military. There will be Queen Victoria, a sexy tango, fifties bopping, elegant gents, twenties Charlestons, a surreal scene, modern art influences, sixties styling, with colour everywhere and lots of movement, and bubbles and balloons, dry ice and a mirror ball, magic moments, non-stop for just over an hour, all punctuated, complemented, by short serious items to create a moving narrative historical context for the jollifications.

The idea catches fire and I get swept up in it. In all honesty it becomes an ego trip. I show off shamelessly, flirt outrageously, shout and cajole excessively. It works! They give me a whip-cracking long leather-weave whip afterwards in recognition of all my exertions. That kind of thing never happened to me! I decide ACT should offer a production as part of the celebrations: something very much about the late 1970s, now, this time of our lives.

Barrie Keefe's contemporary version of Thomas Middleton's *A Mad World My Masters* is the obvious choice. It is raucous, dodgy, satirical and daring, a plunge into corrupt politicking, greed and incompetence, double dealing and graft, totally anti-Establishment. We decide to lace it with Ian Dury's music, its rawness and beat, songs like *Reasons to be Cheerful* and *Hit me, hit, hit me with your rhythm stick*. It cries out for speed and rapidity. And simplicity, especially in the circumstances in which we are preparing it – little time, no money.

We will draw a large chalk circle in the centre of the hall and space ten distinctly different chairs around its perimeter. These chairs will be the 'home base' for each character. Two black screens set back will serve for quick changes and surprise entrances. The Barley Mow, our favourite rough and ready pub, will provide the bar and ply the audience with Ward's Best Sheffield Bitter, no poncey drinks allowed. The audience will be seated, Cabaret style, at small tables around the playing area. Informal and hard hitting, we will open after the last presentation of the Fashion Extravaganza, starting at 10pm and finishing at midnight.

It was tricky doing both simultaneously, but we were making good progress. The ACT group were experienced and needed little direct direction. One problem arose, the casting of two minor female characters. One involved impersonating the Queen, about four minutes on stage – and the one person I knew who was perfect for the part, a mature but insecure student who looked and dressed like H.M., refused to play the role. The other character, in a more demanding and slightly longer role, had to impersonate Angela Rippon, the tall, elegantly sophisticated, first woman to read the news on BBC television, who had recently and famously ripped off her long skirt revealing two beautiful long long legs to the awestruck amazement of Eric Morecombe and Ernie Wise on their wonderful and popular TV comedy show. And there was a Beauty Therapy student, tall and elegant with the features of Angela Rippon. She was the twenty years old flaming Queen of Tango partnered in the Fashion Show with handsome Farouk, the equally tall, intriguingly rich and mysterious Egyptian graphic student. And she said Yes!

I gave her a script to take home for the weekend. She returned on Monday saying her father forbade her to have anything to do with such filth and trash. Apparently he was a Colonel in the British Army based at Catterick Barracks. And he was right, it was filth and trash, it trashed the Establishment right or wrong, but it also held truths, broad brush contemporary truths about society, English society and its power bases, just as did Middleton's original version written nearly four centuries earlier.

I was too pre-occupied to take on the might of the British Army and let the matter drop. With barely two weeks to go I was in a fix, with no idea where to find appropriate actors. Fix, fix, fix!

Then I contacted Jonette who had played Gonzago in The Tempest four years earlier. She was small and a good character actor, she could play the Queen, impersonate her. She said she'd help me out if she could get baby sitters. I'll pay for them I promised recklessly, and then, "Will you play Angela Rippon as well?" Her burst of jeering laughter left me feeling doubtful. "You thinking I'm joking?" I asked, "It's a mad world." Eventually, quite quickly I suppose, she agreed, after we had negotiated an arrangement concerning disrobing as well as baby sitting cover. I had not previously mentioned that in Keefe's version of the play Angela cast off far more than her skirt.

Problem solved, after a fashion. They were small, tricky parts, a chicken feed challenge for Jonette. We worked on her approach to the roles. When she had her costumes, we played around with a variety of interpretations, nothing too precise, but I was happy and she seemed so. Her strip tease went just far enough to be naughtily cheeky. She came to a full cast rehearsal to meet the group, my raggle taggle gang of strong-minded individualists who, strangers to Jonette, probably appeared to be the worst of cod-amateurs as they played their scenes in a haphazard rackety seeming way. The play needed this texture; they were serious and I had confidence they could pull it off. Jonette's work slotted in nicely, and I was pleased with what she had created and told her so.

There would be a full final run through the evening before the first night. I warned the cast it might be a long one.

After supervising the fashion extravaganza's afternoon performance, I arrived early for ACT. They were waiting, ready to go. I started with a gallop, a fun (for some) practice which sparked the actor's brains and served as a warm-up. Round 1 – all the actors start simultaneously and gallop through their own parts as quickly as possible, both words and moves on the set. Collisions and confusions, but Concentration must be kept. When back to their seats they are all winners. Round 2 – we gallop through the text in sequence, not acting but galloping, forcing the mind and body to think and react as quickly as possible. But it's a group responsibility, moves gestures looks generating the ongoing impetus. Back to their seats round the circle and they are all winners. It's a silly process, anarchic, preposterous and hilariously chaotic. I often used it, frequently in the most inappropriate contexts. An Actor Prepares! Jonette found this pointless, confusing and a waste of time, it had left her bewildered. I told her not to worry, suggesting she put it out of her mind as now we started the real thing.

The 'real' rehearsal did not play well, there were longeurs, we realised that swapping the positions of three chairs would make transitions easier, and one actor returned to his base, apologising to all but insisting he had to replay his scene. One actor missed his costume change. None of these things should be happening, theoretically everything was sorted – a run through means you play non-stop, but I knew this lot, the work had been done, we were ready. We finished. "Home to bed", I said.

Simon, I says, this is the countdown, your W moment approaches.

Jonette burst out in tears: how could I be so casual, she had never felt so hopelessly unprepared in her life and it was all so humiliating, and she had tried really hard to master her parts but that had been utterly pointless as not one of the cast was serious in their involvement. The whole thing was a pitiful shambles! She never dreamt she would have to work with such a shit load of Wankers! WANKERS! And there was no direction. No control. And no praise. And no direction.

She wouldn't look at me.

And off she walked, leaving the building with tears of anger still streaming down her face.

Oddly, no one commented on the incident – ever – as far as I know. We all walked off, went our separate ways. We were ready, truly we were.

At the opening performance, our audience was young, celebratory and fuelled with good beer. We were energetic, sharp, harshly comic, fuelled with audience engagement and surprise. They were riding a big one. Rough! Very Rough Theatre!! There was laughter, worry, and cheers. Jonette's husband told her it was the best thing she had ever done, and I do believe he truly believed that. She had fitted in perfectly, enjoyed herself.

<u>Simon blinks</u>.

Ideal casts, Simon? That's the point, the name of the game really. Pig's ears and silk purses. I only know what I know. One actor who worked for me said he always wanted more direction but I was good at casting. I interpreted this to mean I offered him some challenging roles, but didn't praise him. Without praise actors become anorexic. That was my W., my Weakness. I didn't really do praise, but nor did I expect it. That whip was a real surprise.

We took the production to the Pauper's Pit Theatre at the Buxton Festival Fringe and received plaudits. Is that the word, Simon?

<u>Simon says</u> : Yes. Plaudits! What a surprise. But was she right?

I avoid answering.

There is a kind of rider if you'd like to hear it:

<u>Simon asks</u> : About W's?

No, P's, plaudits.

<u>Simon says</u> : Well, that will be nice for someone,

After the run Bernadine came to see me in my office. We had an often quite harsh face-off kind of relationship. She had been a leading player in every production since *Female Transport*. We were sexually involved and had much respect for each other's work, but she never made life easy – there was an element of contest around our times together. Bernadine talked about *Mad World*, and how good some of the characterisations were, picking out two in particular. But Warren wasn't up to it, his two twins didn't ring true. And anyway he's a musician, she said. I know that, I replied, he played on Neil Ardley's latest suite which was Broadcast on Radio 3. Then why did you use him? I told you Bernie, didn't I, he done music for me and wanted to tread the boards. But playing twins! She exploded.

I have a gesture, a hand gesture, which says it all. She returned to her two favourites, and as I write, I agreed with her, absolutely, but, I said, Good they were. The best they were not. Huh! She shrugged and shot a killer glance in my direction. Killed a lot of men with that glance did Bernadine. Who was then? She challenged.

I was, I replied, quiet and steely like.

<u>Simon's</u> jaw drops.

Shots ricocheted around my office, but not a one could pierce my skin.

Simon says, you are a...

No I'm not, I do protest, I do not think I am. At least, let me, and I hold up my hand.

I says, read the review Simon. Which is precisely what I suggested to Bernadine she might do.

BUXTON TIMES – FESTIVAL REVIEW

Simon smiles : He's cherubic when he smiles.

I says, Now then, Simon my boy, Wankers will as Wankers do, no names no pack drill, but I never never ever showed that review to any of the cast, except to Bernie, who had to swallow the whole mouthful thereafter, because I did not want them to know that I was better than them. Outstanding in fact. It's a mad world Simon and, I swear, never did I wish to hurt the feelings of a single solitary soul in it by comparisons, ranking, favourites or bests. But! That reviewer puts me as outstanding, amongst an excellent cast.

Simon says: But you never said you played a part.

That, my boy, is because, I'm modest.

Simon says : You're a...

Simon! Who do you think re-arranged the chairs in the last rehearsal? Who do you think was the one with half his mind elsewhere? I was the one under rehearsed. I was the one who missed his costume change. The longueurs were mine.

Simon says: Then how come you were The Best?

Because I am a master of cunning disguise. I played the Police Inspector who is attempting to crack all the dodgy dealing and fixing that is making the rich richer and the rest sink into the stinking cesspits of our beloved Albion. A Moral Crusader as is. This cunning character I played as a cross between Michael Caine and Graham Garden, the Monty Python who said "biscuits" in a particularly twisted way on a televisual advertisement. And, Simon, I can at this same and very moment hear that very copper's voice creeping up to address you Simey, my Sweetie.

Now then, as you, my dear young friend, will of course appreciate, when facing circumstances involving wily white livered wheeler dealing whippersnappers, along with wolf whistling wind up merchants who deep down are wishy washy wonky wet weekenders and a whole load of workshy wiseacres, a policeman will have to go under cover. Waxworks they was not. This investigation required the services of a master of cunning disguise. And thus, in the one crucial scene, do I become one Mrs Margaret Thatcher, newly appointed leader of the Tories. I wear a scarlet twin-set suit with neat collar and knee length skirt, blouse nice with pearls, nylon stockings, nicely heeled ladies' shoes to best show off my neat, trim ankles, and am embellished thereafter with a well-padded bra, a blonde wig styled for her and make up to suit. Then there's The Handbag, a real handbag of a handbag. And I, that very same Police Inspector, I master the tone, the pitch, the hauteur, the very vocable of madam's speech patterns. And, my son, not one of those Wretched, Wrinkly, Wrecking bastards has any idea who I am really.

<u>Simon says</u>: So you are the...

STOP! I says, STOP there my son, I stare back at him deep into his soul. We have a pact my boy, not sealed in blood, but NEVER, never never say The Best.

<u>Simon says</u> : Absolutely. Yes. O.K. Jack. You're a one and

I am a one, one of the crowd Simon, so just don't say nothing to nobody, right? There's a good lad. Say hello to the lovely Sophie and the kids.

He beams his cherubic smile, slaps the back of his neck with his left hand, shakes his head and takes off his glasses to clean the lenses. Still smiling. Still cherubic.

Ger on wiv yer, I says, up that Bank an don't be late for playschool.

Off he goes. He's a bright enough lad.

Asking a Lot

THE HARD WAY UP, devised from the autobiography of Hannah Mitchell

THIS IS THE TRUE STORY OF THE LIFE OF HANNAH MITCHELL.......
THELMA ROWLEY PLAYS HER HEART OUT IN THE PART OF HANNAH, AND
THE EFFECT IS STUNNING.......IT'S HONEST, DIRECT AND EXTREMELY
MOVING WITHOUT BEING SELF-INDULGENT.......THE STORY OF A
WOMAN'S ATTEMPT TO FIGHT FOR VOTES IN THE FACE OF TORTURE AND
DEGRADATION......SEE IT IF YOU POSSIBLY CAN!
(AUDREY DICKSON, RADIO FORTH, FESTIVAL CITY, EDINBURGH)
21ST AUGUST 1985

ORIGINS – Part of my working brief was to develop theatre at all levels in the county. I was committed to serious popular theatre. The idea of working with locally sourced material was very appealing.

Converting narrative into drama was a fascinating challenge, which I had so far undertaken only in the context of Theatre in Education projects. It provided the opportunity to create theatre from pre-existing resources; literal, material, practical and human.

And I wanted to challenge a particular actor.

THE SOURCE MATERIAL – The recently published autobiography of the now deceased Hannah Mitchell, a Derbyshire woman born in the late nineteenth century and brought up at Alport Castles, a particularly remote part of the Peak District, who, after leaving home, became a leading figure in the suffragette movement, and in later years played a major socialist role in the local politics of the City of Manchester.

RESEARCH – John Mitchell, Hannah's son, readily and enthusiastically gave me the rights to adapt and perform his mother's book.

I read up on local involvement in the suffrage movement, checked up a little on the history of the development of the Labour Party in Manchester, and spent time looking at period photographs of the Peak District, city life and women to give myself the taste of the period.

We contacted a now very old lady in Chesterfield who had been an active suffragette.

THE ACTRESS – Bernadine Turner was the most challenging actor I ever worked with – a young married woman, with two infant sons, who attended a series of workshops and subsequently joined ACT to play a part in *Female Transport*, she continued to work with me for 6 years. Her arrival coincided with an early period in my career when challenge was essential. Every role she took on in that time was difficult, difficult of itself, and difficult for her. It had to be that way. She was thin, pale, very pale, eye-catching but not good-looking, offered an air of some superiority, stern, haughty, outspoken, forthright, forbidding even. She would laugh, but not readily. A practising Catholic, a working class Sheffield lass seeking the challenging roles I proposed to her, voraciously challenging in her sexuality, dissolving away from her marriage, seeking not to damage her sons, wishing to further her education, and hungry for life experience. At some level I always believed she blamed me for all this. At some level, I hope, she may have thanked me for some of it. Bernadine was not easy but our conjunction created some good work.

THE DAY OUT – A car drive into the northerly Dark Peak, and then a four mile trudge to the foot of Alport Castles, the stark Gritstone Edge at the foot of which was the bleak and remote farm in which Hannah was born and spent her childhood. It was a cold day, with a strong wind and sleety flutters of rain. The farm was partly derelict. Some was partially restored as it was scheduled to become a ramblers' overnight hostel. A tattered notice mentioned that it had been the childhood home of Hannah Mitchell. The place chimed with me. I recalled my own childhood and adolescence on the rock-strewn moor-topped Otley Chevin, where we occupied a smallholding, living in a single-storey house without gas, electricity or running water, neighbours three fields away, the nearest shop three miles down, and the daily walk to school three miles away. A stunning, less remote, site overlooking the lower sweep of Yorkshire's Wharfedale.

THE WORKING PROCESS – The creative procedure we undertook was active. The script was not written and then rehearsed, but rather Bernadine and I together, played out passages, located incidents that lent themselves to action, and created dialogue for characters other than Hannah herself. In one short sequence Hannah played her mother, harsh voiced and overworked, scrubbing the pig, the family pig as she hectored her young daughter. On other occasions Bernadine, while not exactly coming out of character, stopped acting and addressed the audience as Hannah, the author of the autobiography. This worked especially well when she recalled the day she had spotted a rambler approaching across the distant fells, who, when offered a glass of water as he arrived at the farm, sat on a rock, took a book out of his rucksack and began to read. Hannah stood nearby, it was so unusual for a stranger to arrive. The man talked to her, read her a poem, and offered her the book, saying he would call to collect it on his return. It was Hannah's introduction to poetry. The man never returned.

THE SET – The performance's set, properties and costume had to fit in a car, to save the cost of van hire.

I approached Charles Monkhouse, the sculptor who had already worked with me on the Beckett productions. Much of his personal work derived from his abiding involvement with the landscapes of the Peak District and the Lake District, which were the inspiration for his very ordered, minimalist and formally controlled drawings and three-dimensional sculpture pieces.

Charles designed and built a painted, gridded 'landscape' box, a low platform, and a vertical two-sided prison cell. These three pieces existed as separate individual elements, or as a single integrated sculpture. They produced a tight playing space of about 10 feet square. I was always happy to face the issues involved in fitting my actors to his sculptural solutions rather than insisting that he meet the actors' requirements. This approach suited both of us. It gave our endeavours an extra edge, and Charles' art added a particular, not obviously theatrical, dimension to the production.

THE TRICKY BITS – Hannah became a militant suffragette. Her campaigning for universal suffrage led to eventual arrest and imprisonment. She went on hunger strike and was one of those unfortunate yet heroic women who were force fed. This I felt, had to be dramatised rather than narrated. However, this whole idea of a sword swallowing act with rubber tubes and some kind of milky slush poured down a funnel was so obviously impractical. Ridiculous, said Bernadine; even she found this prospect a step too far. I suggested we could play with the idea, do a de Niro, go in deep, just so she would know the real experience, just the once, in rehearsal, no one else need be there.

She knew I was joking, and that I was not joking when I said that she should be naked and we could communicate the whole appalling raw humiliation of what Hannah had been forced to suffer.

The actor moves into open space, isolated, she looks towards "an official" (we imagined a female prison warder), and shakes her head, a long pause, her eyes still fixed on the official, trembles in her vulnerability, she glances away, shakes her head, looks back, a longer pause. Tears fill her eyes, she turns away, and slowly undresses, dropping each garment to the ground. She stands naked, her back to the audience.......then a sharp glance, the official has ordered her to turn around.......she does, she has to put her hands behind her back, she does, she has to open her legs, she does, another pause, another order and she steps into the cell, moves to take the sack-like shift that is hanging there, is stopped.....and then is allowed to put it on. All this in silence. And slowly, tearfully, Hannah finds the words to describe her experience in prison.

The scene worked.

How to effect the next transition?

Stand tall Bernadine, relax, show some pride, step out of the cell and tell of the suffragette's eventual success as you dress, tossing aside the sackcloth shift. Women have the vote. Fix your hair, go back to the landscape.

An awesome lot had been asked of her: Hannah/Bernadine.

Now, we faced the second tricky bit. After the prison experience Hannah was in fact weakened, damaged, and suffered a very serious nervous breakdown. I regarded this as another opportunity to turn the dramatic screw, make the audience "share her pain". She spoke jaggedly, showed her anguish, fidgeting restlessly, wild eyed, gaunt, and we pushed it too far, too hard, I now believe. The simplest, most understated means would have better expressed her condition, which was internalised, hidden from view. Words alone would have carried the scene.

Whilst recovering from this appalling depression Hannah remained politicised and totally committed to the Labour movement.

HOW TO END THE PLAY? The older Hannah emerges, wiser, more measured in her responses. We opted for a stillness, reminiscences of marriage, family and political success. She felt her fight for equality had failed, "but at least we had tried" were her words that ended the play.

ON THE ROAD – The production proved very popular in a variety of venues. We applied to the County Arts Fund for support to tour extensively. The Arts Officer came to a performance at Junction 28, a local activity/arts centre. A decent audience had turned out, a section of which was made up with what I supposed to be the Darby and Joan Club. This seemed totally appropriate. A generation who would identify with Hannah. As the prison scene began one old man called out: "Hey up duck, that lass is teking'er clothes off now."

After the performance, the Arts Officer said he did not believe the piece had popular appeal. It was obvious he would not recommend funding. A few days later we received a letter informing us that, as it stood, the piece should not be played in centres funded by the local authority. We carried on regardless. These were the people who paid my salary. So it goes.

In fact, *The Hard Way Up* continued to be performed for two years, and was included in the selection of five productions we took to Darmstadt on our first visit. At about this time Bernadine and I went our separate ways, and she continued to perform it with success for a number of years.

LATER – Five or six years later I decided to revive *The Hard Way Up* as a fitting pendant to *Means Test Man*, an adaptation for two male actors derived from a very famous novel by Walter Brierley set in the Nottinghamshire coalfield during the 1930s. Thelma Rowley, a poet born in Lancashire, who in spite of having emigrated to Australia many years previously had not lost her northern accent, was invited to take on the role. I hardly knew her. I explained that I would accept no compromise, and she accepted this condition in spite of feeling nervous and reluctant about the nudity. The new production was scheduled to go to the Buxton and Edinburgh Festivals as well as playing locally.

THEN, OH, THE VANITY OF ACTORS – I received a visit from Bernadine suggesting that she was seriously considering legal action. Who did I think I was? *The Hard Way Up* was hers. How dare I? She came to my office. How shall we start I wondered. A quickie across the desk? No, she sat rigid, very sour-faced, claiming sole ownership of the piece. John Mitchell had watched her perform and supported the play. John Mitchell, Hannah's son, had sent me a letter with adaptation and performance rights, I replied, holding out the letter. She didn't speak. I discovered the book. I was tempted to say I discovered you Bernadine, but didn't. I thought of the project in the first place, resourced it, effectively created it for you, provided a unique set, booked the venues......
......I know I asked a lot of you. Shall I clear my desk?

ABOUT GETTING BETTER. Since the first production I had developed as a director, learnt many lessons and was exploring ever more adventurous approaches to original work. I felt I was a better director, wiser, and might now have better ideas, do a better job. And, of course, Thelma might prove to be a better actor than Bernadine; certainly her face, her physique and natural manner seemed to me the more apposite. And why should she not take up

113

this challenge, enjoy the experience, the thrill of performing at two major Arts Festivals? Think what our potential audiences would miss if we were not there, and some people who had watched Bernadine's performance might appreciate an alternative interpretation. I hoped Bernadine would realise I was offering a wonderful opportunity to a second actor which I thought should please, even excite her. Perhaps she did realise. I had asked a lot of her. As she left she insisted that the feminist elements of Hannah's story should not be compromised. I agreed; it was me who had proposed them initially.

I have not seen Bernadine since that awkward, unfortunate and unnecessary meeting.

GETTING AHEAD – I asked a lot of Thelma who worked very hard and quickly. Her performance was, of course, different, different in tenor and emphasis, but very effective. One night, early in the run, she performed at Chesterfield Labour Club. I was unable to be there. She took on the evening alone, with stage manager Roger setting up and operating the lights. Tony Benn, our local Member of Parliament, was in the audience. Immediately after the performance he phoned his daughter Melissa, a London-based novelist and *Guardian* journalist, suggesting the piece was outstanding and should be seen in the capital. A few weeks later, *The Hard Way Up* played in a small central London venue.

In Edinburgh each of the two pendant productions was exceptionally well supported and won great reviews. We were particularly pleased to read this:

WHILE still a knowledge-hungry, little-loved girl on her parents' Derbyshire farm in the last century, Hannah Mitchell decides there's only one way for her to go in life--- the title shows where and how.

And through prison force-feeding, family problems, WSPU politics and a nervous break-down, she struggles to finally become a leading Northern suffragette leader, writer, magistrate, and local politician in Manchester.

Thelma Rowley single-handedly shows us Hannah Mitchell's pig-scrubbing frustrated mother, the relations who failed adequately to justify the lack of enfranchisement for women and so fired Hannah with her sense of unfairness, the derisive hecklers and petty court officials.

The highly professional Plan B theatre from Chesterfield devised this one-woman show directed by Jack Blackburn.

Jo Stanley THE SCOTSMAN

Thelma was already scheduled to return to Australia, and, back home secured a series of performances in The Studio of the South Australia State Theatre. She wrote to me. A young and very able director had helped and advised her. They had edited the script to make it shorter. I took this to mean she had compromised.

Playing the Gangster in the Gangster Spectacle

THE RESISTIBLE RISE OF ARTURO UI, Bertolt Brecht

(Learning about acting – Part 2)

BRECHT is the man, the phenomenon, hence the Event.

UI is the production.

ARTURO is me, is the gangster, is the actor, is me.

ARTURO ASCENDANT – ARtuRo Ui, I Roll the 2 R's on the tongue and pRonounce the name with Relish. I Repeat the Roll. The Resistible Rise! ARtuRo. So! I am not a TheoRetician but I do know what I like! ARtuRo!

THE UI INFLUENCE – As a student at the Sorbonne in 1960 I saw a performance of Jean Vilar's *The Resistible Rise of Arturo Ui* at the Théâtre National Populaire. Vilar played the lead role. The production served as a warning to the French regarding the possible rise to prominence of far right politicians, a particularly relevant and potent enterprise at the time. The scale, the nature, the enterprise of this production astonished me. It was my discovery of epic theatre.

THE BRECHT EVENT – Eighteen years later, and I had, for the two previous years, organised a Chesterfield Arts Festival, in my role of Director of the Arts Centre, with financial support from the Town Council and East Midlands Arts Association. Each of these events comprised an eclectic mixed programme of music, theatre, dance, poetry and exhibitions with the aim of offering a wide public appeal. They were moderately successful but would require much more administrative support if the format were to flourish. However, funding policy changed and I realised that a more focused initiative would be more likely to receive financial support. After discussions with Bill McDonnell I proposed a Brecht Event – a programme looking at the range and influence of the German playwright generally recognised as the most significant in the development of theatre practice in the twentieth century. I believe this event was the most comprehensive consideration of Brecht's work that there had been in England at the time. The claim may be valid even now.

THE UI IMPACT – The play is a masterpiece. Some consider it the greatest masterpiece of serious black comedy ever written. In the adaptation by George Tabori which I chose to use, the language, a brilliantly evocative parody of Jacobean dramatic verse with direct reference to both Shakespeare's *Richard III* and *Julius Caesar* as well as the works of Marlowe and Webster, is linked with clichéd American gangster speech, vocabulary, and rhythms, as represented in movies and crime novels. The narrative relates the rise to power of a petty gangster who, using the most blatant thuggery, takes control of the Chicago Cauliflower Trust and then proceeds to extend his power relentlessly. Quickly written in 3 weeks in Finland in 1941 it expresses Brecht's utter hatred for Hitler and the desire to see him destroyed. He had witnessed the appalling growth of politics by thuggery up to 1938 but chose not to depict it directly until Arturo Ui. Subsequently he wrote a number of plays directly concerned with Nazism including *Schweyk in the Second World War*, and *Pointed Heads and Round Heads*, none of which have enjoyed the performance success of Arturo Ui. The basic situation hovers just this side of lunacy, but follows more or less precisely the trajectory of Hitler's rise to power. Headlines punctuate the action. It is the total ridiculousness of the episodes by which a little man takes control of cauliflower distribution that makes this parable of the ignorance, stupidity and barbarity of fascism so successful.

THE BRECHT PROGRAMME

THEATRE	–	The Resistible Rise of Arturo Ui – ACT
	–	The Caucasian Chalk Circle – NEDYPT
FILM	–	The Threepenny Opera – G. W. Pabst
	–	L'Une et L'Autre – R. Allio
MUSIC	–	And so to Brecht – song cycle, Sally Miles
	–	Brecht's Berlin – music from the plays with poetry readings in German and English
EXHIBITIONS	–	German Expressionist Prints – Kirchner, Beckmann, Schmidt-Rottluff, Heckel, Grosz (Victoria and Albert Museum)
	–	Berliner Ensemble – programmes, posters and documentation (Goethe Institute)
		Brecht in Britain – photographs, with accompanying book for sale (Goethe Institute)

LECTURES   –   <u>Brecht and Expressionism</u> – Professor J. M. Ritchie
(University of Sheffield)

<u>German Art and Politics between the Wars</u> –
Peter Knight (M.A.Leeds)

<u>ARTURO IMPULSIVE</u> – Never did I dream when first I saw this play, after nearly two decades, I would come to play my part. In 1979 now I know, irresistibly, that me it is should be this man Arturo. I realised now how great an opportunity the staggering richness and panache of translation into English, married to the facile evil of the protagonist, might offer to the actor. No doubt about that actor – he was me. ME! I run the whole show do I not? You wonder what attracts me? Demagoguery, nothing less. I have this inner drive, to lead, to quest, the unknown territory in the realm of theatre shows. And some have found me manipulative, dispassionately so. And to them I say, don't show reluctance to recognise how right I am. I know the Joker in the Pack, the wild card played both safe and testing too. So now I test me in a major role, all the more to be the influence, the man who's served by others to ensure a show's success. Dynamic of that role I feel it in my bones as soon as I begin to read the script, and relish now the chance to build the role, so knowing, minute by minute, that every minute is just so. I work by instinct, without the alienate of my gang too much, I say this material, will we not belittle.

Slumped when first you see me with sundry folks around: my friends, that some call hoodlums, and the molls. I talk to them. I strain my head and neck, straining high up, into the moll Dockdaisy's groin. Giri looks at me strange, in life, real time, she is his wife. She spreads her eyes, bemused, provocation or does Arturo seek a haven safe? Pah! How deluded can a leader get?

<u>THE BRECHT PROTOCOL</u> – Beware the dread empathy. Brecht believed in epic theatre, a theatre which prioritises the telling of the story which the play proposes. All work on the production is subordinated to this end; it is in fact irrelevant which individual actor plays a part. The actor must share the ideas of the author and include them in the acting, experience them. The actor must not be possessed by his role to such an extent that he offends against the content of the play as a whole, and only sees his own acting ability. A total contrast to conventional approaches, which aim at seducing the audience into total empathic engagement with the performers.

In order to reinforce his belief in epic telling Brecht practised 'Verfremdungseffekt', usually called the alienation effect but which more accurately means making strange. He wished the audience to be engaged, but at a very mindful level, thus becoming especially aware of the social, philosophical and political implications of the stories they were watching. Devoting an enormous amount of thought and energy to achieving clarity of theatrical expression and an exactness of communication was so necessary in the parable we were undertaking. I personally had to hold in balance my impulse to lose myself in the role and the import of the material.

THE UI CHALLENGE – How to make it work. How to direct the large cast and allow them to share the whole experience, go for an extreme comedic effect whilst avoiding a collapse into indulgent farcical behaviour. There are 34 named parts, plus sundry grocers, reporters and gunmen. The core gang were talented, highly intelligent and committed to the concept of the Event. For supporting roles I decided to complement them with a group of mature graphic and 3D design students who had worked with me on the College Centennial Fashion Show.

I was most concerned that our show should not be dull or boring, a reputation with which Brecht productions were frequently tarred. I had sat through a number of disappointing productions, slow in pace, the presentation pedantic, the audience numb.

A few days before he died Brecht posted a notice to the Berliner Ensemble about their forthcoming first visit to London:

"………there is in England a long standing fear that German art (literature, painting, music) must be terribly heavy, slow, laborious and pedestrian. So our playing needs to be quick, light and strong. This is not a question of hurry, but of speed, not simply of quick playing but of quick thinking. We must keep the tempo of a run-through and infect it with quiet strength, with our own fun. ………The audience has to see that here are a number of artists working together as a collective (ensemble) in order to convey stories, ideas, virtuoso feats to the spectator by a common effort."

Perfect, pertinent, advice.

ARTURO INVESTED – Scene 7, two heavies come in with a dilapidated actor. This scene I use to uncover the UR Arturo. The scene begins in prose but soon I'll use the poetry. For now I talk the man to man with this Maloney thesp. This guy's old style – a grandee and no less. I have been informed that my pronunciation ain't quite perfect. Now it's getting to be unavoidable that I should utter a few words here and there in public – especially political type words, so I take a lesson in speech making. Also how to make an entrance. Brecht, he encourages actors to speak with their own accent and find the man from there, but my broad Yorkshire vowels don't chime with gangster talk that comes that Shakespeare way. Maloney bemoans – "Ah the tragedy of the acTOR!" – if it weren't for the Bard he'd be playing

Broadway. Maloney I ask to teach me how to walk because when tomorrow I walk into the room I want the natural look. I want them to notice that I'm walking. I practise then that strutting walk he knows and the crossing of the arms. When I stand I strike the poses, so that my hands are there to see as they cross the upper arms. In front of the big mirror I do the practice. My right hand, my arm, is free now to pop up. I barely hold it down. Down! Down! I strike it down. And Down! again. Strangelove is infecting me. Maloney talks of actors who can sit, but where is the actor who can walk and cups my hands before the genitals. "Then," he sticks a small black square of hair underneath my nose, "all is well, MR Ui", says he. And Arturo is transformed. Maloney speaks the Oration as he calls it that Roman Antony speaks in Shakespeare's play about the honourable men who should be made of sterner stuff. So that's what I have done, me and him we speak the speech together, and Givola's there, and Giri, and my heavies and they lend to me their ears.

A PLACARD APPEARS:

HERR HITLER COACHED BY PROVINCIAL ACTOR, LESSONS FROM HERR BASIL IN ELOCUTION AND DEPORTMENT

That Maloney, he plays The Barker before the show begins. A brash and confident spieling of our goods. Of me he says:

"And now with all his crimes full-blown,

Our top banana, the notorious

Gangster of all gangsters! The furious

Gods have sent him down to scourge us

For all our savage sins and urges,

Stupidities and apathies,

And cowardice, and here he is

The troubler of this world's peace. O phooey!

The one and only great Arturo Ui!

And on he goes, to say some things of me of which I don't approve. That Barker's walking tightrope close to hell. He also plays harmonica, those haunting unmelodic notes for which I ask to mark and point my best Arturo moments, and the deeds what I have done.

THE UI SETTING – I had looked at photographs of productions of the play and found them imbued with a stagey formality, especially the German ones, which seemed to aspire to something verging on fascistic grandeur. They were 'staged' with a vengeance that was to my sensibility alienating in itself – perhaps that was the point. Again as ever, I was both constrained and liberated by the spaces available for the play, and knew intuitively the context in which I wanted the action to be played. The Chapel was not suitable, the Studio too small, we would use the Arts Centre's high spacious and hollow Phase One hall, a soulless space with the pathetically useless small box stage. My inclination was again, not for sets, but a setting, an evocative space shared with the audience.

Eight tall, broad, centrally swivelling panels were erected on a scaffolding frame along the length of the tall bare wall. These gave us the possibility of 14 different points of entrance. One panel, the third from the right was fixed. In front of it, perched at the very top of it, Little Brian was beginning to copy one of the drawings from George Grosz's series Ecce Homo. Both sides of the remaining 7 panels were painted with enlarged black on white copies of the artist's grotesque expressionist images of Teutonic bourgeoisie. As the audience enter, Little Brian is beginning, very slowly, with exquisite care, to paint a final image and will continue throughout the play's first nine scenes. At the far right end Givola's Flower Shop spilled onto the low constricted stage, a glorious abundance of colourful splendour to contrast with the stark ugliness of the black and white drawings, and with Ui's dive at the opposite side of the stage. Here, a scruffy armchair, a rickety table, packing cases, beer bottles, old newspapers, a couple of machine guns, a baseball bat, and the molls, all barely illuminated by a low swinging cold yellow light, was a base for hoodlums, Ui's place.

At the opposite far end of the panels where the audience entered through double doors was Dogsborough's bar. Beer was sold here, and some of the audience sat at small tables, whilst the remainder were ranked facing the panels, near enough to listen good to those wise words Arturo had to say. Again, Hargreaves more than exceeded my design expectations.

The cast were immediately positive in their response to working on this set. Steve Cox has described the excitement of being part of a large cast playing multiple roles, and how he loved watching Reg Shaw, playing Giri, move in and out of character as he entered and exited through the swivelling panels. Ian Rochard, who played Roma, says he *"loved the boldly staged show and felt the beautifully textured blank verse text inspire us all"*. For the first time he became truly confident in his character, and sensed that he moved forward in his development as an actor. Everyone was vibrant; the script was a key challenging factor, but the sense of playing in the right space made the whole creative process a very special experience.

THE BRECHT ADMISSION – He became famous as a playwright and a theoretician, which I am not. Only in his last decade after his return to Berlin did Brecht become seriously involved in direction, and the contact he had with actors brought a modification to his approach. Brecht turned to emphasizing pleasure and entertainment. In John Willett's *Brecht on Theatre* I found the following statement:

> "If the critics could only look at my theatre as the audience does
> without only stressing my theories then they might simply see
> theatre – a theatre, I hope, imbued with imagination, humour and
> meaning. ....Theatre's noblest function is to give pleasure. It
> needs no other passport but fun, but this it has to have."

He asserted that both audiences and actors should take part emotionally in theatre. With actors he still encouraged "demonstration" and separation from the role, but he now urged them towards virtuosity and self-indulgence in rehearsal. Hours were spent not talking but trying. Brecht would say he wanted no discussion in rehearsal, it would have to be tried. This change in approach is a perfect fit for my practice. I always found discussions self-serving and too often circular, so we embarked on discovery, seeking riches, sharing fun.

ARTURO EGOTISTICA – Don't give me that there is no such a word. It's there in front of you to read. Of course there is one such a word – Egotistica – which resonates with me, the most profoundly with the way I feel when playing moustached Arturo, whilst playing with dull Dullfeet's wife as we together meet in the flower shop of my main man Givola. It is a scene of foxy sharp and rhyming repartee, and finger tingle tip, as I recall those moments close to Betty dear, as played by Bernardine. Meantime Givola distracts, then persuades the husband Mr D., whose eyes soon show his days are almost gone. Back off says he, but now too late.

A PLACARD

AUSTRIA YIELDS TO NAZI CAJOLING CHANCELLOR ENGELBERT DOLLFUSS CALLS OFF PRESS ATTACKS

And then quite soon in Scene 16 I meet with Betty one more time on that sad day when we have come to Cicero, the interment of her husband to be done. Beside, behind, above, along the poor man's coffin sited there I draw on all the best Maloney made me learn. And my performance now is so redolent of Richard Three's seductive wooing of that princess dame in Shakespeare's play about the Crookback King. I hunch a shoulder and so I stand like him. I stretch my hand and thus I work on lovely Bernardine. I stretch my hand and close her husband's eyes. I stretch my hand and touch her pale drawn cheek. Ah! the words I use and use so well. And then her words – the strength, the fire, the anguish of a widowed dame. I offer her my friendship and forever.

Never! Never! Never! Never! Never! she replies.

Agh! This learning about the acting game. Tingling tips.

A PLACARD

DOLLFUSS MURDER OPENS DOOR TO RAPE OF AUSTRIA. NAZIS WOO AUSTRIAN PUBLIC OPINION

<u>THE UI TRANSACTION</u> – a pair of thugs rock the high stepladder to which Little Brian clings with real fear flickering his face. He half jumps, half falls. Giri drags him aside. Givola daubs black his face with paint that he was using. He is offered a drink, looks doubtful, it is forced on him. As he is frogmarched away his legs turn weak, his head rolls, his eyes blank, his tongue lolls. He's mickey finned, slumped on a chair in a Court of Law. He is quite innocent of course, but Defendant Fish is charged with arson, a warehouse of the Cauliflower Trust has been destroyed by fire.

The scene is devastatingly clever, brilliantly conceived. Seven short incidents, each defined by a moment's blackout, highlight the rapid insidious corruption of the justice system. It is a key, pivotal scene from which the subsequent narrative is able to devolve. Nazi Germany was effectively without law.

Pressure was building, rehearsal time barely adequate. I was becoming tired, needing a pause to learn my lines, complete and coordinate the whole Brecht programme, arrange accommodation, organise promotions, watch the budget. I suggested to the cast that they should prepare and present the Court. The scene involves 8 actors plus grocers, reporters and the heavies. I offered them 3 hours to block, prepare and run through the scene. I sat in my office, brain pulp, couldn't look at the script, stared at the schedule of events, felt it was worth it – but, wondering, what if…...suppose…….. Bill called; he was rehearsing his radical rock version of *The Caucasian Chalk Circle* in the Dome, the play "with the great message for humanity" as he called it. He was twitching, more frazzled than me, fuming as Charles Monkhouse wouldn't compromise on the massive scaffolding structure he had designed for the Youth Theatre's production. I suggested to Bill he compromise, as we directors survive on that commodity; we can flourish on it I suggest. I could hardly believe my own words, being reluctant to compromise myself. The kids will adapt, I suggest, let them explore the possibilities of whatever structure he creates – he's the Artist. My brain is putty, but sharp enough to allow the cast to do this key scene of the play. The phone rings. Angela my secretary is going home, she generously gave extra, unpaid time. I say yes, not thank you. I drink a large carton of fresh orange juice. A mime artist I booked for the Arts Centre had drunk 2 cartons during his preparation and 3 after his performance. He never touched caffeine. Two unopened cartons stood on my desk. I go for a pee, listen to sound from the set; it is quiet, reassuringly quiet. I step outside and stand on the bridge. There was a chill in the air, but it was calm; the calm called for a cigarette moment. I took a ticket from my pocket and rolled it into a cylinder, placed it between my lips, flicked an invisible Zippo lighter, and smoked, a pretence both settling and soothing. In my life, asthmatic, I never touched nicotine; the faux cig spins arcing and tripling below; somewhat relaxed I leave the bridge and go back in to check how they are progressing.

This was the first time I had walked in to see the set as the audience would. Its impact both amazed and even shocked me into a renewed, delighted, awareness of what we were doing. They were in mid-scene, there was an ugly threatening tension in the room, Little Brian was bruised and blubbing "Ablah-blah-blah", gob wide, head shaking, Givola snarling, Roma leering, Giri mocking, grocers aghast, the blocking was telling the story, the words extra potent, sharp, the look of the scene without any overt violence was viscerally compelling. There are some very nasty people here. Momentarily they freeze, they freeze 7 times for 7 seconds, glaring grinning, grotesque, at the audience, having decided to freeze rather than blackout between the successive short sequences. On one of these occasions they direct their attention at the painted Grosz figures, but mostly it's the audience whose implicit involvement they challenge. "Ablah-blah-blah", and the harmonica wails in the stillness. They show me the frightening dangerous method they had devised to get Little Brian off his stepladder, and assured me, in character, that they would ensure he was looked after, with Giri's foot across his neck. The scene ends in chaos and in tumult, the judge, suborned, reads the sentence in flat voice – Arson, fifteen years' imprisonment.

A PLACARD

REICHSTAG FIRE TRIAL ENDS IN UPROAR.
GOERING LOSES TEMPER IN COURT.
DRUGGED LABOURER SENTENCED TO DEATH.
MOCKERY OF JUSTICE.

The work was outstanding. They knew it. I verged on praise, wondering could the whole show be as effective as this. We moved on.

THE BRECHT OUTREACH – Brecht had spent some time in Darmstadt, the old capital of Hesse, the German state renowned for its artistic cultural heritage. The city is twinned with Chesterfield. I contacted Darmstadt's twinning office to enquire whether there might be any interest in our Brecht Event and was informed that a Bert Brecht-Schule had recently opened in the city. The school was a particularly liberal comprehensive equivalent of an English Sixth Form College founded as an experimental alternative to the long-established and very formal Gymnasia. The school had a very young staff filled with enthusiasm and the desire to strengthen pan-European contacts. Their response to my enquiry was overwhelming: the majority of the staff and pupils wanted to visit us. My apologetic response was that we could accommodate perhaps a dozen, and a group of 8 pupils and 4 teachers, selected by lottery, came for a five-day visit. It was very important for them; the teachers, being the first post-Nazi generation, were all idealists in the cause of a United Europe. I had every confidence that they would enjoy NEDYPT's rock version of *The Caucasian Chalk Circle,* and, knowing that Germans held Shakespeare in the highest regard, believed they would appreciate our *King Lear,* in addition we could offer discussion sessions round the exhibitions, the evening song recital and an excursion to Lathkill Dale in the Peak District. But I must admit to a certain wariness regarding their response to the Hitler/Ui play.

In fact the visit was a wonderful success. We spent their last evening in The Barley Mow, ACT's rough and very ready local hostelry, supping good English ale where the group leader spoke to me. He explained that they had never seen theatre like ours, so natural, so vital and immediate, a striking contrast to Germany where formal theatre traditions ruled, hide-bound by convention, and serious professional actors were virtually state employees with a job for life. They had not experienced the dynamic all-changing theatrical revolutions and explosion of small-scale touring companies that we enjoyed in the 1960s. They had no sense of Community Theatre. It was important that more people should see my work, I must take it to Darmstadt. When I queried the suggestion he insisted that the great added value for German audiences would be the contact with native English speakers.

This was Rainer Lohnes, who has now supported my work, supported me, for 33 years. He hoped I would take Ui and Lear. That was impossible, but I promised to take up his proposal when I had appropriate work ready. Two years later a party of 30 of us travelled to Darmstadt with a coach for actors, musicians, technicians, students and translators, a truck for sets, lighting rig, costumes, sound system and luggage. We were taking 5 productions.

ARTURO SUBLIME – Ah! the itchy glued-on twitchy touch of that moustache upon my nether lip which makes me who it is is me. I am raised up, up aloft on high and see you all below. And there and then I do begin my speech 'cos they are screaming for protection everywhere.

Men of Chicago and of Cicero!

Friends, fellow citizens and all without!

I, Arturo, offer my protection to their Cauliflower Trust. I praise old Dogsborough who was an honourable man, and Dullfeet too, who is, alas, no more, but Betty, his poor widow, she is here who does advise you place your confidence in MR Ui's hands, in these dire days, as she has done now that she's had the chance to know me well in these dire days, a time so hard for her to bear.

Each man is free to vote for me so raise both hands to get protection I am not disinclined to give when I demand a hearty, smarty, happy, snappy YES! And I tell you, I tell you all, I ordered prompt delivery of Tommy guns and hand grenades and knuckles made of brass, rubber truncheons, and new supplies of armoured cars as well, because they're screaming for protection everywhere. I list the towns. Arturo loves his listings – not only Chicago and Cicero, but many other towns – Detroit, Washington and Milwaukee, Baltimore! Toledo! Tulsa! Pittsburgh! Little Rock! wherever else they're selling groceries. St Louis! Boston! Minneapolis! Yes, everybody wants protection now! Flint! Scranton! Trenton! Charleston! Wilkes-Barre! New York! New York today! The World tomorrow!

A PLACARD

MARCH 11, 1938. NAZIS INVADE AUSTRIA. 98% OF TERRORIZED ELECTORATE VOTES YES FOR HITLER

THE BRECHT CONTINUUM – A decade later I took a party of students to see a student production of *The Threepenny Opera*. It was an indulgent mess, full of camouflage-dressed aggressively posturing girls, the songs belted out with no communication of their meaningful content, the whole narrative of the play obscured by showy gestures that served no purpose, the words a scattergun blabber, the music loud and insensitive. I have rarely felt so negative about any production, but this was doubly annoying as it so mis-served whatever talents and aspirations these young students had. A year later I was working with a student group myself and proposed *The Threepenny Opera*. Tony Baker, talented poet and exceptionally gifted jazz musician would be musical director. We would create a straightforward, uncluttered presentation of the script, committed to respect the storyline. The songs would be delivered with a clarity that served the narrative. The music would be honest and simple: Tony on piano, accompanied by 2 students on guitars and some percussion. The songs were given priority, we cast accordingly. Characterisation would be individualised but rather plain, underplayed if anything in order not to draw attention from the narrative drive of the script. There would be no set.

It was a privilege and a pleasure to work on this piece in a quiet way, and in total contrast to Arturo Ui. It was a work of my maturity. I had learned about acting from my performance as Arturo; on this occasion I learnt how valuable and resonant a quiet approach to a very potent script can be. Tony Baker's temperament was a major factor in influencing this aspect of our collaboration. It was different from my usual work, and worthy of ACT.

Some time later, after I had stopped directing, I came across a translation/ adaptation of *The Threepenny Opera* by Frank McGuinness for the Gate Theatre in Dublin. This version has the kind of energetic, wicked, harshly eloquent quality that had so attracted me to Tabori's Ui script in the first place. The role of Pirate Jenny had been taken by Marianne Faithfull, one of my very favourite female singers, and subsequently she issued an album, 20th Century Blues, with a subtle nuanced accompaniment by Paul Trueblood, which I recommend and esteem as a wonderfully singular example of Brecht/Weill interpretation.

At about the same time I created a logo to help promote my workshop programmes. It plays on the twin masks image – tragedy and comedy. A Screaming Shakespeare, stolen from the menu of a German café of the same name, is twinned with a cartoon of a sparky, amused Brecht.

Two heroes!

ARTURO FALLIBLE – BESTED AT HIS BEST – He strips me bare, that Brecht, at my apogee. I play Arturo. You vote for me. Then he makes the man you know rip off the 'tache that made Arturo. I do this act myself. The actor that is me, not me, must speak the final epilogue. So, I rip it off, and then:

> If we could learn to look instead of gawking,
> We'd see the horror in the face of farce,
> If only we could act instead of talking,
> We wouldn't always end up on our arse.
> This was the thing that nearly had us mastered;
> Don't yet rejoice in his defeat, you men!
> Although the world stood up and stopped the bastard,
> The bitch that bore him is on heat again.

THE BRECHT LEGACY – I learnt that I could master a major role, and command the attention of those who played alongside me. I settled, feeling comfortably right in character, enjoying the power.

The Event took place in 1979. In 2012 when writing this piece, I looked out my old copy of the play, opened it, and there was the moustache stuck on the title page – waiting.

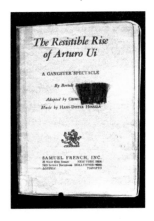

Learning Lessons

KEN CAMPBELL'S SCHOOL FOR CLOWNS (1980)

(Learning about acting – Part 3)

After working to create a body of work and an Arts Centre in Chesterfield for a couple of years, I had established a productive working relationship with John Baraldi, and creative things were beginning to happen. We received an early morning out-of-the-blue call from Nottingham Playhouse suggesting that one or other or both leave and join them to develop a programme of community and Theatre in Education projects. It was urgent, the posts had to be filled immediately, the money allocated, performances scheduled or the opportunity would be lost. This was very flattering, and tempting, as the Playhouse was the leading regional repertory theatre in England at the time (the early 1970s). The call came from Richard Eyre, director of the Playhouse and subsequently of the National Theatre. We chose to continue with our own project.

In his book *Utopia and Other Places,* Richard Eyre recalls the most exceptional theatre he has enjoyed over years, the work of the best directors and greatest actors. However, the one production that best and most excitingly distilled the essence of theatrical experience had been Ken Campbell's *School for Clowns.*

That same production in Nottingham had had an exactly similar profound effect on me. I had long been intrigued by Ken Campbell's approach to theatre, surprised to learn much later that Margot knew him well – the whole Roadshow gang had camped in her garden, long late nights, ferrets, mad jollities round the swimming pool.

George Key, a talented but failing concert pianist who had, wanting to be an actor, attached himself to me, accompanied me to see the Nottingham version of *School for Clowns* I was utterly enthralled by the performances, taken aback, unsettled, left wondering at the glorious unqualified anarchy of the end. George was thoroughly discomfited, threatened, frightened, unsmiling and barely spoke on our return journey. The following day I went back to the show with my two young daughters Catherine and Susanna.

Four, maybe five, years later I had four dangerous clowns. We could prepare our own version.

WEASEL: John Connolly, the erratic punky thug, filled with a psychotic energy.

PUFF: Reg Shaw, the crazily sinister, bland, yet insidiously troubling presence.

PIMPLE: Bernadine Turner, peaked, taut, edgily fraught and sensual, not shagging but clowning.

DIMPLE: Steve Cox, the bewildered white face, timid, fearful, bawling

and PROFESSOR MOLEREASONS: I would be the Professor,

"Good morning, clowns. Where exactly were we when we left off yesterday?" he asks on entering the classroom to stand, cane in hand, behind his tall teacher's desk. "THERE!" shout the four clowns triumphantly pointing in four quite different directions: one high, high, higher, the second at a spot, precise and delicate under the second desk, the third all over round and about with vaguely wandering forefinger, while the fourth, the lady clown, points simperingly with questioning eyes at her own bottom. Professor Molereasons swishes his cane and yells "I cannot teach under these conditions."

It is the thankless task of Professor Molereasons, a remorseless advocate of discipline, to teach the four clowns lessons in clowning. Lessons had to be learned. He opens his large book, finds a topic for the lesson, perhaps –

"HELP! HELP! MY AEROPLANE IS ON FIRE!"

and gives instruction on how to act it out. The clowns start according to instructions, quiet and submissive, but as their enthusiasm grows and invention multiplies, the whole classroom is swamped in an enormous billowing parachute and, amid the anarchy, Molereason's every attempt to teach a lesson is rapidly transformed into utter chaos by the stupidly delinquent efforts of the clowns, who progressively drive their jittering teacher to that point, that very point at the very verge of madness! Loud bangs, pratfalls, revolving doors, exploding objects, boomps and daisies, lost balloons, failed mechanicals, crocodile tears, an all-enveloping parachute, the wrong music, then stopped, locked, silent, waiting to make their next move but can't move . . . until . . . a trigger sets the whole thing off again enriched with utterly irreverent linguistic wit and word play and nonsense. This, their world was compellingly believable and I found my self locked into it.

Here, and then, I learned one of my key lessons of theatre, of acting: that it was possible to inhabit and believe in a theatrical construct, from which there seemed to be no escape and within which there was no assurance. I didn't know what might happen next. Molereasons felt all the real fear of a failing schoolteacher, and could see no way out, no escape. A part of my subconscious was feeling I might never again be Jack Blackburn.

I learnt you could exist as part of a totally convincing, somewhat threatening alternative universe that you had to control but was fast escaping. It was a strange compelling place whose intensity rose to mind bending levels – the bastards, they ran wild, diegetically believable, and then even wilder.

Professor Molereasons becomes so unnerved and helpless, his anger so extreme that the clowns eventually escape into the audience. Hidden there, as he frantically searches for them because they must finish the last lesson, the clowns persuade the audience to come back into the school with them, where they are quickly made up as clowns so that Molereasons cannot possibly find and punish the real miscreants.

It was wonderful. Lost in Clownland. Riotous laughing audiences. The sense of danger vibrant and rollicking.

Children shivered as John joshed them, strong men quailed as Bernadine picked them out and approached with wincingly sensual sniggers, young women paled as Reg stared fixedly, marking every eye blink with "In your pants?", and ghostly Steve drifted aimlessly sad, dripping and loon-like wondering amongst them.

Best fun. A glorious caper from an inimitable snapper-up of unconsidered trifles! *School for Clowns* was a version of an original script by F. K. Waechter, a leading German cartoonist. So after having played the piece off and on for several months it seemed appropriate to revive it as part of a package of productions that we took to Darmstadt when first invited there in 1982. I suggested to Rainer Lohnes that the piece would best play to large audiences in a good space. We worried about how it would be received, but – in for a penny!

Rainer negotiated on our behalf with the City Council and they provided the Orangerie of the Dukes of Hesse. The Orangerie was a magnificent building, long, very long, large with height to take the trees over winter and wide windows to catch all the light. An eighteenth century edifice, no longer used for overwintering citrus-bearing trees, but an ideal venue for classical concerts, formal balls and the occasional international conference. It is immaculately preserved, and there was a platform stage erected for our purpose at one end, with serried rows for the audience stretching into the far distance. And the show was a sell-out: six hundred seats. There would be children, fathers, more children, town dignitaries, cousins, mothers, children, teenagers and teachers and more children, all of them Germans. The clowns were worried. This was our first visit: we were diplomats for British Theatre: would they understand, would they hear at the back, would they keep up with the pace, appreciate the daftness, the cruelty. I said yes, I think, to the clowns. Yes. Go for it. Yes, Remember: the sense of danger must not disappear. I have false memories on occasion, but do recall a clown whispering maliciously: Who won the war? Don't mention the war! False memories.

The newly appointed Director of the Orangerie was full of enthusiasm, thrilled to have something different in her hallowed space. Especially English Theatre. Yes, of course, you can splash a little water, that will not be a problem and climb on the chairs is OK but not the gilding on the wall there, please if you will not touch the gilding. And the bang, you say a big bang will not I hope crash our windows. Let me show the poster I made from your clever programme with children to colour it red. It is good? Yes it is all very good.

And the support was wonderful and the performances dynamic, and the really big bang echoed and bounced around the space, and the stage was swamped with children and even some parents for that last all whelming scene.

Triumphant – we are thrilled.

Then, our next booking was at Camp America. Darmstadt was in the American sector of post-war West Germany and US soldiers were a fairly frequent sight in the city in those days, but mostly they lived their lives corralled in Camp America, a sizeable chunk of Texas, as it turned out, teleported into the heart of Europe. We were excited, Rainer had had a great idea. Yanks kids would love this show.

Arriving at the camp's gated barrier at about 4pm after a lunchtime performance of our *Rehearsal Macbeth* in a school, we were quizzed by a gun-toting GI. The back of the truck was inspected. A phone call made and after a short delay quizzed yet again by an officer, with a gun, who had been called to check our credentials. Bernadine, lady clown, simpered gloatingly at them. They were very polite, but not exactly friendly.

Another phone call, and we were directed to a crèche and young folks centre. A crèche didn't seem quite right.

"You're the theatre folks?" asked the lady who was there. "You're right in there," she said, "settle yourselves, good to meet you. Y'all from England?"

"Yes, ma'am" – we were very polite, no clown residue allowed here.

We settled in a room barely a tenth the size of the Orangerie. After putting up the set there would be literally no room for an audience! "I cannot work in these conditions" is Prof. Molereasons' regularly repeated plaint throughout the play. And now?!! What to do?

We'll do it, I suggest, in among them, that'll be good, work around them, use the whole space, improvise, American kids are very adaptable. OK? OK?

They're paying well, very well! Do you want to eat? We'll mix it with them, them with it.

"Jack, sometimes you ask too much."

"Hold on to your characters", I say, "just hold your characters."

Some of our company had turned up, for the ride; to support us, they said, told lies and exaggerations to even get in, get past the gun-manned barrier. And now, early evening, they were hungry, really hungry so they found their way to the canteen bar at the social centre some barrack blocks away.

"If you don't have dollars ma'am I'm afraid I can't serve you."

"We have Deutschmarks and Sterling."

"This ma'am is territory of the United States of America, dollars and dimes, ma'am, dollars and dimes."

"But . . ."

"Sorry lady. No can do! But you're a very welcome guest here."

Even lovely Margot could not soften the heart of that straight-backed, short-cropped military barman.

And in walked two tall Texans in togas. They wore stetsons and cowboy boots and badly fitting Roman togas. We had arrived on the day of the twice yearly toga party, and they were very serious about it. We wondered: Gladiators perhaps? Christians thrown to lions? Sacrificial virgins? And the whole shebang ending with an overwhelmingly disgusting and gorgeous orgy eating grapes? Texans in togas in Darmstadt!

About a dozen kids turned up at the crèche around 7.30. Four left immediately. We started – "Good morning, clowns. Where exactly did we leave off . . ."

The audience started playing cards. That's what they did in the crèche. We tried to keep going. "Adapt", I said, "Adapt, this is a real opportunity!" But it was hopeless; after barely twenty minutes we threw in our cards, cleaned up, packed up, went back to the bar and watched a large crowd of Texans, of toga-clad Texans, jigging to rock music. We drank tap water, starving, and dollar proofed.

The productions we brought to Darmstadt were *Macbeth Rehearsed, School for Clowns, The Hard Way Up,* a shortened *Larkrise and Candleford* and *Maria Marten and the Red Barn* in Reg Shaw's expressionist Limited Company production. On arrival we settled into a Naturhaus hostel in a forest on the outskirts of the city. We played in the Staatstheater, the Justus Liebig Halle, the Kennedy Literaturhaus and a number of upper schools. We performed morning, noon and night, the pressure was relentless, with new venues and fresh encounters the daily programme. Food became a problem. I faced a rebellion by the 3rd night – We must eat!! It's after 10 o'clock, we've done 3 performances, and you're taking us back to a hut in a forest and we have to eat. ----- Rainer! they want to eat, they have to eat. But how? he asked, so late? and then, yes! the new McDonald's, at the Hauptbahnhof, open 24 hours. Hungry actors gorged on burgers and Coca Cola. Learning Lessons.

Folie de grandeur. A bridge too far? I could write a whole book about these 12 days. But ultimately it was the most rewarding adventure, our new-found friends were so welcoming, so generous in their appreciation of our work.

For 12 years I returned with productions annually, usually 2, one for students and the other for the general public

Coda

John Connolly (Weasel) worked with me on four productions. In later years John and I met infrequently, but for all of us that first trip to Darmstadt remained a defining experience. Some twenty years after the event we were reminiscing on the good old days over a beer, those days when we were young and cockily adventurous. Maybe the Guinness loosened John's tongue:

"I've got to tell you," he said, "it's awful this, appalling really, I blame that weaselly bastard clown I played. We were all so into it, but that first time, in the Orangerie, at the end when hundreds of kids came on the stage to be made up as clowns, I was daubing swastikas on some of their faces!"

Later, I wondered whether, strangely, this indicated something honest about the relations, the conditions of our two nations at that time. We had in my lifetime been so dreadfully engaged in the second world war, and its memory remained alive in our consciousness although only three of us had been alive in the early 1940s. Our first visit to Darmstadt was thirty-six years after the end of the war, and we were all amazed at how much more modern and richer the city was than equivalent British cities at the time. There were so many Mercedes and BMW cars, the women were more expensively dressed, and shops better stocked. Darmstadt was modern and upbeat, whereas Chesterfield and Sheffield were depressed, struggling still.

I am now writing this twenty-nine years after our first encounter, and have visited the city that I have grown to know and enjoy every year since that first time with either productions or a programme of workshops. I wonder if a raw young actor would react the same way today. I doubt it; we have all moved on.

Learning lessons.

The Running Man

LARK RISE AND CANDLEFORD, Keith Dewhurst

The Running Man is carrying a gun, he quickens his stride, an old much-used looking shotgun. It swings jerkily in his right hand, loose, threatening. The Running Man is young, good-looking, smart. He wears two shirts. He glances both ways and accelerates to cross Markham Road. At 7.00pm there is little traffic, and he has little time. He crosses the road. Obviously physically fit, his running relentless, graceful, he must get there, get there soon. They'll curse him, but he will get there, get there on time. The gang are waiting. He's never late. A car speeds past the Running Man. Brakes squeal. It stops, half mounted on the pavement some yards ahead. The Running Man has stopped short, tense and alert. The gun, muzzle down, points at the ground. Three police officers surround the man. One takes the gun. Another holds the Running Man's arm. He remains calm. A third is turning to the senior officer still in the car, and asks, "The procedure, Sir, what shall we do with him?"

It is a lovely balmy mid-June evening. An early summer's evening. Oh, to be in England...

ARTS CENTRE THEATRE
CHESTERFIELD

Lark Rise

Chesterfield has a new shopping precinct, opened a week earlier, with a pleasant open space, central, well lit, which might suit theatre. There had been local controversy over the town centre redevelopment plan: the original proposal had been to demolish the old market hall, the adjacent higgledy-piggledy ginnels of the Shambles and the wonderfully varied townscape of the bottom shops. These were to be replaced with a spanking new shopping centre; this in the era of the most unforgiving stark concrete brutalism. Graham Robinson, who had taken the role of Alonso in *The Tempest,* organised the NO campaign. Members of ACT had produced and distributed leaflets, they had joined the mass-marches against the proposal and there was even talk of agit-prop theatre; we would raise support, spread the word on the streets.

The original town plan was overturned, and now, just over two years later, we are involved in celebrating the opening of a sensibly sensitive resolution of the town's redevelopment programme.

ACT is presenting promenade performances of *Lark Rise* and *Candleford* on successive evenings, a kind of baptism of the new central open space.

The gang's all here in what still remains for me one of the most happily rewarding of projects.

Flora Thompson's sagas of English rural life at the turn of the twentieth century had recently been dramatised by Keith Dewhurst with music and songs arranged by John Tams of the Albion Band.

I had said to them, the gang, and they were a gang in those days, "we could do both scripts you'll get to play more parts, there are forty-two characters in Lark Rise alone, and sing great traditional folk songs. We'll play a range of venues, with the audience up close, promenading. We'll tour the Yorkshire Dales. Just turn up, do the show in those lovely dales villages. And there's that Rainer Lohnes, the German who wants me to take things to Darmstadt. We could, and what could be more English? We could clog dance and sell them Dandelion and Burdock."

The gang had agreed we could.

But?

But! But! NO Buts!

They were persuaded when I explained they could take their kids, we'd use them in both plays.

My daughter Susie would play the ten-year old Flora in Lark Rise, her best friend Irene would play the fourteen-year-old in Candleford, and all the younger ones would enrich the mix. I offered the actors contrasting but fitting roles, and all were content with their selection. Nigel the Fiddler would source the musicians, and Phil Tomkinson would be musical director. And we needed a forge and bellows, and a cottage and a Post Office, and authentic props: a big tin bath, a period bicycle, a postman's bag, pots, pans and platters, crooked walking sticks, vegetables and fresh fish – a John Dory, and a tinker's cart, and an anvil with loud hammers clanging, and a big bound Bible and a ferret. And the band would be in the play, and yes they could and must learn lines. We'd scatter straw, and have bales to sit on. And some were singing as others rehearsed. The whole process was so positive. It was a charmed few weeks, all expectations fulfilled. I can barely remember doing anything, it came together like a dream, a very happy dream.

The precinct performances were a great success. John Tams attended one and gave our efforts his blessing although leaving early for the London train. We tour Peak District villages.

Then we are off to the Dales, Wharfedale, Swaledale, Wensleydale, that part of Yorkshire where I grew up, that part of England which is dearest to my heart. We make our base the tiny hamlet of Horsehouse where we set up camp, cooking communally, sleeping in tents or the barn long and late after drinking in the pub with music and singing. Then off in the morning to promote the next day's venue, whilst others unload the truck for the day's show, and some busk to raise a crust and encourage the public.

Muker, Hawes, Kettlewell, Lofthouse, Redmire. Until, finally, Middleham.

And I explain, I announce to the gang, my Great Idea. Middleham is scheduled to be an early evening performance in the town square on the Wednesday. The town will be in bunting-bright celebratory mood, and I have met the local dignitaries and they are in favour, very much so, of my great idea for that particular day, the particular day! (THE DAY of the marriage of Prince Charles to the lovely Diana Spencer).

The cast assembles, some look sceptical, some doubtful, others downright worried. We have a shared history. They are suspicious.

Lark Rise finishes with a circle dance and the audience joins in and the whole thing is joyous and jolly and fun. Well, you can, as they all must realise, step a circle dance in straight lines, and, prior to the performance we will gather-er-you will gather, with the band, on the Council Estate, and you will all progress straight-line circle-dancing to the town square, and that will be our additional contribution to Middleham's rejoicing, which will attract an audience and that's the Great Idea. There'll be free beer.

I had not realised how far it was from the housing estate to the town centre, nor how slow and repetitive straight-line circle-dancing is, far slower than walking pace. Nor had I realised how tiring it is to circle-dance repeatedly three-quarters of a mile in a straight line. The gang were cursing. I heard them, cursing those DAMNED ROYALS! with fixed smiles on their faces; but, arriving at the Square they were delighted to be plied with Marston's Best and Old Peculier by the waiting audience: a mostly drunken audience, and the most mostly drunk were jockeys and stable hands who joshed and squeezed bottoms, laughed raucously, and made the most indecent proposals to our lovely actresses, whilst a coven of bold brash blondes whistled and "fancy a fuck, kid" embarrassed the actors.

What to do?

Not the play.

I scurried around, frantically pinning cue notes on lampposts and litter bins, suggesting the bit with wotsit, play bigger, play bigger, don't worry, you're losing your characters, cut this, and that, don't worry, it'll be okay if we can just/ Bernadine looks me straight in the eyes darting hate beams/ if we can, if, if... Collapse of stout party!

We couldn't. The whole thing became crazily, joyously shambolic. We gave in, the cast caroused, the kids ran wild, the Old Peculier worked its wonders. Our gang joined their gang, and all caroused together, vying, vying for... once more into the breach, dear friends! and some toasted Charles and Di whilst others shouted them down, sang the Red Flag and the Marseillaise, spat on all Royals, and roared the night away.

Some photographs of the tour recently came into my possession, and a review and a letter. Looking at them stirred thirty-year-gone memories. Everyone looks fulfilled, sharing, happy, travelled players, just what it all should be about. I looked again at one photo, more closely, and yes, there is my father in the audience, and my mother I know was beside him, but she is hidden by Margot with Reg's daughter on her lap. And I recalled my parents driving up to see *Candleford* in Lofthouse. "Well done, Spratty."

Our last performance was in Youlgreave, where my family had moved to live on Bankside the move being managed by June whilst the girls and I were up in Yorkshire.

A few days later I chanced upon Paula and Margot sitting in a coffee shop at the precinct in Chesterfield where we had played a month earlier. I joined them. The emotion was palpable. Cold Turkey/Hot Turkey? Coming down, still filled, thrilled with the drug of those days together.

In November we leave for Darmstadt with a revised, much shortened compilation of scenes and songs from both plays. *Lark Rise/Candleford*, being a promenade production, needed space. We played in the vast cold concrete openness of the foyer in the new built Staatstheater. Again we were overwhelmed. This time by the attendance of over a thousand people, family groups, children, students who had come to promenade and drink. One scene kept their attention – two labourers (Steve Cox and John Connolly) return from the fields to take a bath in the farmyard. Zillah (Sheila Harding) fills the bath, pouring cold water over them,

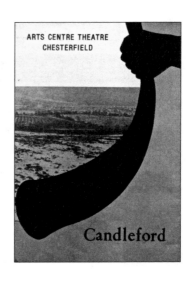

deriding their manhoods. Butt naked they shivered their complaints. Eyes popped, seeking out manhoods.

I have included the following review as it presents an interesting consideration of what may be termed 'community theatre'. That phrase may be said to have defined my role, my whole raison d'être. The item is

of particular interest as it was written by a man professionally involved in theatrical education for presentation to a meeting of the Drama Section of the National Association of Teachers in Further and Higher Education and was subsequently printed in their newsletter.

LARK RISE IN DERBYSHIRE

A review of the production by the Chesterfield Arts Centre in Wensley, by Alan Clarke.

So much of what goes under the name of community theatre is neither of any recognisable local community or of real relevance to the community it is supposed to be for. It was a real enjoyment and relief therefore to experience the Chesterfield Arts Centre's presentation of *Lark Rise*, based on the novels of Flora Thompson and imaginatively adapted by Keith Dewhurst – originally for the National Theatre. The location of the hall itself was ideal for this warm picture of a late 19th century rural community; up the hill from Wensley village green opposite the old church, conveniently chiming almost exactly on cue. Behind, an idyllic hillside and one of the few fine evenings of early summer.

Although the play itself is an account of a hot summer's day in Oxfordshire during the end of the last century, its relevance for a village setting in Derbyshire of today was not lost: the long kitchen table and straight-back chairs, the trestles for dining, clog-dancing and selling dandelion and burdock during the interval, the tin tankards, the pedlar's handcart – all smelt of simplicity and poverty. And this was the key to the production's credibility: it managed to achieve a fine balance between sympathy and sentimentality. Despite the impact of such village characters as the lunatic being taken off to the mad-house, the simpleton showing his 'nuts' to the ladies, the village bore chanting his traditional folk song to the disinterested pub regulars, the village gossip on her rounds, never stopping still for a moment – despite these humorous eccentrics, at no time did the production lose its sense of reality. We felt the ordinariness of the people, the unenviable hardship of their existence, the sadness of their neglect. One of the most emotive instances was when the city pedlar tried to interest the villagers in his bric-a-brac only to find them too poor to take even the cheapest wares from him; the village's 'honour' is only saved by the young soldier spending 11s. 6d. on a china set for his betrothed's 'bottom drawer'.

Even more to the company's credit was that it itself stemmed from a local community: local teachers, students, an engineer, a postman – some of them never having acted before, including the four children who were a delight not only for their freshness but also their subtlety in portraying their roles. The music too – updated traditional played on a fiddle, accordion and guitar – gave the bitter-sweet emphasis needed to counterpoint the action. I could have wished for more direct audience involvement earlier than the two whirling circle dances in which we were all caught up towards the end – the 'promenade' aspect mentioned in the programme was not fully developed in this performance – but this is a small reservation compared with the wider enjoyment experienced by us all.

The following pieces by long-term members of ACT give a broader view, with alternative significance.

Sheila Harding writes:

We're touring Lark Rise and Candleford in the Yorkshire Dales, camping out in a field and driving through a stunningly beautiful countryside to perform in village halls. There's a whole community of us, a band as well as actors and technicians, some children too. After a couple of days this starts to feel like some sort of alternative existence: like one of those Eastern European theatre collectives, where theatre is life and vice versa. It's blazing hot, we're eaten alive by midges and no-one washes much. We spend the mornings putting up posters and handing out flyers, the afternoons setting up in dusty halls with cramped little kitchens to change in. Not many people come. It's the experience of being part of a working community which attracts me; seeing performances, ability and relationships develop, and sometimes splinter, in conditions which can't be replicated in twice-weekly rehearsals. I find it challenging, a bit dangerous.

Steve Cox writes:

ACT was a loose community of people who had a common interest and passion for theatre. It wasn't just the plays themselves that were fun, it was the whole process of forming a company with everyone having a common purpose and together, creating a story from the page and sharing it with an audience. It was probably obvious to other people but I hadn't realised that the audience was part of the process or at least, how much the audience contributed to the performance. I suppose the whole thing was greater than the sum of its parts.

It seemed to me that Jack's interest was always about how individuals would or could interact in the story. In fact, looking back, his direction was often quite loose, bringing in the thoughts and ideas of the cast in a quiet organic way. It was also quite forgiving. That is not to say that there were not tricky moments. In this diverse mix of people, there were some who could dominate, pull focus and become stage pirates. Some who would always do more than others to build and strike the set and some who were always 'missing' when there was work to be done. This all added to the mix of the company and offered an extra challenge when a play was being toured.

From Ian Rochard:

Being a member of Arts Centre Theatre (ACT) changed my life, both personally and professionally.

Most of my memories of this show come from the week spent touring the Yorkshire Dales. We camped in a field (there were over thirty of us), with very basic facilities, most notably a chemical loo. It was the first time I realised just how noisy sheep can be first thing in the morning. The weather was beautiful throughout. During the day we promoted the shows by having the band play the music whilst we encouraged members of the public to join in the dances.

The shows were very successful, with enthusiastic audiences following us around the Dales for repeat performances.

My lasting memory however, is of a separate chance event, which was to have lasting repercussions for Anne and me. She and Jack were sitting at either end of a bench outside one of the venues (Lofthouse, I think) where we had just installed the Candleford set. Jack got up from the bench and the sudden release of weight caused his end to fly up, depositing Anne on the ground. Although there appeared to be no damage at the time, we later learned that this accident was most probably the cause of my daughter's premature birth. She was seriously jaundiced at birth and then contracted a blood infection. For several days she was considered unlikely to survive. The foetal bloodstream had leached into Anne's rhesus negative system and the resulting antibodies had caused Anne's body to reject the baby. Because of the antibody issue Anne required weekly sessions of plasmapheresis during her second pregnancy, which left her physically drained. However, after numerous complications my daughter did eventually pull through. We named Lemady after the song, sung by Ken Richardson, which opened Lark Rise.

Hark says the fair maid
The nightingales are singing
The larks are winging
Their notes up in the air.
Small birds and turtle doves
On every bough are building.
The sun is just a glimmering
Arise my dear.

Rise up my fair one
And pick your love a posy
It is the finest flower
That ever my eyes did see.
Yes I will pick you posies
Sweet lily pink and rosy:
There is none so fair a flower
As the lad I adore.

Lemady, Lemady
You are a lovely creature,
You are the finest flower
That ever my eyes did see.

Didier, our son, who was born by planned Caesarean section at thirty-four weeks, tiny (under 2lbs.) but relatively healthy, sang this song at Lemady's wedding in 2010 some thirty years later.

The Running Man stands in Court. He is guilty. He wears a suit, well-polished shoes, two shirts and a tie. This is an occasion. He stands in the dock. His solicitor explains the circumstances of the incident. The Running Man is of good character, he is the director of a Theatre Company, highly regarded in Derbyshire. The shotgun is used as a property in a production of *Candleford*, it helps set the mood for a scene where the Lord of the Manor is about to go hunting. The fox-hunting scene is, of course, a separate issue, as we are considering the rabbit-shooting scene, in which the Running Man, ahem, director, had intended emulating the Rabbit shooting scene in Jean Renoir's film *La Règle du Jeu*, which incidentally is regarded by those who know about such things as one of the greatest films of all time, but whose shocking immediacy ahem can hardly be represented on the stage in live performance without... ahem. One magistrate raises an eyebrow. My solicitor quotes a legal clause regarding the use of firearms in live performance, and explains that the Running Man had borrowed the shotgun from its licensed owner, his father-in-law, who ahem........ The case is hopeless it would appear. The Clerk of the Court turns and whispers with the three Magistrates. Heads nodding, one glances up – not the pretty one. It would appear that said Running Man is GUILTY on two counts: holding no licence to possess a firearm, and being in possession of a shotgun in a public place without the necessary and statutory gun case covering it.

I wait.

I watch the nodding
> the whispered conversation.

The Clerk of the Court advises

I watch the nodding
> the glances
>> more whispers.

Case dismissed!

I thank the Court. I thank my solicitor.

The costs of the case will be met by my Union.

Back to the Gang.
> I get Brownie points!
>> And Ridicule!
>>> Gangland!
>>>> Gang Culture.

INTERLUDE

Make believe is a necessity.
Question realism – prefer to
experiment with characters
behaving out of character,
and with the lies, inconsistency
and total confusion of daily
life.

PETER BROOK

INTERVAL CONVERSATION

I suppose it came down to instinct, emotions, feelings, in the end, but the core, the essence of my work was WORDS, the love of words, the spoken word, words aloud: the searching intellectual complexity of Howard Barker, the midlands dialect of D. H. Lawrence, the gobbledegook of Count Backwerdz, the hill-billy sing-song of Lizzy Strater, the tensioned allusiveness of Pinter, the squark of Mr Punch, the evolved degenerate English of Riddley Walker, the snarly hard rockjive of Sam Shepard's *Tooth of Crime*, the Jacobean metre and rhythms melded with the Chicago gangster speak of George Tabori's translation of *Arturo Ui*, the northern vernacular of Jim Cartwright's *Road*, the poetry of Shakespeare, Bogart's laconic whole hill of beans *Casablanca* comments pirated into Biggles so awfully awfully Received English, the elegiac tone of Doctorow's *Welcome to Hard Times* – and so many others. The wonderful, masterful writers who create human lives! Without words, without the writers of those words, there is no theatre.

Myself not a talkative person. I can and do enjoy talking, but by nature tend to be a retiring listener rather than a spontaneous talker.

INTERVAL ASIDE

Never ask an actor to bring the goat for the show on the back seat of your beloved, bright green, trendy Citroen 2CV because he will drive your car into a ditch and blame it on the goat for jumping into his lap when he was negotiating a particularly steep and bendy road.

INTERVAL COMMENT

Photographs were not important to me; we were making a live art form. W. B. Yeats wrote that whatever is begotten, born and dies is greater by far than monuments of unageing intellect. That was my position; when one show was over I was ready to move on to the next. I tended to feel there was an element of ooh! Look at me! about theatre photography.

I now think this was wrong, perhaps from no more than nostalgia. When I prepared an exhibitions of photographs, NOT BE ALONE, I was able to trace images of only eighteen of the eighty-two productions I created. Some of those are rich and memorable, images that have triggered new memories and some of this writing. They can also have the useful purpose of ordering my response, as well as that of other people to the work. When a friend saw the photograph of a pile of three naked women's bodies with another in the act of being executed and asked: how did you get them to take their clothes off?, the kind of direct question I have never faced, I was able to say: because they believed in the work.

INTERVAL ASIDE

If you have a stage manager/technician with a tendency to be temperamental to the point of threatening to beat you up, avoid being confrontational and depute the best-looking actress to keep him well supplied with Mars bars.

INTERVAL TRANSLATION

This is a free version of Régis Debray's preface to Claud Confortès book about his life as a metteur en scène and actor: **De Theâtre et l'Eau Fraîche.**

> Theatre is not like a trade or an occupation, but rather is a way
> of life, of ethics, of 'morale', a gamble with the stuff of life. You
> are not one of a profession, but one of a family that engages the
> entirety of the individual, his memory, fibres, loves and dreams. In
> these respects theatre is closer to poetry than to any other cultural
> activity, nearer to the bards of antiquity than to the conjurer,
> theatre is welded to the very nature of our humanity, rather than
> being our prop, prosthetic or other mechanical appliance.

The book was lent to me by Aline, his cousin, who was my neighbour in Cereste. Reading his account helped prompt me into writing this my own very different story.

INTERVAL ANECDOTE

Eric Popplewell totters upsy downsy, stops, then down touch the ground, a little rush and arrives down the Bank to the side of my house. He waits to take balance at the top of the steps, descends in a rush, swivels to a stop and shakes his head with a look of surprise. He has developed Parkinson's disease, but in no way allows this to stop him leading a full life. He's here for the opening of NOT BE ALONE, looks at the theatre series of photographs, meets my daughter and immediately tells her that I hit him. She looks puzzled, but not shocked, not amazed, she knows her dad.

He really thumped me your dad he did. Hard. Shocking.

His voice is strange and strangulated. This heightens the import, the nature of their encounter.

But you came on without your ears Eric! The worst thing a Bottom can do is come on without his Donkey Ears! I should of fucking killed you!

Eric always blames Brian who did carry him on for that scene. He maintains that Brian picked him up too early and just dumped him on the stage.

This anecdote is very live.

It lives on.

You never hit Brian, he says.

You're the lucky one, I reply.

INTERVAL CONVERSATION

No, no, no, no, no, using Space is crucial, it's the airy element that ultimately defines the nature of your production.

But of course I quickly got over, or adapted to, the fact that they never would build a properly designed Studio Theatre. It meant there was no reason to create work that fitted a particular defined area. It enabled me to explore a variety of different formats, allowed us to determine the size and shape of space that best fitted our overall design and concept. We played in spaces from the most closely confined and intimately shared with the audience, to large all-enveloping environments within which the audience were scattered in individual knotted groups, to the occasional promenade production without fixed seating as such. Very, very rarely did we have a traditional fourth wall set-up with the audience in serried ranks looking at the performance face on. The idea of playing on A Stage became increasingly uncomfortable to actors accustomed to occupying A Space, (although the Farndale Actresses squealed with delight when they learnt, they realised, they were to perform their production of The Scottish Play on a proper raised proscenium stage with curtains that opened and closed.)

Some of my best memories are of those productions where the actual playing space was shared with the audience. These include *The Tempest*, *Lark Rise and Candleford*, *Dusa Fish Stas and Vi*, *Riddley Walker*, *Line One* and *Welcome to Hard Times*, in all of which the audience were integrated into the playing area, thus inhabiting that same imagined world for the duration of the drama.

In character you can become very attached to a space when it is right; it becomes your territory, your imperative, you have no wish to be anywhere else.

INTERVAL: QUIPS AND EMBARRASSMENTS

J.C : He persuaded me to ride a real motorbike around the stage and through a wall in one of the anarchic scenes. We had such fun, Jack keeping us all on our toes by giving a different Professor Molereason's performance each night. Learning lines was not one of his strong points.

Ph.C.: I remember the time he wrapped his head and face in gaffer tape. Round and round. We had to cut it off with scissors. I don't know what he was trying to prove. Something about bondage perhaps. Or commitment.

B.S : I felt uneasy with Jack, he was quiet and sometimes I would arrive at rehearsal and he'd be sitting on his own. I would shout a greeting and he'd ignore me. I think he was the same with everybody. I got used to him eventually and learned to love him. Early days it was almost fear I felt.

J.C : I can't remember him giving praise very often, and when challenged about this he would say "You don't need me to tell you if you're good or not . . . you should know yourself".

INTERVAL CONVERSATION

Moving is not the problem. Moving at the right time with the proper intent is the problem. Moving to suit the pitch of the words, so that words and movement together convey the necessary dramatic sense. I hate wandering actors. Inexperienced performers feel the need to assert their presence on stage by moving; they haven't discovered that still, inner gut strength that allows them to simply be there. My dramas were full of action and movement, but I was determined that these would never overwhelm the words. I found myself restraining and controlling the urge to move, in the cause of clear imagery and an audible text. This might seem paradoxical, contradictory – lots of movement yet limiting it. What I am trying to address is the fact that movement must be significant and defined, serving the dramatic impulse rather than happening simply for the sake of changing the picture.

INTERVAL ASIDE

If you can't sing in tune, and I can't, don't muscle in on a number which is being developed with subtle harmonies just because you're playing a part in the play. The cast members will despise you for it as they did me in *The Tooth of Crime*.

This in spite of the fact that when thirty years later I met Mick Simmonds, our musical director, who had arranged and performed around the world, he said it was the most rewarding and thrilling music he had ever played.

They should have stood me at the back, with a tambourine, with specific instructions not to bash it.

INTERVAL QUESTION – Can acting be sexy?

In the opening scene of *Road*, a teenager is preparing herself for a night out with girlfriends whilst holding a contentious conversation with her elder brother. He is working on a car engine. He is dirty, dirty minded, coarse and uncouth. They insult and bad mouth one another. From the text I felt he had had at least his fingers inside his sister's knickers. There needed to be sexual tension in the atmosphere if nothing more. During one private practice of the scene Sandy tensed momentarily, tremored twice, opening her mouth, looking at her brother, almost smiled, slowly blew out her breath and relaxed slightly blushing. There's a pause. The brother shoves the engine clattering over. *"A glorious tribute to Jack's creepiness"* is Rochard's description of my performance. I never achieved the same effect again.

In ACT's version of *Nana* I played a sexually predatory aristocrat who in one scene buys sex with a prostitute who is a friend of Nana. I met Kay to discuss how we should approach this, get comfortable with one another, know if and where we could touch, and how to engage in what should be an ugly, depraved encounter. How should we start? She said, you can do what you like, which showed her confidence in me, but in no way put me at ease. She was in costume, she had a pretty face, nicely pert breasts, nicely rounded derriere, shapely legs, baggy knickerbockers. She lay on her back, raised her knees and spread her legs. What to do? I was standing at her head looking directly down the length of her body. I raised my hands to slide them down her face, and her neck, to caress her breasts, perhaps squeeze a nipple, but barely had I touched her when I noticed her foot, her left foot. I slid my hands the length of her body as I moved to take her foot, her left foot, which I raised to my lips and kissed as I unlaced her shoe. Then I press that left foot against my cock and fuck and fuck and fuck her foot whilst deeply inhaling the scent of her shoe which I hold clasped across my mouth and nose. After climax I turn aside and toss the shoe at her, offering no payment.

The idea came from Dennis Hopper who in the film *Blue Velvet* uses his asthma inhaler similarly to enhance his sexual experience.

In fact it was a totally unarousing encounter, both in rehearsal and in performance. A missed opportunity? I wonder. The audience were suitably disgusted.

INTERVAL: MORE QUIPS AND EMBARRASSMENTS

R: Abiding memory? – Female Transport, being told off by Jack for smoking while we waited to go on. I soon came to see his point, but at the time thought his comments rather harsh.

J.H.S:...that day he had complained of a dry persistent cough which threatened his rendition of the very vociferous Arturo Ui. My only suggestion, as I know nothing of the demands on an actor's voice, was to try a proprietary cough mixture ... He was able to find an appropriate formulation which contained ipecacuanha, an ingredient always kept in our stock of remedies in the pantry at home. And so, Arturo Ui is taking an occasional swig of the cough elixir concealed here and there in the scenery, the ipecacuanha doubtless adding an extra dimension to the crazed rhetoric of a dictator in the throes of his (ir) restible rise.

C.D: That river he made me stand in up to my chest, and then crawl, was freezing really really freezing cold. When he let me get out I just couldn't stop shivering. He ran a hot bath for me in his house. I remember the bathroom, it had a dark portrait on the wall, it was unusual and typical.

J.C: We were a community theatre group who took theatre to the community. Comedians had a mixed cast of about nine actors. A few things stick in my mind, one was seeing Jack licking the blood (red food colouring) off a female mannequin's right breast.

INTERVAL QUESTION – What was your last public performance?

Reading Cordelia's lines in a skilleted version of *King Lear* offered as a rehearsal presentation to trainee English teachers in Darmstadt. Knowing this would be the last time, after ten years of regular successful visits, that I would bring productions to Germany, I had decided, in the cause of encouraging future generations, to bring a group made up of students, with the exception

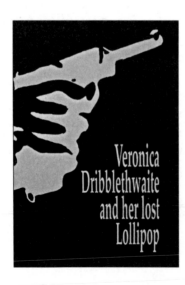

of two senior members of ACT. The decision proved disastrous; the group did not gel, and the presence of the man playing Lear was particularly disruptive as the group were aware of an incident involving him the previous year which I now realise I handled very inadequately. I should not have allowed him to continue working with us. The support show we had devised, *Veronica Dribblethwaite and her Lost Lollipop*, was an indifferent Five-Go-Adventuring romp which I had envisaged as something like Dennis Potter's *Blue Remembered Hills*, but which remained pure Enid Blyton.

There was an outbreak of group hysteria at our base, the University Guest House, to which I called the ambulance service. They looked, laughed cynically, and walked away. Later a nasty spitting incident broke out and two of the party had to be separated from the rest. I had succumbed to the pleading of one particularly weak, failing, student on the grounds that his life had been shattered by the recent divorce of his parents. His behaviour was appallingly immature, his work worthless. The girl playing Cordelia took to her bed, even before the first performance, sobbing pitifully and claiming that she was sick, sick, sick. I explained to her that the only reason an actress doesn't perform is because she is dead. She claimed to be dead. I think she was pregnant, by the wrong man, and simply could not bear the trauma and stress she found herself in. But it was a gutless performance.

Our return journey to England was cold and embarrassing. Good ones had pulled their weight – the bad pennies and my failure to handle certain situations led to a very unhappy last tour. The whole thing was ridiculously wasteful.

And as to my performances as Cordelia, playing the part with script in hand? Commended. Highly Commended in that it gave the rehearsal presentation format increased validity.

Oh! How are the Mighty fallen . . .

INTERVAL ASIDE

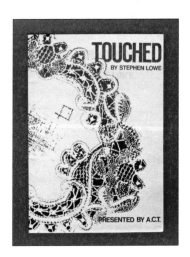

Don't let an actress drink real gin when acting a scene of attempted abortion involving a 1940s tin bath tub full of hot water, a large bottle brush, some unlikely looking instrument and a bottle of gin, as Helen did during her final performance of *Touched* by Stephen Lowe. She just about made it until she bowed her head for the final applause, when she immediately collapsed into staggering eye-glazed, nervously giggling drunkenness.

Some have called it Method Acting.

I have no idea how much gin she had drunk on previous occasions.

Helen was a great character actress who claimed to suffer acute stage fright before performances.

INTERVAL CONVERSATION

Working all those years, yes, and always either wanting to, or having to, find new resolutions to the questions of creativity and the changing times. So, no, if you ask me I will say I did not have a system. My forte was making use of other people's talents. I would suggest, come along, come along with me, and many people did and we got there. Theatre is not like painting or writing or music where you can leave product on a shelf for years or throw it away. If a group of people have been invited to commit themselves to a work of theatre you have to finish it. Only the most exceptional of circumstances allow you not to. I learnt this early, the hard way, in my twenties when I began trying to make films and left every attempt more or less unfinished.

However, there is one system quote that I have tried to live by. It's William Blake:

> I must create a system,
>
> or be enslaved by another man's.
>
> I will not reason and compare
>
> My business is to create.

I am so fortunate, that during my working life I was allowed the freedom to more than less live by this tenet.

INTERVAL: AND MORE QUIPS AND EMBARRASSMENTS

I.R: .. my next role was as Roma, Ui's henchman in The Resistible Rise of Arturo Ui. I'd lost a lot of weight since Jack had last seen me. He wasn't particularly pleased as he thought my character should have as much bulk as possible. His was the only negative comment made to me about my body shape, but it's a nice indicator of his single-minded attitude towards his work.

T.O: I remember him standing scrunched up with tension, stamping his left foot and yelling with frustration as he tried to get Ariel's song out, and that was at the last rehearsal – he was in costume!

J.G.: He talked about using every fibre of your being on whatever action you made, and demonstrated this by 'dying', taking about three minutes to die, keeping us riveted as the horrible scene unfolded before us. Would he never actually lay down and stay down!

INTERVAL EXPLANATION

The type of work we produced more usually involved men in major roles than women although women were perhaps more influential. I love working with men, love their manliness. But do not fall in love with them. Two very good friends have written very generously about our time together.

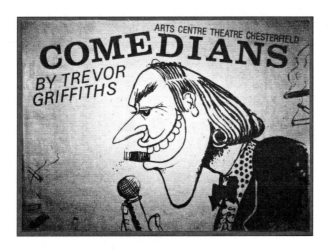

Steve Cox:

Of all the high points of my life, and the most enjoyable and memorable experiences so far, some key moments are from my time with ACT. The experience of performing in an ACT production was different to anything I had expected. Unlike my experience later, the plays often had a large cast: sixteen actors in Arturo Ui with multiple roles. There was nothing in the way of casting Nazism. I'm not sure how Jack coped with the creation of the plays. Complex would be an understatement. I think that my favourite role was in 'Comedians' by Trevor Griffiths. I loved delivering the Northern Irish comedian's stand-up set. Every time we performed, I learned more about the play and about my ability to act. It was a brilliant experience.

I gained so much confidence working with Jack. As a direct result it enabled me to develop in my career in ways that wouldn't have been possible otherwise. It also led to a further eighteen years of professional acting.

John Connolly:

I first started working with ACT after a chance meeting with Jack Blackburn at Chesterfield's Hipper Centre. Jack was running some drama workshops for teachers and asked if I wanted to be in a play he was to direct. This proved to be a life changing decision. When Jack told me the play was Comedians by Trevor Griffiths I immediately agreed, and was so excited to be cast in the role of the punk Gethin Pryce. Jack is such a good director. Not only did I enjoy working with him but I learned so much about both acting and directing from this man who should have been working in full-time pro theatre rather than the Arts Centre's Community Theatre group. He had a way of getting great performances out of actors.

It was life changing when I decided to do a play with Jack Blackburn. Working with ACT has been one of the most enjoyable times of my life. Working with Jack gave me the opportunity to develop as an actor, a director, and to meet so many wonderful people who have become a big part of my life.

INTERVAL PHEW!

I must slip out for a few moments. The bathroom. The Gents. To spare my blushes. Another round, perhaps?

INTERVAL ANECDOTE

*It's **Tuesday afternoon.** I'm sitting across the desk from Jack in his office in Chesterfield College. No one else has responded to his attempt to recruit a day-time group. It might be difficult with just you, he says, what do you want to do? I have no idea; it's embarrassing. He tells me about the sort of thing he usually does. But they need more people, he says. I'm on the point of apologising for existing and getting out. There are some Alan Garner short stories 'The Stone Book Quartet' I think are quite interesting, he says, reluctantly it seems to me. Do you want to go away and have a go at adapting them? (S.H.)*

INTERVAL ASIDE

As performance approaches always carry a Swiss Army Knife. Preferably the most sophisticated model with every imaginable gadget and appliance – all the usual tools, plus a pair of scissors, tweezers, a tiny ball-point pen, a compass, a tooth pick, etc. Keep the blade sharp, you never know whose throat you might decide to slit, and make yourself fully aware of the multiple uses of the thingy designed to remove stones from horse's hooves.

Some recommend a comb, but I never bothered myself.

INTERVAL JUSTIFICATION

Yes, of course I should have been running the R.S.C., it's just that I couldn't make myself available. I had work to do, and, for a few short years, in my small way, I was 'world famous round here!' I never wanted to see my name in lights, being wary of adulation of any kind, although ambitious and determined to succeed in those areas in which I chose to work. I found it a wonderful privilege to be embedded in a College of Art, staffed by practising professional artists, whose raison d'être was artistic and original creativity. After the inevitable shaky start which involved mutual misunderstanding I won the respect of these artists: they supported my work and many worked with me, providing ideas, inspiration and artefacts that originated beyond the common culture and practice of theatre. This context and support network was refreshing, stimulating and rewarding. I think it benefited and suited me more than if I had been embedded directly within a purely theatre-based context.

INTERVAL HOWL!

Aaah! Marcello! The 8½ Syndrome was often hovering, always there, like a haunting side partner just biding its time, just waiting, with gleeful wicked grin to tap a shoulder, invade the brain, alter being – and then me, knowing that now, after that last piece, now, just at this moment in time, and for however long, there is nothing there. Neither inspiration nor imagination nor creative pulse, no prospect, muses all dissolved, deserted, alone, locked in, energy drained, lollipops lost.

It's awful. I've shared time and place with groups who have realised that we've hit the wall, nothing forthcoming in spite of all their support, their suggestions for new direction, their recommendations of scripts, their offers of respite. I have worked on loopy explorations, lazy improvisations, pointless gaming with exercise and text, knowing deep in my heart that it was mere floundering, helpless floundering in a search for oxygen, desperately, drowning, fearing I might never surface.

Although very rare occasions, they seemed everlasting, despairing. But they were, in reality, quite short in duration.

One day, with a finger click, a silky oh so smooth knees bent quick few steps and a tilt of my wide-brimmed hat and we would be back on course, the road clear. Inexplicably we could begin again.

I have worn wide-brimmed hats for many years. Comfort, Image, Pretension, Homage – just like Fellini – who did after all have the excuse of shelter from the blazing Roman sun.

Or, just like Marcello in the movie, all to do with Style, Image, Presence.

Aaah, Marcello! che sera sera.

INTERVAL REVELATION!

I said to him (in no uncertain terms): Don't you ever ever give an actor direction or any rehearsal expectations? He said: I do it by osmosis. I said: I'm not sure what that means. He said: Nor am I.

We carried on working. (B.S.)

INTERVAL ASIDE

Never, never ever, start back late.

ACT 2

Being Widowed and ? Emotional Intelligence

THE WIDOWING OF MRS HOLROYD, D. H. Lawrence

DUSA, FISH, STAS AND VI, Pam Gems

Sheila Harding writes:

> Not all of my experiences with ACT have the same intensity. It's a foul night and I've set off straight from work without having time to eat. We're performing The Widowing of Mrs Holroyd, in, I think, Bolsover Library. The set is an unwieldy beast, Nigel is struggling to rig the sound and lights from a single power point and making a melodramatic fuss about it. Although I like the play well enough I'm not enjoying my involvement. I have a minor part which I feel to have learnt and been directed in a very conventional way. I hate my costume. There is nothing like the involvement I feel with work we have devised or adapted, or texts we have had to grapple with or present in a new way. There are three people in the audience, one of them is the librarian, who has to be there – this may not be literally true. It's certainly how it feels. After the show we struggle out into the night; thick snow is falling, settling fast on the empty car park and I have a twenty five mile drive home.

Strange how the passage through a slice of life can be so different for those involved.

When I started this collection of writing I had no idea where it might take me or what it might do for me. When the young Sherlock Holmes was asked by a taunting fellow pupil what he wanted to be in the future, he replied – Not be alone. A year ago I put together an exhibition of photographs that I called NOT BE ALONE. It featured a selection of images from ACT productions ordered under the titles of DANGER and EMOTION. The sense of danger that must not disappear, together with truth to emotion, these were the twin templates that underpinned the foundation of my work. Danger and Emotion. Being alone is something I don't find easy. I felt I needed another project.

The impulse to write quickened and led me to consider my working life. A fortunate few enjoy the privilege of making their living by directing theatre, and my experience has had its own individuality. I had meagre resources, but these were more than compensated by the artistic freedom I enjoyed. Poor theatre is an honest trade. What has surprised me, even though I expected, wished, even planned to be subjective in the writing, is how much my personal life has meshed with the work. Also, I now realise that what you end up remembering isn't always the same as what you have witnessed.

This account of *The Widowing of Mrs Holroyd* was begun in La Placette, the house which we bought in Provence ten years ago. It seemed important and necessary to begin thinking, note making, drafting, on the third anniversary of Margot's death. That anniversary will, for me, always be, not a date but a day, the Tuesday after the first weekend in July. For nine years we had spent that weekend at St Sulpice in Paris meeting the potters and ceramic artists whose pieces we had been selling at Pots from France Exhibitions at Bankside in Youlgreave. The original idea, providing a way to pay for trips to France, had been Margot's.

In early July 2008 we learnt that Margot had but little time left before a virulent form of leukaemia, which we had battled for two years, would take her. Aware that she had but a few days remaining, Margot was determined to make the trip to visit our many good friends at Les Journées de la Céramique. At two days notice colleagues organised the trip, we travelled by Eurostar, arriving on the Thursday, the fair's opening day, and settled in to the adjacent Hôtel Récamier in Place St. Sulpice. On the Friday morning we walked up to the nearby Luxembourg Gardens – a sentimental journey. We watched the children sailing toy yachts on the pool with sticks to trap and turn and relaunch their vessels. A band played in the distance, and way beyond, the scale of the Montparnasse Tower recalled the day we got lost trying to locate the Cartier-Bresson Foundation. T'ai Chi was practised, slow and graceful under the shade of trees. The donkeys and ponies, awaiting small riders, tail whisked away flies, and waited, heads bowed, in seeming melancholy. The occasional blast of a Gardien's whistle cleared errant tourists off the grass. We enjoyed ice-cream. We enjoyed being there, it was living and peaceful.

Margot was very weak. I realised she could not repeat that walk.

In the afternoon we met Malcolm and Sheila, who arrived from Normandy to join us every year. They could barely comprehend the news I gave them that evening as we strolled to the Pont des Arts. Margot was resting in the hotel, but had been so bright, laughing and looking perfectly well while we were together.

She spent most of Saturday in the hotel, fatigued, trying to conserve energy, and rose late afternoon, practised her French with Champy and Anne Verdier in the Café Céramique, and suggested we stay for the outdoor communal evening meal, but managed only the first course. Margot said goodbye to Paris, to France, to les amis.

I held her close throughout the night.

On Sunday we returned home – our last shared adventure.

On Monday Margot visited the hospital and returned for a blood transfusion on the Tuesday. As she walked down Bankside on her return I knew that she would never walk back up again. She died, not easily, that night.

When she first came to work with me twenty-seven years earlier, Margot Saunders Bartlett, a proud Scot, was forty-three years old, a mature degree student at Nottingham University. Bernadine was studying theatre on the same course, and they, together with two other mature students, were looking to broaden their experience, as they found insufficient challenge in the practical projects they were offered in their final year. I suggested to Bernadine that we might tackle a production of Pam Gem's *Dusa, Fish, Stas and Vi*, an important breakthrough play about the lives of four contemporary women. As work experience it would count towards their final degrees, and I would add an interesting extra project to my planned programme.

It proved to be one of the productions over which I felt I had little control.

As a group, their combined experience of female lives, dealings, traumas, marriages, births, sex and work and cheating, makings and breakings was broad, extensive, colourful and dauntingly more than enough for the play. Finding themselves together in a context of barely mature students they had, even though temperamentally very different, bonded to create their own tight but somewhat fragile small group dynamic. Female chutzpah overawed me.

Bernadine was insouciant, spiky and bored – our personal and working relationship which had been so productive was moving towards a break-up point. Sylvia, now a successful novelist, was a tangle of nervousness, seemingly fearful of not getting it right. Paula was mostly high, stoned, away or utterly exhausted – which fitted her role but not good working practice.

Margot seemed haughtily distant, awkwardly strained and unnecessarily self-asserting. I found myself unable to relate to them individually and uncomfortable in their company.

I created for them a tight, four-walled, box set of a walled room placed squarely isolate in the centre of a large open space. They would share the enclosed volume of their room with an audience of no more than eighteen persons. The audience would enter by the room's door, find their way through personal belongings to perched seats from which they had fly-on-the-wall views of the play. The four actors researched their roles themselves, selected appropriate clothes and personal items to suit each character's identity. One day I suggested they went on a shopping trip in character, It was a get-out clause shifting all responsibility to them.

The performances were erratic and nervy; they had wanted to be challenged, but perhaps acting in such an enclosed space within touching distance of the audience was a step too far. I felt they were unhappy with the piece. I was. It was dull. They were not dull, but their performances were. I failed to challenge and change them.

However, I must have done something right. Sylvia chose to concentrate on her writing, but the others continued to work with me, touring Yorkshire with *Lark Rise* and *Candleford* and opting to be part of the company that made the first tour to Darmstadt.

We prepared a *Macbeth Rehearsed* presentation for Germany. Margot shared the role of Lady Macbeth and suffered an obscene grizzly murder as Lady Macduff at the hands of the three witches. She was exceptionally attractive, sometimes beautiful, intelligent and worked with dedication, but in performance remained unconvincing, reserved, couldn't relax into comfortable playing. I would see her stop, look pained, stiffened, yet radiant – slowly eventually, she did begin to laugh, then to show off and be silly. Drive too fast, drink too much.

Then the real Margot arrived.

I happened to chance on her in a café with Paula a few days after our return from Yorkshire with *Lark Rise* and *Candleford*, and they invited me to join them for a drink. Their memories of the tour were so real, so ripe, so rich! Raw emotion swamped me as I sat beside them. Over the years that followed I came to recognise, to seek out that sheer emotional force field, mostly positive, but sometimes hatefully negative, that Margot's engagement with life generated.

I needed a trigger to bring me to *The Widowing of Mrs Holroyd* because to write about it is difficult and complicated. I am getting there crabwise. The third anniversary of Margot's death, a sense of my being widowed, a memory of that engulfing emotion, have proved to be that necessary trigger.

D.H. Lawrence's play was a tipping point production. A relaunch of ACT. The core of the first generation of the company, the gang, dispersed to pursue their lives and careers elsewise after the return from Darmstadt. The time had come. It had been ten years, we had done as much as we could together. Tim Anger left to work with 7:84 Theatre, John Connolly and Reg Shaw to form their own companies. Hargreaves and Steve Cox concentrated on their careers in education. Bernadine moved to Sheffield and worked with Yorkshire Art Circus.

And my life was changing: I was forty. Thatcher's Tories ruled, values changed. As a family we moved into the Peak District to Bankside, the house where I still live. A couple of weeks after the tour of Germany I lost the position of Director of the Arts Centre I had created. I struggled to accept and adjust to this loss of status, felt insecure, unsure of my next move and couldn't move. June Billie, my wife, was seeking to change her life, making plans to do voluntary service (VSO) in Bhutan. My daughters Catherine and Susanna were maturing, preparing to go to university. Lollipops lost, I didn't know where to what how to if and whether or not.

What to do?

What to do?

I do remember that I did know I wanted to direct a second D. H. Lawrence play ten years after *The Daughter-in-Law*. I remember that I knew it would be *The Widowing of Mrs Holroyd*, and that I would use the same music, a link, a nostalgic reference, a tribute even, to the first production.

But I don't remember,

> I remain unsure
>> of what part of me
>>> – instinct, delusion or nascent lust –

led to my asking Margot to take the role of Mrs Holroyd, the bitterly unsettled miner's wife who becomes involved with another man before her husband is killed in a mining accident after which she becomes reconciled to the love she had for him as she bathes the naked damaged corpse which has been returned to her.

It is a major role in the only one of his plays that was produced in Lawrence's lifetime. He regretted that last scene of the bathing, believing it to be misjudged, a too theatrical device crudely designed to garner sympathy. He was right, but I believe the play to be stronger for it. The scene can be downplayed, a deeply felt unacknowledged love dawning softly and gently with neither drama nor histrionics.

Martin Wiltshire designed the set, a simple open kitchen, with the first six treads of a staircase, that was very sparsely dressed. Brian Sargent played Holroyd, Alan Williams the other man, and Ollie Wilmot from *The Daughter-in-Law* played Holroyd's mother. Two children, a boy and a girl aged eight and nine, played the family's children. Two drunken giggling local tarts, Sheila Harding and Jacky Williams, overplayed their flirting encounter with Holroyd in his wife's presence. Their caricatural emphasis heightened the gut-wrenchingly coarse embarrassment of Mrs Holroyd's situation.

I was proud of the production, feeling that we had come close to the essence of Lawrence's experiments with dramatic form and technique described by Raymond Williams as being

> based on one of the variant forms of naturalism: the play which gets close to ordinary experience, not only by taking ordinary situations and probably characters, but by using these to embody crises of immediate relationships, with an emphasis on ways of speaking, minutely observed and reproduced, as the social reality of a particular dimension of life.

In performance Margot's interpretation was a revelation. She drew such profound emotion from the role, so convincingly, with such impassioned sensitivity that she drew tears from every audience. It was astonishingly moving.

> *I was moved by the whole production, Brian Sargent has written. Another thing that comes to mind was the brilliance of the opening of the play, Margot hanging washing and talking to her little girl and the lights creating a sunny scene and then the music – the first time I saw it at dress rehearsal I was entranced.*

I wanted to know the actress better.

I fell in love with the woman.

It was not easy.

There was mutual hurting even while our love was growing.

Not easy.

It came from left field. Unexpected.

Some months later I asked Margot to become my lover. We stood tremoring in the force field of her emotion.

Our marriages foundered.

We shared our lives and work for the following twenty-six years.

It was not easy, but it was a wonderfully rich rewarding relationship,

We fought. Of course we fought, but never split.

Margot was such fun to know, quite the opposite of my early perceptions. She was comic, sensual, caring and committed, extravagant yet dedicated, with an adventurous buccaneering devil-may-care ésprit, tempered occasionally by fear, even panic, scared truly fearfully scared of cows and mice and high places. The emotion thing raking me raw.

It feels strange. I am choosing to be correct, describing her with a degree of formality that belies her essence, her vitality.

She should be splashed in multicoloured abundance across the pages, with exultant sweeping curves and joyous conjunctions, with darting jabs and dangerous dark hiding marks, with a misting grey for apprehension, with sunlight and passion! And a lurking, a lurking endgame.

When I started this writing I had no idea where it might take me or what it might do for me.

I'm finding out.

In my life women have been fresh water.

I have had two Great Loves.

The first was June Billie, the sweetheart of my youth, mother of our children, the wife with whom I shared twenty-six years of tempestuous, heartfelt loving life.

Margot was the second.

Two Great Loves!

And a Grand Passion! With the Greek who sat beside me.

And a Searching, Deeply Explored Engagement! with Bernadine.

And Muse 1 – Pippa, when I was starting!

And Muse 2 – Claire, when I finished!

These women defined much of who I became, of who I am. And this is where deciding to write about *The Widowing of Mrs Holroyd* has taken me.

To realising and accepting the fact of being widowed myself. Knowledge of a kind I never dreamt of knowing when I directed the play.

To honouring the women I loved, those who so inspired, supported and shared their lives with me. I knew the four intimately, met and mixed with them in such a range of contexts and endeavours that I feel I have been as close to them as possible for a man.

I know we all keep kernels of privacy.

I am widowed.

I had no idea what it might do for me.

Emotion can and did run wild in productions and real life. Emotion discovered, explored, experienced in both the working process and performance, and in our shared personal lives.

I am widowed.

I live alone.

It's always been a kindness, a gentility and a certain social grace (difficult for a Yorkshire man) that has been reasserted through women.

? They say I am inscrutable.

? Emotional intelligence.

?

I'm not sure what it is. Could it be something that equates to wisdom, in the realm of shared relationships? Possibly, that is what I have come away with? It seems somehow apposite, having relevance to the ways these relationship have deepened and enriched my understanding of the possibilities between a man and a woman. In my case, the work we shared was the key that unlocked those possibilities.

? Emotion

I can say no more.

> Emotion is not a theme. It is the central fire
> and the external glow, but it is not a theme
>
> (E. M. Forster)

I am thoroughly widowed.

I value emotion.

I frequently misquote the following :

> Nothing matters in the end but the quality of the affection-
>
> that has carved the trace in the mind;
>
> What thou lovest well is thy true heritage.
>
> What thou lovest well shall not be reft from thee.
>
> (Ezra Pound)

What the Dickens - The Song Solution

OLIVER TWIST – Charles Dickens

EXPECTATIONS – Not the cluster of black clad figures in a gloomily lit space huddled over a panting screaming woman who gives workhouse birth to a boy child and then dies. Not at all the expectations of audiences which have come to think of Oliver Twist in terms of "Food, glorious food" and the fact that "We've got to pick a pocket or two".

EXPECTATIONS – Not the gloomy prospect of suddenly losing my job, Director of the Arts Centre and Community Theatre programme that I had initiated and built up over a decade. Not at all the expectation of a man who has recently returned from a successful tour of the Yorkshire Dales, who has just moved with his family to the house at Bankside, Youlgreave where he still lives thirty years later in a particularly appealing part of the White Peak, and who has put before the Academic Board the proposal that the range and quality of the work had now reached a level to be worthy of faculty status; a proposal passed with the 100% support of voting members present.

EXPECTATIONS – Not the writing on the wall when I was asked to prepare a job description for the new post. I was interviewed and, this being, the managerial minded 1980s, the job was offered to an administrator. Not at all the expectation that a man might lose his job after an eight minute interview. I found this very difficult, knowing the Centre the new appointee had been running previously as I had visited it several times in my role as an assessor for the Arts Council of Great Britain.

EXPECTATIONS –It was suggested that my forte was creative work, hands on engagement with people. I accepted this whilst hating the fact that I no longer had the boss role. In the long run it has been for the best: becoming a suit was not my style.

I determined to make the best of that suggestion. I would explore the role of 'metteur en scene', which did suit me, in new directions. I would hang on to my freedom of operation, and as ever in my working life would not be bossed. For the next decade I would hold them to their word.

After the return from the first tour to Darmstadt the gang, with whom I had worked so productively, dispersed. We had done all we could together, strains were beginning to show and the time was ripe for those who wished to extend and explore their experience in different areas. Two of them set up their own theatre companies, some pursued acting with varied success, others settled back to 'real' work and family life.

I was left with a core and we had to begin again. At this turning point I felt impelled to create more original work, involving the group more deeply in the process. I had pursued this method many times on smaller T.I.E. projects and it proved to be very rewarding. Now the idea was to apply the practice to major productions. Using all our collective skills as an ensemble we would go further in terms of ambition, scale, rash adventure and daring experimentation. We would have great expectations!

So, on the understanding that we had no money, and therefore no sets, costumes nor sundries, a new ensemble came together.

After the gang ensemble became the buzz-word. But, to paraphrase Orwell, "all were ensemble but some were more ensemble than others" and I got to play the Big Pig every time.

I'm not sure how the idea to adapt a Dickens novel germinated. Some of us had seen the R.S.C. production of *Nicholas Nickleby*, a five hour long performance that was a ground-breaking presentation. I believed that on a smaller, simpler scale, using direct narrative as and when necessary we could create a powerful, easy to tour (no sets, no costumes) version of a Dickens novel drawing on the wonderful richness of language and dialogue, amazing characterisation and dramatic plotting. We selected *Oliver Twist* on the basis that it was shorter, had a less complicated plot line and being perhaps his best known novel would readily attract audiences. And there would be no performance rights fees to pay.

There were seven of us initially, eventually eleven actors would perform the twenty characters involved. I allocated chapters to each of the devising group, suggesting that they come up with the essence of each using narrative, dialogue or any other means of theatrical representation. This initial experiment provided interestingly varied responses to the material, but with them came the quick realisation that all were too long, and tended to be cumbersome, we needed essential streamlining, streamlined essence. Rather than spending time re-scripting we began workshopping the material, building blocks of apposite and dynamic drama, this being my favoured method of working. It produced promising ways forward: we realised ways to evoke the darkly oppressive Victorian underworld, pinpointed peripeteia, when the plot took a new direction or threw up a surprise, discarded whole chunks of descriptive filler and locked on to characterisation. As so often in the ensemble the play cast itself: Rick Burns, young, angelic, a perfect blond victim Oliver; Ian Rochard as Fagin, oppressive, seductively manipulating the lost boy in a foggy city; Helen Owen, a sparky and grinning guilefully gesturing Artful Dodger; bluff snarly; Alan Williams, cruelly menacing as Bill Sikes; Sheila Harding for Nancy and lovely Rose Maylie played by the lovely young Sharon; Brian Sargent and Margot expostulating round and ridiculous Mr and Mrs Bumble. The whole cast effectively picked the parts that fitted them. I was determined we should play true, dilute Dickensian stereotypes and caricatures, wanting real people not pre-conceived ideas of how Dickens should be spoken and performed. In actuality it proved difficult to get the pitch right. I chose to play Monks, Oliver's villainous half-brother, twisting my face into an ugly deceitful manic grimace, with greased flat hair and wearing a long black plastic rain mac which I jerked tight around me at every confrontation. I think I probably thrashed around with a walking stick as well. It must have looked very peculiar.

And it was thus that I broke all my afore stated rules. I believed in it at the time, but it was a horribly overplayed caricature and surface performance with neither depth nor reality. None of the group made the mistakes in performance I perpetrated. I wouldn't have allowed them. I only had three short bits, and I was the only one to enter and leave the in-the-round playing area, every other actor staying on stage to contribute by body language and facial expression to the tempo, tension and mood of successive scenes even when not participating in them..

We were soon struggling with the narrative, progress was slow, the whole thing having a stop start raggedy quality, very shapeless and very erratic. There was great energy and focus in certain scenes, the playing was totally committed as is testified by a powerful selection of black and white photographs taken by a photography student using us for a work experience project. But progress was too painfully slow. I had so much still to learn about adaptation on this scale, having totally underestimated the need for a prior prepared detailed skeleton script. If we were to avoid an Orghastian prospect of at least six months rehearsal through workshop based exploration, something had to change.

And it did. Jack had one of his great ideas – not the greatest as it turned out – The Song Solution/The Wedding Cake.

A four minute song can encapsulate an entire life history. We were bogged down in the central section of the novel – if, post interval, we began with

a song it would surprise and enliven the audience, cover several chapters, moving us rapidly on to the final dramatic encounters and outcomes. Remember? Essence of streamline?

Jacky and Alan Williams were musicians and songwriters. I suggested they undertake the Song Solution whilst we quickly dramatised the ending. After a weekend break they returned with the song. The complete version, which we never attempted, would have lasted not four but at least forty minutes. All the necessary narrative was there along with the unnecessary. It was endless folky rhyming quatrains totally without variation of tone, light or dark shading. It had a jolly singalong repetitious narrative monotony that was magnificent in scale but effectively unusable and in no way matched the requirements of the piece we were trying to create. I shortened it drastically, interspersed narrative interludes, a sweetly uncomfortable solo by Rose Maylie, and a ridiculously overblown intervention by Monks. And that was it, and I believed that none of us truly believed in what we were doing here.

Short acted sequences took us to the 'happy ending' – Nancy brutally strangled, Bill Sikes dead, Fagin condemned gibbering, and Oliver Twist living happily ever after in the bosom of the lovely Rose Maylie.

The production opened that year's Mansfield Festival and was very well received. We played the piece with some apparent success. But in reality we/I failed.

One primary school teacher who knew my work, organised a trip for the pupils and parents of two classes of ten and eleven year olds. At the interval so many parents sat, with dead eyes, strained expressions. At the end, a smattering of applause and the theatre cleared quickly. We had not met their expectations.

However, it is revealing to me, how positively others recall this production.

I just loved pretending to be that small child in his lair – no lines just pretending to be a kid, which wasn't difficult for me. Apart from the 'wedding cake' I don't remember much, other than Ian was a scary Fagin.

Brian Sargent comments on the workshopping process and recalls playing several small parts including one of Fagin's kids; and particularly enjoyed Mr Bumble's scenes with Margot. He says he can no longer remember the reason for *The dreaded WEDDING CAKE!* I cringe at the mere thought of it and refuse to offer any explanation.

Sheila Harding writes :

We're adapting Oliver Twist. I'm not really engaged with it; things are bad at work, and at home and I'm tired. Jack has given us homework – a chapter each to read and present. I've struggled all week with mine but nothing will come together. Everyone else seems to have found a way in – a visual image, a song, a monologue.

What do you mean you can't do it, woman? Jack has a good line in scornful incredulity for times like these. He gives me another few days.

I try again in what time I can spare, mostly the small hours, but nothing works and I am tempted to miss the next session, pleading the pressures of real life. Then, out of desperation something clicks. In my chapter, I realise, all the characters are desperate, everyone is afraid of something or someone. I present fear, and it works, it makes sense and I feel confident about it. I don't remember whether any of this survived into the show, just my step forward in the process of interpreting a text.

Several years later during a pub conversation, when I expressed my doubts, Sharon Burns told me it was exciting and involving for her, being the first time she had undertaken a major ACT production. She particularly enjoyed the work on adaptation of the novel, and the challenge of playing more than one part. The whole process was a new experience and she retains warm memories of the parts she played.

Ian Rochard comments that :

"The show was advertised as dramatic storytelling played in the round in a tightly defined space. A lot of time was spent giving it the physicality which jack wanted. I remember a lot of work on the 'wall' which we constructed with our bodies for the burglary scene at Chertsey, and being part of a pile of coffins in Mr Sowerberry's undertaking premises and much vocal work to create an appropriate soundscape for the piece.

The action was continuous and the scene changes needed to be extremely slick, which took considerable practice. Our dependence upon each other and the ensemble creation and presentation produced a very tightly bonded group of performers.

I felt that my own level of performance improved markedly during the course of this project. Playing larger than life characters seemed to suit me.

They say we learn more from our faults than our virtues. And I had certainly demonstrated faulty judgement here, failing both to comprehend the complexity and scale of what we set out to do, and to make any adequate assessment and preparatory schema before we set out. They say that expectation is the better part of realisation, but my expectations had been sorely misplaced and were left unrealised. I was disappointed and low at the end of the run, but if you stay in the valley you won't get over the hill, and I determined that this production offered a way forward, an approach to original ensemble creation that we had to pursue further. We would learn from our mistakes, and, forgetting the hills, take on some mountains. If we make no mistakes we make nothing.

Easy to understand?

POMMIE

Barbara and Alistair Scrivener recall memories:

It was very dark. I could hardly see anything but slowly I managed to pick out strange shapes, and then realised the shapes were men, standing very still. To the left an old woman sat on a stool, dressed in black with a white crocheted shawl over her shoulders. Slowly she rose and spoke. I can't remember the words she spoke but the tale she was to unfold was, for me, one of the most moving scenes in the play.

She was retelling the tragic happenings in 1932 at the Mawstone Mine on the edge of the village. It was here, at one of the very last working lead mines in Derbyshire, that 8 miners became trapped underground after an explosion. None of them survived.

There are many lasting memories but this is the most poignant. I doubt there was a dry eye in the whole audience. Standing figures in blue light lamented by a solitary wife, over voiced by the tape of a surviving miner of the period.

This was one of 12 scenes in the play called Pommie (the nickname of Youlgreave) directed by Jack Blackburn in the summer of 1986. (Barbara)

It all started like this..........A letter arrived at Youlgreave vicarage from a number of Americans who were coming to "look up their roots" as Americans do. The carved tomb of Thomas Cockayne in the church led to a proposed visit from the American Branch of the Cockayne Society whose request to visit Youlgreave gave birth to the idea of a performance to celebrate the occasion when the letter was passed on to me. (Alistair)

We visited Jack Blackburn and suggested to him the possibility of some sort of pageant. This did not interest him, but he said he would work with us on a village play from ancient to modern times.

* * *

I was delighted when Alistair and Barbara asked me to help create a performance in the village where I had come to live 4 years previously. Village plays, living memory theatre and community drama were growing phenomena in the 1980s. Perhaps in some ways a response to the Thatcherite claim that there was no such thing as society. I had already contributed to the production of a historical play in the village of North Wingfield and closely followed the progress of a living memory project at Junction 28.

This new invitation was an excellent opportunity to extend my experience. I wanted villagers involved at every level, which included writing the scenes that required specific scripting. Seven people took up the challenge of researching and writing a scene each: I took on a couple myself and prepared linking narrative. First drafts were skeletal, basic information passed between 2 or 3 cyphers, but the writers quickly learned how these might be fleshed out with character traits, incidental action and tangential dialogue: "Nar then listen to me wilt tha' for a change." "No, I won't; tha's had thisay let me tell it as it were." "Ah shut it – tha knows nowt", etc. And of course, the same technique is equally effective with the upper classes "Forsooth, I wouldst that thou wouldst list me sire" "Nay, sir knave, not I, for thou hast spoke since cockcrow as it were." "Pray silence fool, thou knowest naught of that which thou dost speak." – as she scratches her bum, etc., etc.

And it was fun to meet and plot and thicken every scene. I wanted a balance of seriously dramatic and comic scenes with as much lively action and visual stimulation as possible, the whole punctuated with music and song appropriate to the chronological succession of the scenes.

Youlgreave has a particularly large and impressive church where the play was to be performed, and I wanted us to use the space as adventurously as possible. The project had the support of Derek Gibling the vicar, and the Bishop of Derby gave his blessing. We were able to remove some pews, install raised platforms, fix screens and set up a complex sound and lighting rig which did not interfere with the architectural integrity of the building. The scenes began to fall into place.

* * *

Barbara and Alistair Scrivener continue:

The idea for the opening scene of the play grew from the premiss that there were a number of interesting historical themes that would work well dramatically. The idea that took hold was to trace the early growth of the village from key wood or stone carvings. For example, the carved pagan image of the bat creature in the parish roof became a 'Chinese Dragon' that screamed its way into the nave as a symbol of disorder, to be confronted by the arrival of Christianity; a musical sense of harmony provided by a viol consort, the Plant family of Bakewell.

From this starting point the script developed, laboriously it seemed. However, somehow a play materialised. BUT next were needed actors/actresses.......from a small Derbyshire village. It was amazing where they all turned up from and even more amazing to find so many people with undiscovered acting skills! The oldest performer was in her late seventies, the youngest were infants from the village school.

And so the play took form under Jack's expert directing powers. There was a dog on stage and a real hawk. The costumes looked authentic, we had early music with viols, and men, women and children all dancing and singing, portraying scenes of past life in the village.

There was a duel which was incredibly realistic with swords flying in all directions up and down the central aisle. This memorable scene resulted in the death of Thomas Cockayne, and the death-scene was very moving.

Another memorable scene was the opening of the first tapped well in the village in 1829. Since that time we have been proud to have our own private supply of good fresh spring water. This was a hilarious scene presented as a Mummers Play with Judith Green dressed up as the well and all the lines in rhyming verse. It was acted by many of the local lads of the village, who on performance nights had to be extracted from the nearby hostelry to which they retreated in order to gain courage to play their parts, and they certainly brought the 'house' or rather, the church, down!

In the end we had 79 actors and singers and musicians on the stage performing, plus another 30 offering backstage and front of house assistance. At the very end every single one was on stage singing the finale song specially written all about Pommie being a fabulous place.

Each performance was a sell-out and the Americans were most impressed. It is fascinating looking at the video of the play now, some 28 years later, seeing youngsters who were eight, nine or ten then who are now thirty-five years old, many married with their own children at Youlgreave School.

Charlie Watson describes his involvement in the play.

Easy to understand – we're going to do a play about Pommie, you're going to write it and you're going to act it.

Not easy to understand – how?

Easy to understand – I'll direct it.

Again not easy to understand – but how can we write it if we can't write, let alone act if we can't act?

The measured intensity of those blue eyes, the hit of the coffee, the shared shuffling, the start of some ideas, Jack sliding that line he does so well between little boy quiet in a corner and full-on in-your-face telling.

Not easy to understand – but who on earth's going to come and see a bunch of am dramatists despoiling the venue of the church by their well-meaning venture, popping out historical tablets of Youlgreave (Pommie) in some vague attempt to be both informative and entertaining?

Easy to understand – Jack says bollocks who cares if nobody comes, it's worth doing and we'll be the richer for it.

Not easy to understand – time, time, time to write the bloody thing, or that bit of the bloody thing that was given to me, rehearsals, rehearsals, rehearsals, full-time job, young kids, walking to be done, birds to be watched, and pubs to be drunk in.

Easy to understand – fine, don't then, I'll get someone else.

Not easy to understand and easy to understand – ego gets tripped, challenged, smarting I find myself saying OK I'm in.

And so we came to do it. We actually did it. I got to play Sir Thomas Cockayne and fought a snarling, clatter of a sword wielding fight the length of the nave with my friend Paul viciously attacking as I parried every thrust, every sweeping slash. I got to die. He struck me with a cruelly savage blow. I staggered to my death at the foot of the altar steps. We floated and were buoyed by Jack's confidence, encouragement and sheer belief, we began to trust each other, then to enjoy each other, and emerged with a pathetic pride in what we achieved and the sheer how of doing it.

And the church was full. And we had to do another performance.

Self-discovery and all that but a helluva good time in the making.

Looking back – easy to understand.

And slowly the Pantos come together

SHADOWS

They call themselves 'Shadows'. They know they are a theatre company. They tell me they chose the name themselves. A company, all friends together. Just like Shakespeare was, one says. Like a family. I become one of the family.

BRIAN cares for Ada, he moves with slow, careful precision, treading very carefully, it could be on eggshells. He takes her elbow, tentatively, as she turns to sit down, looks at her, enraptured, sits beside her, unshaven and unwashed.

ADA is the oldest, by a long way, in her late sixties. "Yes, Jack love duck I can do it all, you know." "Yes you can Ada." "Thank you, Jack." She is very gentle, slow of speech, the only one who can read with confidence. "I make all my own meals now Jack duck." Very careful, insecure. Apparently she was 'a bad girl' all those years ago when bad girls were put away in Homes. Now, fifty years later, totally institutionalised, they are trying to help her into a degree of independent living. The panto is a small part of that process.

MARY takes on the role of the Bossy One; she's large, bottom heavy, bustling; stomps around the stage moving things, getting them right, talks with a deafening nasal twang, can't help herself, continuously bossing with vigour and a dash of vengeance. Fierce vengeance because, "Aie towld d'em nort to BE thear agen!" and I try to reproduce the echoey boom of her voice as I write this.

CHARLIE "carn't", he never can, he is one of the best, understands what a play is, has a wide range of reference but "carn't" always "carn't" – "Cos I'm into my flat next month, and I have no time." – "I've my training day on Friday so I carn't." We want him here on Wednesday afternoon. "And carn't with painting and decorating at Tech. I come to Tech. for two days now."

CAROL craves attention. Roly poly rocking from foot to foot, one wall eye distracting, distressing, "I'm doing alright aren't I? Remembering words?" and she is except her mother, very caring, often accompanies her, and I can tell from her baleful eye that she doesn't really approve of my forthright approach. One day I'll learn that she was not the only one.

MICHAEL, white stick, near blind and boyish jolly offers this, and that, and the other, brings records cos we do music, and tee shirts, and is proud to have lots of stuff we can borrow, and a mother who is very pleased now he is in the drama. "Can she come, Jack, can she, can she come tomorrow to see me? She'll watch me Jack." "No, Michael, not tomorrow but next week. The Panto starts on Tuesday at 7 o'clock, and Wednesday and Thursday. Ask her to sell some tickets." "With my sister?" "Yes." "Oh, Great!"

PAUL VICKERSTAFF has Downs Syndrome, he is very kind, very positive and enthusiastic, but has apparent difficulty in speaking without slapping his forehead and wait, wait, stress building something locking and visibly tightening until slap-slap – "I've got it. They're idle!" "Good, Paul, yes Paul, spot on, they are sometimes." He loves writing, will bring newspapers to rehearsals, opens them searching for crosswords and fills the blank spaces with random willy-nilly words he has learnt to spell correctly. He does this with a proud distinct panache. He is Paul Vickerstaff, never just Paul.

DENIS – steady, organised, going to Mansfield, Ashbourne, Castleton, Matlock, Bolsover, Dronfield, Clay Cross spends his days riding on the buses, buys his own ticket, takes his lunch box, gets off at the stop. He is working quietly, methodically touching successive fingers, thinking and admitting he can't remember all those words.

BRIAN, arthritic, will be a plumber in the Panto; every year Brian asks to be the plumber – he's got overalls and we can use his keyboard.

GWEN, born again Gwen, who comes with her Bible and talks OVER! and ABOVE! and ASIDE! from everyone, and will not SHUT UP! her words, slashing, saliva propelled through the studio, often insulting, always intemperate scatter-gun talk. The most socially dysfunctional of the group. Yet, amazingly she plays the piano, all the old pub type songs. And she had just MARRIED!

"Yes, she's not bad at all," concurs her new very very serious husband, KEVIN, and continues, "I'll get my deputy to chair the centre meetings. I won't let you down Jack." I realise he's supporting his wife, wishing to deflect attention from the tantrum we all know will come. "I really will Jack, I'll attend all the meetings. I know it's important to come to all the rehearsals," and I can tell he's already worrying and a little confused about how to fulfil his responsibilities. Always impeccably dressed in a smart suit and tie, hair brylcreemed neat, moustache, thick-lensed glasses, he has the appearance of a 1930s bank clerk, and the manners to go with it. "Yes, she's not at all bad on the piano," he repeats. And he's right, name a tune, and Gwen hammers it out, hard, and very very fast. 'We're all going on a Summer Holiday'; that's the song, Gwen it's what we do in the Panto. She belts out 'I've got a lovely bunch of coconuts'. "Gwen!" and she won't listen, talks over me, shouts, stamps, slams the lid shut, begins to cry, very loud. Kevin stands aside helpless. "Gwen, it's summer in the play." I barely dare approach her. "We all know the words. I know you know how to play it. Come on." I want to SHOUT – and SWEAR. Suddenly she turns round with a flounce and plays the tune. The group clap. I nod towards Kevin, "Yes, she's not bad at all." But we're not ready. We hadn't sung along with her. Begin again!

RONNIE EDWARDS – opting out, opting in, and out and in again tunelessly blowing on his harmonica. He keeps hurting himself. We have a routine. I rub the sore point, it hurts more, then I pump and squeeze his shoulders man to man, hold his thumbs and gently pull as we count up to four. The procedure always works, like magic. He is very unreliable, except, he's always at the front of the queue and asking for extras when we go down to the canteen, as we do after every rehearsal. The food is probably the reason Ron joined Shadows.

ROSIE – the bouncing full-on dwarf dashes across to me and shouts and blurts with great independent spirit and cocky confidence how she is organising her day's leave from Remploy. And she agrees now, she will go in the trunk, in the dark and lid closed and carried on if Paul Vickerstaff promises the men won't drop her. But for all that brave front hers must be a lonely life as she never takes tickets for friends, or colleagues or family.

SEAN – pale-sick and dirty, epileptically fitting, watching, waiting for his turn.

JOHN BROWN – a small, smiley, grinny rotund bubble of a man, who tries to overcome his partial deafness for us, just a little, shouts his ideas, and acts evil with relish, nasty grinning super evil. He always want to play The Baddy. Stumbly, greedy, John the Shitter sneakily kisses LIN.

A couple of years previously, in order to support the independent living project, we had decided that Shadows, like ACT did, should have a residential weekend end for bonding and the final rehearsals and the adventure of it. They would pack their own luggage, buy the food needed to cook for ourselves, and we'd borrow Social Services mini-bus to go to Glossop and make a smashing pantomime. However the Glossop Centre refused to give us permission to use their premises, citing a number of reasons, all valid in their own way, including the fact that a number of teenage visitors had tragically died there some years earlier as a result of a malfunctioning heating system. We argued our case. Kate Gard, the social worker who supported Shadows, was extremely angry: this decision flew in the face of all we were trying to do. She went to the top, committees met, but all to no avail.

So I offered my house, Bankside, for sleeping as and how, for cooking if and when, and for working booked the Village Hall. The group arrived Friday evening and we all ate fish and chips from Youlgreave Chippy followed by an early night. There were nine of them, and Mary laid down sleeping rules of who sleeps where and why, and the house was taken. I chose my small garden pavilion.

Saturday went well; we worked after breakfast, had a walk on the dale with picnic lunch, then more work, cooked an evening meal, cleared up, practised songs and went to bed.

The following morning, early, Paul Vickerstaff came down to me in the garden. Looking very concerned, he slaps his forehead and says, "John Brown has done it again." I don't understand. "He's done it in the bathroom. Come on." He takes my hand and leads me upstairs to the bathroom and there stands John Brown wearing his pyjama top and large floppy underpants, his face switching from cheeky grin to real concern. There stands John Brown, barefoot, trampling on his pile of shit. "You should use the toilet, John", says Paul Vickerstaff, slap.

The following year we broke the deadlock with Glossop, drove off through the wilds of the Dark Peak with eleven Shadows. Everyone was primed and John Brown had sworn, "cross my heart, Kate" he would not do bad at the Centre and yes it was not nice to do bad in Jack's house, "Sorry Jack cross my heart." And Jack had issues and tensions enough on his mind, but everything went well. There was a pub up the road so we decided to call in on the Saturday evening. The men bought their drinks at the bar and the landlady was a delight when they struggled to work out the money. (Shadows had been refused entry to a pub near the Studio in Chesterfield.) We relaxed.

Where's John Brown?

Three soft sausages of shit on three steps down the staircase, and at the bottom, standing in front of the Gents door was John Brown with a final dollop trickled down inside his trouser leg and settled on his shoe. The landlady was wonderfully understanding. Glossop is a tough little town, perhaps she'd had to handle worse things. Kate, the caring one, flamed, incandescent with anger, made John clean up his mess, hoiked him to the Centre, put him in the shower where he cleaned himself, his clothes, his shoe. He was not allowed to work with us the next day. He was contrite, sad, and cried.

Apparently it was a technique, both the before and the after, that he had perfected and played with mastery. I wondered why he'd never done it during the Panto performance. That would have been really evil. Grrrr!

Life went on.

When we re-convened for post Panto workshops after a winter break Paul Vickerstaff arrived early. "We're all sad, Jack." "Oh, why?" "John Brown's gone." "Oh, where's he gone?" Slap head once – twice. "He died. He was deaf."

John Brown had sneakily kissed Lin and grinned at me, soft and devilish.

LIN – This is where it becomes both difficult and amazing for me. Lin had joined the group four years earlier with her boyfriend, who was brashly awkward and just not interested; after just three visits he never returned, he went away. Whereas Lin stayed although she also was away, away, away some-other-where, locked in, or just staying in, away far away. She barely moved, would not speak, twisted her neck, wrung her hands, wraith-like, angulated, wretching, seeming to suffer, would hint at a smile but never made eye contact. She was delivered, alone, lived in a care home rather than the Centre. I found this very strange and difficult, a new kind of difficulty I

didn't comprehend. Apparently Lin always knew when it was drama day, had her coat on in good time for her pick-up and money in her purse for the canteen. Ask an actor to create a seriously brain-damaged young woman and I dare bet they would act out a Lin. Nineteen years old and a stereotype of an inexpressible gone wrong.

She always had a role of course. I would lead her into position, move her when necessary, accept an off-beam mouth movement when she tried to say yes, give her something to carry, ask her to hold hands, lift up a song sheet, bash a cymbal. And when we came to the sad bits (Shadows were very good at sad bits: they loved them) Lin would move over to stand beside me and shoals of sadness swamped us.

Then gradually, as we progressed through workshops and struggled through rehearsals, a glimmer of dawning surprised me. Was I the dumb one? Some of the group seemed to barely understand when or if they were acting or what, indeed, a play was. But somehow, by a strange osmosis Lin made me realise that she knew exactly what was going on, what we were aiming for, where the cast should be in any scene. She knew when the laughs came, and if someone totally missed a cue, which happened repeatedly she would cross the stage and nudge them or nudge me when I slipped up. She knew when Gwen should play and Rosie jump out of the trunk and Kevin lose his silly spectacles and everybody cower at the scary thundering crash bang wallop. And it wasn't just so simple, she was following and sharing and being there with me, for me. A Shadow Muse? I wanted her there, it was easier then, somehow more bearable and eventually she would look me in the eye, and sometimes she tried to speak in chorus, and the odd sound came, and she was utterly involved.

So this was the Shadows cast for the Panto, except that year we were doing a play, a kind of Morality about how we are all the same inside and all ultimately want the same things: a job which we can do with confidence and satisfaction and feel well rewarded, a home of one's own, nicely appointed, and good friends, and love, and somebody to fall back on. We watched the film E.T. together.

It was Kate's idea; she felt we had to move on from the Pantos, should address real issues that faced the group. She was my best help and support in this activity and organised the schedules, doing necessary research and workshopping their own ideas until I was able to create the show with them. She became increasingly involved and proud that this group project was derived from their own ideas, from their own lives. She insists, again and often, that I must honour their research, must get the ending right, and the meanings across. She explains, cannot over-emphasise too much, that we all, she, me, the audience and cast, we all ARE the same inside and deep down have the same needs and desires. So I do agree, and I say I will, and I like you Kate, we make a good team, and Kate relaxes and smiles and settles to enjoy our work on this new venture when she realises that what she wants can happen. Two Art students design and paint with three of the group a successful manageable set to work on, which helps the actors to feel that this time it is really special. And we will perform in the Concert Hall where the seats are raked and more comfortable, and not in the Studio.

And when I ask Kate to act, "three cheers for Kate! Hip Hip" slap, shouts Paul Vickerstaff, and the company cheers and laughs and there is Lin, touching them one after the other and she is laughing, and Kate thinks it's a great idea. And best of all she loves the fact that the cast really does know what they are doing, and why, and are remembering points and pointers that I forget, and thinking of songs and solutions for every scene. Her caring nature is a great support to me as I tire, flag, flag, flagging with the last long rehearsals as I'm working on two other productions at the same time. When she knows we will make it she gives me a good bottle of good wine. In my mind Kate's steady building work has been worth more to Shadows than any number of my marauding raids.

As we sit with wine Kate says, "We used to have meetings about you. We thought you were so rough and uncaring. You upset them. We kept thinking it wasn't good for them. We wanted to have a meeting, or not do any more."

"Why didn't you?"

"Well, we decided you delivered, they always finished with a pantomime and afterwards it seems alright, worthwhile. No damage done. Perhaps. Probably. But now you've changed."

"Actors are cattle," I say, mockingly quoting Hitchcock, "and you acted."

"You have changed."

"Have I?"

In 1979 Bet Heathfield who had played the mother in Lawrence's *The Daughter-in-Law* had approached me on behalf of a group who wished to put on a pantomime. That group was Shadows. We all started to build from Ground Zero. In the following years we produced nine pantomimes for Christmas and three original plays. And these were supplemented with an annual series of Spring Workshops.

Then Kate got a promotion, she was moving to Nottingham. We went to the Director of the Arts Centre and explained the situation. Rather than contacting Social Services, she approached an elderly do-gooding lady who said she preferred to work alone, not with Mr Blackburn. I didn't argue. Two months later Shadows was no more.

So I wish you first a sense of theatre; only those who love illusion and know it will go far

AND I AM THE SAME, RE-CREATED FROM RIDDLEY WALKER, Russell Hoban

On my naming day when I come 12 I gone front spear and kilt a wild boar . . . Walker is my name and I am the same. Riddley Walker. Walking my riddels where ever they've took me and walking them now on this paper the same.

I don't think it makes no differents where you start the telling of a thing. You never know where it begun realy. No moren you know where you begun your own self.

RIDDLEY WALKER

Adaptit by the nacters of Art Sentafearter from the woal story tol by Russell Hoban

At Malx-morial in Sheveeld Feb 2 ohwunwun I riddley-ing ree-cauld that time back way back set. Afta I telling 2 telling 3 telling a wundras footchers werld gon rong set!! The huck nosed reddle ead were Malx-maid Sheelah stuk in a kage. And Malx-made were the making of that Apocklips-tick set.

Such was the set's success and our satisfaction in the opening performances of our re-creation of Russel Hoban's novel that I decided to extend the run although realising we would then be missing an actor for a small but crucial part.

Mal volunteered.

"You're deezynaman Malx-made," I says, so stick to your last but Mal insists and forget it I says you don't act but will he says with lines I says to learn I stress knows them he insists and speaks word perfick out and loud YOU'RE DEAF! I shouts what's that he mocks ear cupped DEAF, DEAF DEAF, I'll hear he says and costume I asks you wait he says and BED? I asks sleep he replies not a night's work he grins and bests me at last and turns to leave and I says keep fotoing!

Mal returns the following morning having created a newspaper-bleached wonderful hand-made two-piece suit, ragged yet right, with white-splashed wellies, red-tinted shades gaunt drained face, isotope blank, and fitting smart topper. He plays the part formally, with conviction and assured aplomb, dropping and dying at the WUN BIG WUN. He cast a white shadder.

At Malx-memorial this is the tel that gets em Riddley laffs, and sadness cos he's gone. The deezynaman, that Bestoss got him.

No optimism

only endurance

and moments of indestructible humanity.

Then, into my head pops another goner, long gone. Croo-siffighing Rick is the tel. The set had a massive block of a wooden cross laid slantwise centre space and grappling Riddleys hold Rick across it while a Hevvy's loud thud hammer blows six inch nails into his palms letting the blood splattering capsule burst red ooze darkening down as feet are tight lashed fast. The cross, his body across it, is horizontal hauled, hoisted high, and up and higher and higher still. Left aloft he's hung above the audience and there remains, dead dangling left until the WUN BIG WUN, left until the audience has left and the theatre cleared when actors caring, gently, and slowly, lower him down to earth.

Night after night, arms aching, back scored, sore, feet numbed, neck cricked, pain, victimised, he could barely move when released.

Rick played the victim. I treated him as one. A talented poet and successful novelist, a sensitive and brilliantly perceptive writer and regular reviewer in leading literary periodicals, he produced a script of *Wuthering Heights* when I mentioned that ACT might work on the novel, a script which I never read and barely acknowledged. I accepted his design for a poster, but with little grace – it was not the poster I wanted and I didn't explain why. My brusqueness upset him. I never commented on his novels although I read a couple and enjoyed them.

His marriage failed. He moved away, remarried, had children and, believing his books were underappreciated, killed himself.

Rick played the victim.

Type casting.

Time passing.

Memories surfacing.

Who could no he were that delkit. I never wantit im ded.

I said, 'what if you wer me, Fister? What'd you do?'

He said, '. . . You're myndy don't you see. You ben lernt to read and write and all ways thinking on things. Trubba not nore I aint starin but I wunt want to be like that it ain't no way for a man to be.'

Sensing the scale, and wondering how to master this project.

- Set in a remote future and composed in an English nobody ever wrote or spoke, this short, swiftly based tale juxtaposes pre-literate fable and Beckettian wit, Boschian monstrosities and a hero with Huck Finn's heart and charm, lighting by El Greco and jokes by Punch and Judy. It is a wrenchingly vivid report on the texture of life after Doomsday. (New York Times)

I came to this a long way round.

- The voice of Riddley Walker is the strongest, most desolate and bewildered in modern fiction. Language and thought and landscape ring more true than any other vision of the future I have ever come across. You should know that Riddley Walker is difficult, dangerous and harrowing. (Cosmopolitan)

I took time, sitting an egg, warming it.

- What is marvellous about Hoban's creation is the effect it has, how it draws us into an atavistic dreamworld to which we intensely and instinctively relate, and it does so in a language all its own that soon becomes ours. (Publishers Weekly)

I played a long game.

– A hideously plausible picture of what our world would become if we went down the nuclear road to the bitter end . . . Within his dark parable of death and rebirth, told in a language that attempts the impossible and achieves it, he is telling a "littl Shynin Truth".

(Sunday Times)

A slow wait, waiting . . .

-It is so perfect in its conception that a corner of the reader
responds with awe and even an anguished delight. Perhaps a work
of real genius. (Los Angeles Times)

And then, I hatched it.

We'd try

Believe me

We could do it

There is a fine distinction

       between over-reaching

         and faulty judgement.

I had had a plan, which was to adapt Russell Hoban's enthralling and
compelling children's classic *The Mouse and his Child*. But we were too many
for that, the group should be kept together. After having failed at *Oliver Twist*,
we had learned lessons and it seemed a reasonable gamble to overreach.
We had to be challenged, hence Riddley Walker. We would force ourselves
to search out unlikely solutions, master a language, test limits of extreme
physicality, create a sub-civilization, challenge an audience.

I applied for adaptation rights only to find that they had already been
licensed. So our work would have to be an experimental endeavour, an
educational exercise using the book as source material and inspiration, rather
than a commercial project.

Nothing ventured – I told them read it.

Workshops began in dark places, seeking to become physically expressive,
get touchingly close, lose inhibitions, explore animality. We work on snarling
force and gross gestures. Women versus men rugby scrums collapse in piled
heaps as grimacing faces got increasingly fierce. Obstacle courses built from
old junk demanded shared teamwork, brought bonding and daring and
damage and pain. Biomechanics built stretching and strength. All savage and
howling we practised the dogs to seek out a way to a Bernt Arse Pack. We
planned to make puppets, researched all Big Bangs, measured the space, and
looked up St. Eustache, talked in found language and wore smelly pants. The
taste and the texture and throb of the piece. And I knew we could do it, but
weren't getting there.

I called a pause

Time back way back befo people got clevver they had the 1st knowing. They los it when they got the clevverness and now the clevverness is gone.

Everything has a shape and so does the nite only you can't see the shape of nite nor can you think of it. If you put yourself right you can know it. Not with knowing in your head but with the 1st knowing. Lissening for what's coming as well.

The pause proved a long one.

I needed help, to find a structure, distil the narrative, select the action, re-think fundamentals, devise a strategy, make the right choices and create a script.

Stories – you want stories.

Another day.

Another time.

Light relief was the new agenda, and I knew just what. *The Farndale Avenue Townswomen's Guild Drama Society Production of Macbeth* proved sublimely appropriate, and challenging in a totally converse register. Fun and Foolishness played Pitch Perfect which we toured through the Derbyshire Dales.

> Riddley Walker weren't no talker
>
> Didn't know what to say
>
> Put his head up on a poal
>
> And then it tol all day.

Well you know 1^{ce} the kids start singing at you that's a cern kynd of track youre on nor there aint too much you can do about it. Making the kids stop singing wont help its too late by then youve just got to clinch your teef and get on with it.

Three months later we begin again.

An This is My 2nd Tel of It!

Sheila Harding writes:

Riddley Walker is like some strange twisted circus show, full of wonders and horrors. I've no idea what the audience makes of it. As I watch from Granser's cage, crouched in a horribly uncomfortable position, I'm still excited by it. There are moments of tremendous poignancy and lyricism. The spaces between the hulks of rusted metal, the rough wooden beams and the torn webbing which constitute the set, seem vast and lonely. There is danger, confusion and horror; smells, not just sights and sounds; a sense of life on the edge. The people I know so well and have been working with for months are transformed.

Sheila played in thirteen ACT productions; false crookt nosed, boxed and grinning fiendishly, face bright reddened, wears a corset as a disjunct hat and was the part of Granser. She sent me this snapshot when I lost my way trying to find a way, a way to write about our project as my Writing Pause lasted almost as long as the original Production Pause.

In the same pause-period I happened to mention to Charlie Watson that I was finding it difficult to describe *Riddley Walker*. He reminded me that he had seen the production and I suggested he might write a response. He posted the following:

If your experience of amateur dramatics is accompanying your mother to a local Christmas version of Oklahoma in some remote Suffolk Village Hall, then you can imagine my reaction to this question;

"Do you fancy coming along to see a play I'm in?"

Even though it was from my new friend Paul, there were some follow-ups that needed answering.

"What is it?"

"It's called Riddley Walker"

"Riddley what?"

"Riddley Walker"

"What's it about?"

"Hard to explain really"

"Where's it on?"

"Chesterfield Tech"

"Oh"

"Yeah, it's in the basement"

Hardly auspicious. But because it was my new friend Paul, a left field type of new friend, I succumbed.

And I'd met the Director, Jack, who lived in the same village. Another left field type, potently creative, quiet yet intensive, enigmatic, a bit scary. Intrigued by how he might do it.

So I went.

And 2 hours later I left.

And in between I'd had the most stunning theatrical experience of my life.

A maelstrom of speech, plot, character, costume, sound and vision, all woven together by some impossible thread, inexplicable to explain, constantly compelling, and quite, quite extra-ordinary.

I saw Paul become someone else, and Sharon, and Margot, and Ian, and the others, and I now knew not only what Jack did, but what he could do.

The troupe were astonishing, professional to a tee, committed, spirited, given over to the performance, and forming a bond with the audience that it was impossible to break away from until the end.

An end I didn't want to come.

See! The 2nd tel of it is not by me at all.

Does a script exist? I ask, knowing we would not make a play of it but rather re-create a version of the "woal of everything there is in inland way back, time back" and bring the audience into it, and find and show The Littl Shyning Truth.

Casting about for ideas, Casting thoughts. More physical workshops – women's parts are scarce! The women will play Riddley, five women Riddlers walk the story, with focus on the small one, Sharon, the most boyish, for action; the others work in chorus. And will find The Littl Shyning Truth.

I know wot I wanted be.

The leader of the Bernt Arse Pack, bare, balls barely covered in the tatters of a charity shop fur coat, charges barking onto the tight-held spear of littl Riddley – that's me kilt skweeling dead in the opning moment. That's my part!! Out of the way early. I wishes I'd painted my balls blue: we had a lovely make-up team.

Then it wer mosly uvvers.

Green-headed, blanket-wrapped Eric crouched high atop the structure – menacing muttering and lonely.

Muscle-flexing Hevvys strut and lurch and watch and chuckle, bodies blacked.

Mutton-cloth Eusa-folk wriggle maggot-like, Goodparley is held, Big Ian's eyes sucked out, eyes held aloft by sleight of hand, raw dulled real sheep's eyes.

Mr Clevver, half-life size, a clattery jointed 2-dimensional avatar with litlpoynty beard and the horns and all is voiced by Paul.

Out of a coffin another teller tells with pointing stick the legend of St. Eustace projected up the wall.

Post-nuclear Mr Punch, bleached grotesquerie screeches babble to hoarse-struck lissners.

Rochard tels a tel

Riddley Walker was a hugely ambitious show. I played Abel Goodparley, a terrific role, which I found very demanding, both in memory and in range.

What I recall of the show relates to the performances. Each one left me drained. The sense of being immersed in Riddley's world was almost overwhelming. The most enjoyable sequence for me was when Goodparley and Orfing, the 'Pry Mincer' and the 'Wes Mincer' stage the allegorical Punch and Judy show which tells how a figure named Eusa, in a time long ago, became greedy for 'clevverness', using technology to put the 'Littl Shining Man' of the atom into two pieces. The least enjoyable, having my eyes sucked out by the maggot-like mutants the Eusa folk and spending the rest of the show in a state of blindness, my normal glasses replaced by a pair with lenses thickly painted out in bright red. I had had an acute sensitivity on the subject [of blindness] since the age of 13, when I had lost the sight of my right eye, following a detached retina. What made things worse was that the sheep's eyes which we used in the play to represent my own, putrified progressively during the run, to the point where it would make me nauseous to be anywhere near them. Toward the end of the play there is a massive explosion. We hired a huge sound box, which produced a deafening effect. When it went off that was the cue for a Peckinpah-style slow-motion death.

The narrative drive is the seach for the secret of The Wun Big Wun from time back way back when iron could fly and picters came on the air. And so we had the Bang Box: steel, solid, reinforced and grilled because they find a way, and we needed the best loudest BANG aloud in a public space.

I said, 'yes but what about the bang how'd it go?' He said, "Wel the hevvys took the yellerboy stoan and the other greedy mints and they done that mixter like the dyer tol them which they packt it in a iron pot and they had what they callit a fews . . .

The audience shuddered shocked. I know one man fainted but that was at the blinding, another who said he believed it impossible was fixed, stock still with wondering.

And years later someone asked why did I want to shock them and I didn't want to shock them, but do believe that one part of theatre's purposes is to propose shocking themes and material. That is drama. Disorder reigns – is resolved one way or another. The Ancient Greeks felt the same way. And so did Chekov, who worked to get rid of the gun but knew the sense of danger must not disappear,

The actors said they found themselves there, locked themselves with imaginative intensity into the funny, haunting, terrible and unsettling drama with its "wrenchingly vivid report on the texture of life after Doomsday", that is "suffused with melancholy and wonder".

When we gone out thru the gate there wer a kid up on the hy walk sames I use to be up there all times of nite when I were a kid. For 8 he wer may be. Sharp littl face liting and shaddering in the shummying of the gate house torches. Sharp little face and he begun to sing:

Riddley Walker ben to show
Riddley Walker's on the go
Dont go Riddley Walkers track
Drop Johns ryding on his back.

And I am the same.

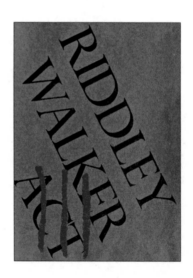

The Uses of Literacy

MEANS TEST MAN, Walter Brierley.

Tha' mun do as tha' will, Sidney lad, but tha's noan goin darn t'pit.

The novel by Walter Brierley, published in 1935, describes one week in the life of an unemployed Derbyshire miner Jack Cook. It concerns the seven days before the monthly visit of the Means Test Man, the inspector who will assess the family's economic needs. Written out of the author's own bitter experience, the novel received both critical and commercial success, with six thousand copies being purchased in the first twelve months and a second print run following. It was recognised by some as an English equivalent to Steinbeck's *Grapes of Wrath*.

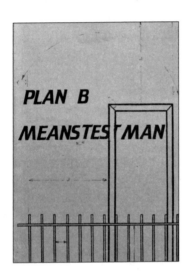

I invited Sharon Burns to work with me on its adaptation as a two-man companion to *The Hard Way Up*, both of them being intended for the Buxton and Edinburgh Fringe Festivals as well as touring Derbyshire. Brierley's son, who in fictional guise features in the novel as a young boy, allowed us generous performance rights. The plan was to follow each successive day, as the novel does, with the Jack Cook character as a pro-active narrator, and using the second actor in a succession of secondary roles leading ultimately to the meeting with the Means Test Inspector on the last day. Jack Cook's wife and his young son play large important parts in the book offering many opportunities for dialect dialogue and dramatic confrontation, but I wanted to develop an approach that highlighted the man's situation, a man whose whole life is being defined by long-term unemployment.

Brierley wrote of his own experience:

Though both my wife and myself are physically healthy, walking as we do about the Derbyshire countryside on Sundays and some days in the week, the prolonged strain of living on the edge of domestic upheaval, and the fact that our social urge has to be repressed, has ruined our nerves and given us an inferiority complex. For myself, the dependence on the state for money without having honestly earned it, has made me creep within myself, losing faith in everything except my own capabilities, closely examining, sometimes even suspecting, friendly gestures, seeing, whether it exists or not, selfishness behind all striving for position in politics, or trade unions or cooperative societies . . . one is afraid to come out, ashamed, idle.

In this piece of writing I wish to describe thoughts and implications that arise from adapting this kind of book rather than the actual process of producing a drama. It is about the Uses of Literacy, the ways our literacy defines and causes us to relate to the events and circumstances of life, the kind of work we undertake and the presumptions underlying that work.

My father was unemployed for long periods during the 1930s; this delayed my parents' marriage, and presumably therefore the date of my birth. A distant twice-removed relative had offered to get my dad a scholarship to the Grammar, but that's not what our kind did so he left school at fourteen. Being advised by his father never to follow the family tradition and become a miner, my father learnt to drive, a skill admired amongst working men in the 1920s, and he found short-term delivery jobs from time to time. The one which I particularly envied him as a young boy was being in charge of refilling the Wrigley's Chewing Gum vending machines, which were bolted to the walls outside virtually every corner shop in the working class areas of Leeds. To do this he drove a specially designed three-wheeler van (one wheel in front, two behind) with Wrigley's Gum Keeps You Fresh in fancy brightly elaborate writing on its sides. He finally got employment as a furniture van driver, holding the job for about two years before being called up to join the army when war broke out in 1940. I was six weeks old when he left to fight Jerry as a lorry driver.

In the 1980s serious unemployment returned to England with the market and privatisation policies of the Thatcher Government. In Chesterfield, a very Labour oriented town, the large new town centre multi-storey car park was adorned with a large banner showing the current local unemployment figures, which rapidly increased each week as large local industrial enterprises went onto short time or laid off their workers. The atmosphere in the town certainly changed, an air of anxiety, of wondering whither next dominating life in general. It was during this period that I decided to adapt *Means Test Man*.

At this same time the miners' national leader Arthur Scargill called the coal industry out on strike. I was aware and concerned, knowing some key figures personally. Trevor Cox, Scargill's lieutenant, had employed me to teach courses on Cinema at the local branch of the Workers' Educational

Association and his wife had supported my T.I.E. projects. Peter Heathfield, general secretary of the National Union of Mineworkers, was a friend, both his sons had been members of our Youth Theatre (NEDYPT) and I had suggested that his wife Bet should choreograph the College of Art Fashion Shows after she broke my nose during a movement workshop. (My still bent nose gives me a certain something they say – manly character? , , , perhaps, or just that hint of crooked danger that women find so fascinating? . . . perhaps NOT.) Bet had played the mother in *The Daughter-in-Law*, and now concentrated on activating the miners' wives movement which became such an important support factor during the prolonged strike when life became not just seriously unsettled but potentially dangerous. She is a woman I have admired a great deal.

Scargill refused to hold a ballot for the strike, believing the threat of mine closures and destruction of the industry to be cause enough. The Derbyshire miners stopped work, whereas the Nottinghamshire miners, working in adjacent pits, refused to strike without a ballot. This was at the crux of the battles that ensued. But even with a ballot I fear the coal industry would not have survived in its current form. In the event pits were closed, and unemployment figures in our area grew even higher.

The eighties were a very difficult period for my work as the whole attitude to arts provision changed. Resources and funding became scarce. Management speak and practice became of primary importance, seemingly the criteria by which successful work was measured. The Theatre Assistants I had employed to run the Youth Theatre and contribute to the development of Theatre in Education, real people who did real creative work, were replaced by facilitators, good at shuffling people and papers, attending meetings and listing numbers. Administration took over as our actual creative output plummeted.

Five years after the production of *Means Test Man* I became redundant, was unemployed myself at the age of fifty-two and certainly at the top of my game. My situation was cushioned as I qualified for a pension which would cover all basic living expenses, but for the next three years I found my life to be as unfocused, meaningless and worthless as ever my father or Walter Brierley had found theirs.

I even had my Means Test moments. In order to qualify for an extra unemployment benefit I had to attend day-long Looking For Work seminars. These were held at The Rutland, Bakewell's posher hotel, where we were told on our first meeting how generously the hotel had provided their conference space, and then instructed that we were not to use the bars or lounge for lunchtime purchases of drinks or food. HOW ARE THE POOR UNWASHED! I was introduced to a computer program and told it would help me find work. I nodded, said Hello Computer and held out my hand to shake and open our discussion. Being computer illiterate I didn't know that computers don't discuss. After inputting a wealth of personal information including studies at the Universities of Cambridge and Paris together with, I thought, a solid, rich and varied CV, the computer came up with two suggestions:

1. Box Office Sales and Pre-booking,
2. Theatre Technician (Lighting).

I tried to say there's nothing vaguely technical in my skill base – this last, 'skill base', a term I had learned from the computer – but reply came there none.

The man and woman running the seminar explained that they fully understood our situation as they themselves had been unemployed before getting their current jobs. They were working from a script, pretty well word perfect, and I accepted that I was, as their computer had indicated, a rather special case. At least I had qualified for my extra dole money, and understood even better Walter Brierley's withering response to the Means Test Inspector's arrivals. I was totally floundering, put on weight, developed a paunch, watched too much television, drove aimlessly through the Peak District appreciating nothing and simply could not focus.

Three years of wallowing in a vagueness I hated, then I gradually built a new life, although I never again directed a work of theatre. Now, twenty years later, it still seems quite ridiculous that a part of the solution to the country's economic problems was to stop me working and pay me a basic living pension, index linked, from the age of fifty-two. Like Walter it was not so much the low income that hurt, it was the fact of being unemployed.

When I look back at our production of *Means Test Man* it raises questions I was unaware of at the time. I realise now that I faced a dilemma and made possibly crucial misjudgements which relate to The Uses of Literacy. In 1957 Richard Hoggart wrote a book with this title about change in aspects of working class life. He identified the grammar school boy (note boy not girl) as a recent phenomenon, a working class child who, having been to grammar school and educated beyond the normal parameters of his cultural origins, finds himself in strange territory, whilst still identifying himself as working class but having aspirations quite different to those of his upbringing. I was precisely such a product of the 1945 Education Act. When I was a student at a small teacher training college in 1958, I was identified as a prime example of this new phenomenon and encouraged to read the book. Speaking with a broad Yorkshire accent, having only working class cultural references, eighteen years of age but looking fourteen, I arrived wearing my dad's, several sizes too large, demob suit, the suit he had been issued thirteen years previously in 1945 when he returned from four and a half years' captivity in a German prisoner-of-war camp. A lounge suit was specified for teaching practice and

Sunday lunch, but there was no way my parents could afford a new one, and, we never ever used the word 'lunch': breakfast, dinner, tea and supper if you were lucky were our eating arrangements. I was literate of course, but the uses to which I put my literacy were in the realms of working class culture although I was becoming increasingly well read with an instinctive sensibility for things artistic. "Tha's allus got thi 'ead stuck in a book, Spratty lad", my dad would say. The gulf between my world and that which I had entered was made manifest in many ways. One day my tutor told me that they had arranged for me to see the college doctor. I duly went to the surgery; he asked me to drop my trousers and saying "Excuse me" felt my balls, then muttered "Sorry, but I don't know why they sent you." The following day, my tutor, alongside a colleague, blushed with embarrassment as he apologised: "Jacky, we're so sorry, but we thought that maybe your balls hadna' dropped." He was a friend, he remained a friend, and knew I was in a relationship with the brightest, prettiest girl on the campus, June Billie King, who became the mother of my daughters and my beloved wife for twenty-four years. And he knew I captained the rugby team on occasion, even though by nature I was quiet and retiring. He could not see beyond the broad accent and that unfashionable ill-fitting lounge suit. 'Lounge' was another word we never used, and I hated to be called 'Jacky'!

So it goes.

But already my home world was beginning to recede, and by the 1980s, although my allegiance to working class values remained as strong as ever, I could not honestly claim to be in any way a member of the working class. However, wishing to demonstrate that allegiance was a part of my reason for choosing to adapt *Means Test Man*. It was very apposite for that time; the word Solidarity was in the air. Yet this was a false premiss. The last thing a long-term unemployed person wants to see is a play about the utter demoralising futility of their situation. A trip to the theatre might offer momentary distraction and address the problem but is unlikely to offer any solution, although left-wing companies like Banner, or 7.84 have done wonderful work for many years focusing on issues to do with terms and conditions of work from a pro-active working class culture based position. Theatre remains primarily an art form that caters for a particular culture of literacy. On its publication *Means Test Man* was criticised in a *Daily Worker* review from this very standpoint, as being 'literary' and appealing to a literary coterie, rather than pursuing a more proletarian ideological stance. Ernie Woolley wrote:

> The weakness of the book, recognisable, perhaps, only to those who
> have experienced long term unemployment is that the unemployed
> worker who sits timidly at home waiting for the investigator is
> not the rule, but the exception . . . A book which brought out this

fighting spirit of the unemployed would have been a much greater use to the working class.

Being unemployed brought out no fighting spirit whatsoever in me. The view expressed does not in any way devalue the book's achievement, but does give food for thought, about the selection of material which an author chooses to present. Theatre tends to be similarly, perhaps more pertinently, selective given the constraints/expectations of a limited playing time.

For example, we made no mention of the fact that the family do have some savings, nor that one day is largely concerned with Jack Cook walking to Derby and back for a new suit. Another example of the consequences of a production decision is illustrated by my going for the theatrical punch as opposed to a straightforwardly simple statement. I had one of my GREAT IDEAS!: Jack Cook meets a local man, an occasional poacher, who offers him a rabbit he has trapped; this is wonderful, they will eat rabbit stew for dinner tomorrow. We had a dead rabbit available for every performance, and as Jack recounted his exploits of that particular day he would gut and then skin the animal. This was real, real life, meat, real meat red in tooth and claw, not ready cubed and vacuum packed in tight sealed plastic, but meat prepared as we did in my youth on the Chevin where we kept geese, hens and rabbits for meat, for food. The effect of the scene was not to draw attention to conditions of life at the time, but rather to the fact of a cuddly furry creature being dismembered. The smell could be bad, it wasn't easy to watch, and one or two members of the audience left. Members of one student audience accused Brian Sargent, who played Brierley, of being a murderer. We decided to gut in advance but kept the skinning.

The sequence needs careful consideration. It was definitely a coup de théâtre, as was Chekov's pistol shot and Lawrence's decision that Mrs Holroyd should wash her husband's dead body on the stage. I had of course drawn the line at killing a live rabbit during this scene, by such decisions are the limits of the uses of literacy defined. One (One!?) becomes more refined in sensibility and raw facts are preferred by filtration. Others enjoy dog fights in preference to theatre.

We never played to an audience of unemployed Derbyshire men. We did perform in Waingroves, the village where Brierley was born, to a small select audience who happened to know and care that he was a famous son of that place, and later we performed in the drawing room of a large Georgian terraced house in Edinburgh's New Town during the Fringe Festival.

Brian Sargent writes:

The other bloke, the Means Test Man, was Eric Popplewell. A staunch left winger – I recall going to Chesterfield Working Man's Club with him for a pint after a rehearsal because the miners' union leader Arthur Scargill was going to be

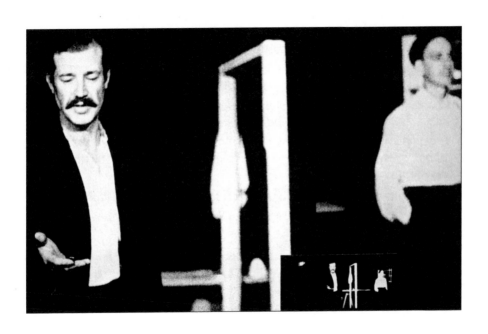

there. Being a copper I wasn't sure. If they found me out!! It was at the time of the miners' strike and the police were hated by the miners. A singer songwriter with very left wing tendencies, Eric's claim to fame was playing guitar in a show that featured a well known performer. He's still around. Anyway Jack was very excited by this performance – so was I for that matter and really enjoyed the experience. There were a lot of monologues and me and Eric could support one another, and we needed that when we got to Edinburgh performing in a very small space with the audience on our toes – we could have shaken hands. In the play I had to skin a rabbit which Jack got from a gamekeeper. He likes his realism! Not only skin it, but clean its innards. It was decided after the first performance in The Pauper's Pit in Buxton to clean the rabbit before we went on stage and just skin it. Less smelly. Jack couldn't get a rabbit at one performance and I peeled sprouts. It didn't seem the same somehow. Also for that play, each run we did I had to get off to the charity shop and buy a load of cups. I had to break them in every performance – my anger scene. One night, inevitably it didn't smash dramatically but bounced. It didn't have quite the same dramatic impact.

There was also a touch of fate in this play. It was set – as was the book – in Waingroves, Ripley, a place I had never heard of then. I have now been living there since 2004 just round the corner from the house that the author had lived at and a few yards from Brierley Terrace, a row of houses built by the Council and named after the author.

I was chuffed with the review for Means Test, felt like a proper actor. It played a part in my acting career until very recently as I used a monologue, the Sunday one, as an audition piece quite regularly. I can still remember it – I think.

(Brian trained and worked as a professional actor after leaving the Police Force.)

The two following reviews are from the Edinburgh Festival :

Life of ex-collier on the dole.

His wife is too ashamed to be seen walking with him on the afternoon stroll he wants so much, his nerves are so bad that they feel as if they've been taken out one by one and grated like cheese. This is the life for an ex-collier on the dole, 1934.

Skinning a rabbit, tearing up newspaper squares for the lavatory, getting over-angry at his child, the miner (Brian Sargent)

Edinburgh Festival

----

finally has to face the Means Test Man (Eric Popplewell) to be assessed for benefit entitlement.

Sharon Burns adapted Walter Brierley's novel which just two members of Chesterfield's Plan B Theatre turn into a poignant and totally human suggestion of dole existence – then and now. Extraordinarily good sets by Charles Monkhouse.

Jo Stanley

The Scotsman

MEANS TEST MAN

Plan B Theatre Arts Centre, Chesterfield.

DEPRESSING subject, but a moving two-man play about the lives of unemployed men in North England mining communities in the thirties, and the ghastly system that allowed them no welfare money until after a home "inspection". Sharon Burns, who's with this amateur citizens' company, has adapted it cleverly from the book of the same name written in those dark days by William Brierley, and the theme is strongly relevant today.

The intimacy of the tiny theatre at Lister Housing Association makes it an ideal venue for a performance full of insights into despair. Excellent direction by Jack Blackburn brings out an especially sensitive and moving portrayal by Brian Sargent of the haunted young husband on the dole. So good are he and his partner, and so real the atmosphere, that they make you "see" the young wife offstage.

George Duthie

Morning Star

I doubt that any other Fringe performance could have garnered better reviews than we did. On its own terms *Means Test Man* was exceptionally highly regarded.

Making a Montage

AFRICA

Back to childhood.

When I was a lad Africa was dark. Darkest Africa.

My cigarette card collection included a set: *Peoples of our Empire*, with exotically varied images of our colourful subjects, including the Black Africans.

I read the Tarzan books and watched the films at Saturday matinees in Rothwell Cinema, fixed a First World War bayonet to a broom stick, practised the yodelling chimp call, and stalked my enemies, usually black men,but occasionally bad whites through the jungly wooded north-facing slope of Otley Chevin.

When we took the bus to Leeds, for special shopping, one treat was to go for a mid-day dinner at the Civic Restaurant, set up during the war to provide cheap self-service meals for the working class, in the basement of Leeds Town Hall. But the real treat was to see and touch the large stone sculpted lions which guarded the main entrance. (When we were working on *Africa* Ian Rochard cycled from Chesterfield to Leeds to see and touch these for himself.)

At the age of eleven I passed my scholarship and went to grammar school – where there was a library, and at the far end, piled on low shelves were stacks of back copies of the *National Geographic* magazine. Most intriguing for a young grammar school boy who barely knew that girls existed were the photographs of Africans. The men wore loin cloths like Tarzan – the women also! – you could see bare breasts. In the early 1950s this intriguingly erotic illicit thrill seemed dangerously scandalous. A closely guarded secret I never dared mention.

Such childhood experiences and memories were seminal to the origin of the most controversial piece of work that ACT ever undertook.

I decided to do *AFRICA*. A dream of Africa. An Africa of the mind. And to take it to the Edinburgh Festival in 1986, together with the new production of *The Hard Way Up* along with its recently completed companion piece *Means Test Man*, and, for pure entertainment value our three Biggles adventures.

Ian has reminded me that a contemporary source of inspiration was the beautiful impressionistic film by experimental film maker Peter Kubelka, *Our Trip to Africa*

which matched his images to sounds from a completely separate context (sync events). Our show sometimes did the same, most notably in the scene in which cocktail party chatter is interspersed with images of big game hunting.

The premiss was that *AFRICA* would be a montage, the intention being to challenge ourselves and our audiences with an original production which would present notions and ideas of Africa through the eyes of a group of white liberal-minded performers of a certain age not one of whom had actually set foot on the continent.

The premiss was mine.

- ACT shuddered. We know nothing!

Precisely.

- So how on earth . . . we're all WHITE!

Precisely, and we all have ideas, knowledge, political notions, literary references, a consciousness of Africa as a place so strangely different and alien, dangerous even, that surely . . .

- They challenged me. Called it arrogance.

Had they never heard of The British Empire! Too young?

- How could we do Africa? That was arrogance.

We, the Brits, have done Africa with a vengeance for centuries. We will be honest, I assured them. Yes, we are working from a base position of unreliable knowledge and will acknowledge as much in performance. I proposed a theatrical montage, not a narrative, but a structured presentation of some of those elements that we white Europeans of my generation have absorbed about the Dark Continent.

- They remained unpersuaded.

Sheila Harding sent me the following snapshot, which highlights the ambivalence felt and the issues we were trying to handle:

A group of nine or ten people are sitting on the floor of the black studio. We are working on Africa, pulling together our own personal images and a big, disparate collection of literature. We're at the stage when some idea of structure and overall tone starts to emerge, and not everyone is happy. For several evenings there are long, grinding arguments about the ethics of presenting a Western view of Africa; about stereotyping; about whether presenting racism is actual racism; about whether there is any value in what we are trying to do. Underlying this is a more than usual amount of doubt about Jack's judgement.

There's a lot of physicality getting in, violence and scenes of exploitation and some very skimpy costumes, which he seems to relish.

Later, I acquire a role in which I have to take my clothes off. It seems justified in the context and I agree, unprepared for how vulnerable I will feel, not so much in performance, but in rehearsals, where things are always less controlled, more personal. One evening Jack points a camera at me and pretends to take a photo, and I am furious.

When the first performances come round we are under-rehearsed and so a lot of the rawness, unease and vulnerability are still really there and seem to give the piece a special quality, which persists, I think, even when they become transmuted into technique.

Faute de mieux, I prevailed, and the decision proved particularly fortuitous, as, on arriving in Edinburgh, we found that productions deriving from African experience were very much a feature of that year's Fringe Festival. Zeitgeist was the word.

How do we work?

Ian Rochard described his experience:

It was my first experience of a piece developed from scratch – via brainstorm, improvisation and research. I found much of the process extremely challenging. The physicality was particularly hard to master and one move, a kind of synchronised squat jump in response to the crack of a slave master's whip, impossible. I remember a rather deflating session in Youlgreave Village Hall where everybody but me gradually got the hang of it. Several scenes were created purely through improvisation, a process with which I have never felt entirely comfortable – too much surrender of control, I suppose. I was much happier contributing towards the finished script, where I could work at my own pace and reflect upon what I was producing. An example of this was The Complete Gentleman (a scene based upon a Yoruba folk tale included in Amos Tutuola's fabulously titled "The Palm-Wind Drunkard and His Dead Palm-Wine Tapster in the Deads' Town" which was written to be delivered in the style of a pompous art historian. Having said that, the significant achievements for me were all physical: representing various elements of the natural landscape in a Victorian explorers scene; as a wild animal in a hunting scene; as a tribal chieftain, clothed in loin cloth and head-dress only, displaying his absolute authority to two British envoys by walking across a carpet of semi-naked female bodies, before ordering their execution. This last experience was a huge breakthrough for me, as I had suffered all my life from a very negative body image. Several other cast members found the experience of appearing semi or wholly naked as liberating as I did, although, needless to say, it caused an awful lot of trouble at home!

We research: texts, images, objects, maps, photographs. We brainstorm: famine, apartheid, exploration, slavery, big game hunting, colonisation, alien values, traditional story telling, drumming and naked bodies. We choose areas of particular interest. I want them nutshelled, no flabby wasted words or actions. Ideas begin to gel. It becomes interesting. It becomes possible.

- The preparatory work is completed.

The stage is wide, open, a selection of authentic African masks and instruments hangs in the centre. To the left of the central playing area is a crudely welded raw iron **A**, eight feet tall, with a number of viciously pointed iron spikes sticking forward from it. Beside the A stands a white colonial. To the right is a tall, narrow, vertically barred structure which represents a prison cell. Behind the bars a more than life-sized carved Kaffir head lies sideways on a waist-high wooden block. Beside the block stands a white South African guard who gently, rhythmically, cynically taps the head just behind the left ear with a leather pouched tennis ball sized lump of lead as the audience enter. The guard quietly questions the head in a crudely realised Boer accent. He is quoting from the novel *Store up the Anger* by Wessel Ebersohn, which inspired this, one of the two sequences which punctuate the whole montage. It is a painful account of the death of Sam Bhenghu, a young black in South Africa, and a powerful, eloquent testimony to one man's struggle against anonymity and defeat. Lying in a prison cell, Sam's injured brain flashes his life before him in a series of violent, sad and lyrical episodes.

The second sequence is derived from Robert Tressell's working class novel *The Ragged Trousered Philanthropists,* in which The Bread Game serves as a parable of the way capitalism exploits workers. A very thin African woman in gloriously colourful traditional dress crosses to the iron A carrying a heavy load of large loaves of bread which she has baked. The white colonialist takes the loaves and spikes them onto the A. In return for the bread the woman is rewarded with a particularly ordinary length of cloth which she accepts with gratitude. Throughout the performance the woman returns at intervals to purchase bread for which she pays with items of her clothing. On her last return she offers her tiny rag of a loin cloth, her sole remaining garment, for which the white man scornfully tosses her a small chunk of bread which lands at her feet. A half- dozen large loaves remain impaled on the iron A as the woman walks off, naked and starving.

These two recurrent sequences dealing with the awareness of famine and apartheid, subjects which, in the era of Band Aid and the emerging political success of the Anti-Apartheid Movement, dominated media awareness of Africa in the early 1980s, serve as a kind of framing device for our other montage items.

The first episode dealt with Exploration. A satirical Pythonesque scene in which the pith helmeted, awfully awfully brave and pompous British tramped through jungle and savannah dismissively noticing elephants and gorillas, naming newly discovered countries and planting Union Jacks whilst wondering where all the dratted natives had gone to because after all they couldn't be expected to carry the pianoforte themselves. The men were loud and officious, the women were louder, and altogether made of sterner stuff. All this to the ominous background sound of drumming as they settle to take a cup of tea.

I fear we didn't push the surreal ridicule far enough.

The second episode was similarly satirical. Our two younger, fit and beautiful actors stripped out of their European clothes to become a leopard and a gazelle in the Big Game Hunt. They were both shot, Paul and then Sharon, with a shattering fusillade of cruelty and great rejoicing. As they lay twitching their lives away, the hunters quoted laudatory passages glorifying the Big Game game from Hemingway's *The Green Hills of Africa*.

A slavery episode followed in which one dissenting slave in the chain gang, the most sexually desirable female, was quickly and unceremoniously buggered by the slave master. It was crude – it had to be. However, this was a bad decision; sexuality became the issue rather than the fact of slavery. It would have been theatrically more effective if the victim had been the oldest ugliest man, which may not, however, be truer to human nature. Again I remain unsure whether this sequence was adequately thought out.

Next the Missionary Wife, all neat in a flower frock and sun hat, told, whilst neatly nibbling a Rich Tea biscuit, of the trials and tribulations which she had endured whilst trying to support her husband's efforts to bring Christ to the naked god-forsaken heathens. She told it plain, straightforward with neither frills nor caricature.

During these sequences the actors had been little by little ridding themselves of their western garments. We had looked at the old *National Geographic* photographs and compared them with the work of contemporary photographers including Leni Riefenstahl which illustrated that a culture might well, in a hot climate, have little need for clothing, and be naturally, proudly, present in the flesh. I suggested we might do the same. This was a provocation both to ourselves and our audiences. Each actor would choose his/her comfort level of nakedness. But whatever they chose they must be there as if naked, proud and rightfully so, no self-consciousness.

The play ran without an interval. We needed a calming moment, which was provided by a contrasting suite of traditional African tales, in which the seated women rudely mocked and derided their menfolk whilst the men postured and danced, recounting stories of foolhardy courage in the face of daunting odds, claiming bragging rights.

Then, a difficult episode about cultural differences clashing incomprehensibly in a kind of nether world at the heart of darkness. An African king has his wives executed in order to demonstrate his power in front of the alien visitor, the white man. I have two particularly powerful photographs of our interpretation of this reputedly factual historical event. One is of the pile of virtually naked female bodies whilst the final wife is being killed in a particularly brutal way as the king stands with passive indifference to one side.

The image is very striking, but I remain unsure about what point I made, if any. We are all red blooded under the skin, few of us are really tested to the extreme, and nobody's perfect. The cast were very brave; they accepted every challenge with which I faced them. But when performances began they remained doubting, I knew that belief, real heartfelt belief was not there. We played in Edinburgh to mixed responses. They were generally kind but somewhat dubious. "Very intriguingly different but entertaining none the less." Faint praise. One commented on gratuitous nudity, but that was clichéd stock response. It angered me. The only full nudity is for a few moments at the very end, moments which are totally justified, understandable and acceptable.

To end: Sheila stands, stark naked, weak, starving, breadless, and gestures towards the iron A where the majority of the loaves she baked remain impaled. Martin stops his gentle, insidious torture, pockets his cosh, and casually rolls the head to the ground. The negro has descended

into inchoate madness

Job done

Frame closed.

Then I had one of my GREAT IDEAS! The ANC theatre company (Mandela's African National Congress) had arrived in Edinburgh from Rio de Janeiro as part of the world tour of its anti-apartheid political sketch and music show. I suggested we take time out to see their show (GREAT IDEA!) and then invited them as guests to see ours (second GREAT IDEA!), Disbelief verging on fear glazed the eyes of my cast; they scorned and belittled me and my outrageous great ideas, muttered and moaned, but then accepted that, as we had been honest in the creation of our *AFRICA*, it would be an act verging on white supremacist apartheid if we were not prepared to show it to politically motivated black South Africans.

We went to their more or less sell-out performance, enjoyed and appreciated its energetic infectious commitment. It was very accessible and without theatrical pretension. Afterwards I talked with their director, who promised that he, with some of their company, would gladly visit us the following day for our afternoon performance.

A late performance of *Biggles* that very evening somewhat distracted ACT from its African concerns. However it struck me as strangely coincidental that our madly comic version of Flying Officer Bigglesworth's adventures, a paean to British all-round ascendancy and Empire, was mining similar ideological territory as *AFRICA*.

Needing a large space for *AFRICA* we were performing in a school hall on the outskirts of Edinburgh which was quite difficult to find. The following day at about 2.30pm we had an audience of about a dozen, and the ANChad not arrived. I made excuses, promising that the performance would begin in fifteen minutes, which it duly did, but still without the ANC, and then, ten minutes later, fourteen of their group arrived. Quickly I recapitulated the opening narrative sequence which established the parameters of our project, this being essential if they were to make any sense of what we were doing. Then we played on. And I am a little ashamed to admit that with fluttering stomach, heart in mouth and meaningful looks in every direction I oozed encouragement and confidence to the cast. I doubt they noticed any of this. They played well.

After the performance we invited our guests to the nearest pub. We stood with our drinks in a crowded huddle, not knowing how to relate comfortably. Their director talked with me about the way we used the wooden head, the lead-filled pouch and poignantly appropriate texts to indicate the situation they were so well aware of. It was an important meeting we had.

When I reconsider the differences between the work of the ANC group and ours the more I become aware of the gulf between us. They were totally politically motivated with strong and necessary commitment to their cause. Their theatre was agit prop, neither hectoring nor solemn, but a matter of jokey confrontations, ridiculously incongruous situations leavened with songs and a spirited joie de vivre. They took pleasure in communicating with skill and simple presentation.

We, ACT, were a group of well-to-do Europeans making something big and ambitious and a bit experimental in form, all of which could seem pretentious, the product of a group with no truly deeply felt concern about Africa or, in this case, Apartheid. I know my intentions were very serious about the work, but we were coming at it from a very safe place and the suggestion that it was an indulgence is not easy to refute.

Two reporters from the *East Africa Journal*, white Caucasians, attended this same performance. Their subsequent review was scathing. We had succumbed to the "temptation to be patronising", had offered a "succession of meaningless sketches" and indulged in "gratuitous nudity".

A part of me can fully understand and accept these judgements. But I feel they are made too easily. And now I could be accused of special pleading.

However, I feel it necessary to challenge the assumptions on which they are made.

When attempting to create work about cultures that are known only at second hand, and are essentially alien, it is difficult and perhaps nigh impossible to present interpretations which cannot be judged to be patronising. From the beginning we set out our position of no real direct knowledge. We researched at length and were serious in our intention to create **our** *Africa*, not simply offer statements of fact. The cast might say it was **my** *Africa*.

The succession of sketches were, by intention, a montage of incidents. Generally speaking a theatrical sketch is satirical, more or less comedic, and usually mocking some aspect of human nature. Our Discovery of Africa sequence did have the temper of a sketch.

A group of pith-helmeted and knotted handkerchief wearing awfully braying English explorers discover The <u>Victoria</u> Falls and sundry other natural wonders whilst carefully avoiding stepping on logs in case they are sleeping crocodiles. Of course, they stop for tea and tiffin at four, before continuing their dangerous trek, offering beads to all and sundry the while. They boldly seek out savage animals, including hordes of chattering monkeys and, inevitably, in these pre-Darwinian Brits' all-conquering times, ape-like humans.

Pointed Ridicule!

The following sequence, Big Game Hunting, had an utterly different tenor.

Sharon, the persimmon girl of my memory, is young, fresh, so lovely, poised and delicate as the gazelle. Back stretched, head set, her eyes flash and query. The persimmon gazelle steps by, her torso, her hair, her slim legs stepping with grace and care. A harp strums. The creature freezes, dead still, waiting, paused, and I think her cocked head is set with bright black eyes to look hard straight at and through me.

Rifle shots racketing around the drully dumb acting space echo falling as she jaunts jerking and clings and breaks and falls as five shots found their target leaving her ripped and struggling stretched again, clobbered, staggering, dying, as three hyenas gross, powerful and threatening stalk, tear and devour the gazelle. Almost naked, a ravaged beauty is held aloft and brings a chiming halt across the stage as bloated indifferent white hunters mouth Hemingway's raw and disturbing description of "the vicious hyena" feasting on its prey.

This scene is not a sketch as I understand sketches.

As to the gratuitous nudity? All theatrical nudity can be dismissed as gratuitous. After all theatre existed successfully for centuries when nudity was forbidden by law, although the nude remained a staple of fine art.

I used total nudity on four occasions out of eighty-two productions.

The first was in *The Tooth of Crime*, Sam Shepard's Rock tragedy in which the female character undresses in a pathetically painful attempt to connect with the man she loved.

The second occasion was in *Lark Rise*, for comic effect, when two farm labourers desperately try to hide their nakedness from the female servant who brings fresh buckets of hot water as they take an outdoors bath after a day's sweltering labour in the fields.

In *The Hard Way Up* the scene of undressing serves to illustrate the appalling treatment of a suffragette leading to imprisonment, force feeding and ultimately a devastating nervous breakdown. An experience which Hannah Mitchell transcends; she comes through strengthened.

In *AFRICA*, where Ian Rochard, gigantic, old, crossing a bridge of bodies hoarsely spits an authentic chant and curse against "You! Dressed People!", only one actor becomes totally naked in the sequence where I adapted a version of The Bread Game from Robert Tressell's *Ragged Trousered Philanthropists* to illustrate how an exploitative system gradually leads to the most desperate of circumstances. A woman who has made and supplied bread to a trader has to barter her last item of clothing to avoid starvation.

The rest of the cast chose their personal level of minimal clothing, a bright G-string, a ragged halter, draped ribbons, woven rope, and looked proud and confident as they one by one cast off their ridiculously colonial/Empire Building attire.

Back in England after the Festival we gave a few more performances which did have some real belief.

Our last performance of *AFRICA* was to a group of University of Nottingham Theatre students. In a following workshop they seemed to be universally positive, commenting that they had never seen anything like it. One found it overwhelming. This group reacted to the theatricality, the event, rather than the content. They made no mention of the content. So it goes. Failed again. Fail better.

Ultimately, I remain glad that we did plunge in, that I risked looking foolish, and our work seeming of no significance. The extended reading undertaken during research was valuable and enlightening, our discussions, although contentious were thought-provoking and very worth while. The people who worked on *AFRICA* with me were brave in taking on its challenges, in using both their minds and bodies so generously.

I write here about my commitment to the work, but proved myself weak and failing in one respect on our return to Derbyshire. The village of Rowsley was the best in the County for welcoming our work, they organised decent-sized audiences and always more than met our expenses. I decided *AFRICA* was not suitable for them, we didn't in fact take it to any village venue. This was pure short-sighted stupidity on my part. When the chair of the Rowsley events committee asked why I had not brought *AFRICA* to them I mumbled "experimental" and "nudity" and "not a proper sort of play" and she went incandescent – how dare I presume they were in any way less suited to anything I might put together than an audience at the Edinburgh Festival. Chastened, I apologised. This is, possibly, indicative of the way my ego forced itself onto this production, which, in spite of that, remains in my memory one of the most genuine collaborations ACT ever undertook.

Getting to Grips

LINE ONE, Volker Ludwig and company

TRUMMI KAPUTT, Volker Ludwig and company

MAN OH MAN, Volker Ludwig and company

Get on your glad rags, Margot! She looks across. Treating me? No, work! In glad rags? Yes, your car, you drive. Where to? South, Pommie to the South Coast – I've decided we'll stay over, enjoy the sea, the seaside, go into Dorset, visit some potters. She smiles, then, that lovely lighting laugh that so delights my life. It's our summer break and we have time and space for one of those short, spontaneous, surprise adventures you so love, my love. She kisses me. I hold her at arms length. Gripped. It's work. Work! I repeat. We are off to Bournemouth to see a production, called *Line One*, by a company based in Berlin. Yes, Jack, work! Jack, anything you say, Jack! I release her. She kisses me again. I maintain a cool, manly indifference. That's just one way we play it. In the good times.

As Margot drives us southwards I explain that the company is called Grips, a theatre company dedicated to creating plays that address the issues which affect children's lives in the modern world, that are about the richness and complexity of their lives, but which are neither childish nor patronising. They present no fairytale rosy Disneyland images of a clean-cut world for kids who are cut to be clean. The plays are about children, and as such are of equal interest to adult as to young audiences.

The purpose of Grips Theatre is "emancipatory education".

Volker Ludwig, founder and director of the company, has stated:

"We want to show that our conditions are changeable and to help audiences to see this. In this way we hope to show different possibilities and to foster critical thinking. Primarily this means that we want to encourage children to ask questions, to understand that criticism is their undeniable right, to enjoy creative thinking and to gain pleasure from seeing alternatives and making changes."

The word GRIPS is slang, difficult to translate directly into English, meaning a combination of wit, common sense, ingenuity and imagination. To have GRIPS implies that you can use your brains to master any situation.

En route we stop for a coffee and wonder where, on a GRIPS scale of 1 to 100, we would position Hitler. We decide he was low in wit and common sense, but showed incredible ingenuity at devising Final Solutions, and the most amazing imagination in believing he could build a Thousand Year Reich.

At the time it was still strangely difficult to get away from the 'Don't mention the War' syndrome when considering things German. But the fact that my father was a prisoner of the Nazis for four and a half years, the fact that part of Berlin remained a western conclave surrounded by the Soviet-controlled East German Communist government, and even the fact of the existence of Grips Theatre, are all factors that keep knowledge of consequences of the war lodged in a part of my mind.

At the theatre the plain, empty stage is set with a row of ten chairs. Ten actors enter wearing a mixed medley cross-section of clothing from top posh to downright and out. They begin to dance, simple and carefree, and then to sing a lively scene-setting song: "Come and Ride the Tube Train" "Linie Eins".

Line One is set on the Berlin Underground line, Linie Eins, which crosses the city from west to east and in so doing passes through a whole section of the city from residential to industrial and from middle class to immigrant working class districts. As Nathalie, a girl from West Germany, travels the line in search of her pop star lover, she encounters characters from mixed and varied cultures and situations which illustrate the tensions and preoccupations of a major modern city. The play is light hearted, but far from comfortable. The performance is punctuated with songs which arrest the play's action to comment on the contexts of Nathalie's experiences. This practice relates to Grips' origins: it was founded by members of a Cabaret Theatres group who had realised that children's theatre was locked into a fairy-tale mode which, unlike cabaret, had neither immediacy nor relevance to contemporary social issues. Their practice derives from the Learning Plays (Lehrstücke) of Bertolt Brecht, but I found their work much more rewarding as they managed to invest the chosen subject matter with entertaining contemporary formats.

The company remains true to its origins in that their plays are presented in cabaret style, that is overt performance, not subtle underplaying, a marked degree of telling rather than implying, and songs with highly imaginative lyrics to provoke consideration of the action rather than to evoke inner emotions of the characters. For Margot and I, the production seen in Bournemouth was very successful in its portrayal of Nathalie's quest, and also in its simplicity, its accuracy of class/tribal depiction, and in its clever juxtaposing of quite distinct group experience.

We found the production revelatory. Instinct had impelled me to travel to see it, and now I was able to talk with Volker Ludwig about his work. He generously offered me the rights to the English translation at no cost, suggesting that although set in Berlin I should adapt the language to make it relevant to the time and place where I worked. Additionally he would be very supportive of my producing other Grips' scripts, again insisting that I adapt the language, especially of Grips' early plays, using phrases and slang expressions current in the vernacular of the North Midlands. He also advised me to make any necessary alterations to the song lyrics to maintain their contemporary relevance.

The quality of the Company's work is universally admired, especially for its research and production methods whereby children and young people are consulted at every stage of development of a new play, and every effort is made to engage and entertain audiences without playing down to them. Grips may be regarded as the most influential Children's Theatre Company in the world at that period, the 1980s. However, being committed to a left wing stance it has frequently ruffled the sensibilities of the German establishment. When, some years later, I took an ACT English language version of Grips' *Trummi Kaputt* to Darmstadt, my producer Rainer Lohnes received an angry letter from the parent of a teenager asking how he dared organise a visit by a company representing such a Socialist Left Wing Collective Political Philosophy and all that it stood for to perform before young audiences. We were playing to audiences of 300+ in the Justus Liebig Halle and feeling we offered not the slightest Revolutionary Threat to the wholesomeness of German Society, and we returned the following year with *Man oh Man*. I suspect, as is so often the case, this father had never seen a Grips production.

More recently, when leading a Theatre Workshop with trainee teachers of English at Frankfurt University I happened to mention *Line One*. Most of the trainees had attended performances of the play as teenagers, one had taken parts in a school production, and another, a young woman in her mid-twenties, a native of Berlin, recalled the Grips production, saying that it has been a defining formative cultural experience of her school years. She had seen the production seven times in three years.

On our return to Derbyshire, *Line One* became ACT's exciting new project.

Trudie Barber would play Nathalie, whilst ten other actors, six male, four female, would share the remaining fifty-one parts between them.

A five-piece band (Guitar, Bass, Keyboards, Saxophone, Drums and Percussion) led by Paul Stone, with arrangements by guitarist Phil Wright, was assembled.

Martin Wiltshire agreed to design the production, poster and programme. Grips' production had played on a bare stage, but I wanted an underground station. In discussion with Martin we came up with a plan that included two platforms, one with a snack bar cum newspaper stall and two open carriages, diagonally filling Phase One Hall; the boxy stage served as a raised crossing between the platforms, whilst sundry static clothed figures (sculptures in effect) created the sense of a heavily populated environment. The audience was to be seated along the length of the two facing platforms.

Both actors and musicians found it totally rewarding to work on this production. I find it difficult, at twenty-four years' distance, to describe the richness, the pathos and comedy, the punch, of the tapestry of action and music.

Ian Rochard recalls *Line One*:

I really liked this show – the set, the lighting, the costumes, the sculptures on the platform, even the screening of the band. I felt I created some reasonably successful characterisations and received quite a few audience compliments. For once, I managed to feel reasonably comfortable with the improvisations we undertook in initial rehearsals, despite my awareness of how easy it all seemed to some of the others – particularly Martin Aistrope (who was still with us at that time) as a drunken Glaswegian. As usual I struggled with the physical side of things, particularly the opening dance number, which needed to be really sharp. I think I more or less cracked it eventually and loved both the moves and the business with the newspapers, during the morning commute. My favourite sequences were as Herman delivering the song 'Joy to be Living' and playing the 'caring daring' Widow Agathe, in one of the show's few genuinely funny scenes.

A wonderfully satirical song expresses the shared longings for "fifty years ago", i.e. the 1930s. It is sung by The Widows, rich, fur-clad, bourgeois ex-Nazis. Its chorus goes:

We caring daring Widows

Defend and keep Berlin

Or else we'd all be Russians

Revolting, left wing.

There'll never be our equal

We're not like common people

We're caring daring Widows

We're grievance-airing, undespairing

Swastikaring, grudges bearing

Brown underwearing, vice foreswearing

Caring daring Widows!

Words Words Words. The temptation is to use words like 'brio', 'panache', 'full on', tempered by 'sensitive', 'subtle' even perhaps 'sublime' when you're sitting on an underground station platform and hear these songs, and watch the panoply of sundry comings and goings of Swigger, Lady, Lumpi, Busker, Turkish Woman, Dally, Office Worker, Married Woman, Lola, Social Democrat, Old Woman, Trudi, Krischi, Boy in Raincoat, Ulli, Bambi, Business Consultant, a Tamil, Deaf Old Man, Widow Kreinhild, Andrea, Mücke, Boy with Walkman, Inspector, Stefan, Drunk, Plaster, Dietrich, Confused Man, Corpse, Chat up Merchant, Junkie, Dilly, Widow Lotte, Angry Man, Marie, Pregnant Woman, Andrea, and more, more, all travellers on Line One, all encountered by Trudie Barber, open-hearted, attractive, lost and learning.

Words – Then:

No! Not 'sublime'.

That is one word too far.

Too slant to be true.

In the two following years I directed a pair of early Grips plays which we produced in a simple format to enable us to tour them to Germany.

Trummi Kaputt, an explicit Socialist critique of exploitative conditions under capitalism and their consequences for children, is a play which proposed ways that children might respond to the pressures put on them by their parents.

Jason's mother shouts at him because of her working conditions. Bobby Trumm cannot relate to other children because he is spoilt and indulged by his father, who owns the factory 'TOYS BY TRUMM' in which Jason's mother is employed making unreliable toy robots, and where she feels like a robot herself because of the monotonous nature of her work. Then Mr Trumm modernises his factory so that toy robots are made by real robots and Jason's mother loses her job, whilst Bobby Trumm discovers the fun of street games as he sees even less of his father. The play relates how the children work together to help their parents to understand and resolve these problems. An erratically intriguing remote-controlled Trummi robot was built by a particularly talented art/engineering student. Trummi needs to be the star of the show.

For these productions original songs and tunes were composed by members of the cast and arranged by Tony Baker, who accompanied us on the tour.

The second play, *Man Oh Man*, examines problems of the adult world, particularly those most affecting women, seen from a children's perspective. The women members of the Grips ensemble played a major part in the conception of this play, leading to long discussions of women's oppression and workers' mentality. The play effectively brings the disparate elements of children's, women's and workers' oppression into focus.

Pete and Christy live happily with their mother sharing housework between them. Suddenly things begin to change in their lives. First, the landlord comes and says they will have to leave their house for another one. Then mother invites a work colleague, Mac, to the house and announces she plans to marry him. The children are pleased; he seems to be a good man.

Three months later, after the marriage, the children realise they were wrong. Mac is strict and bossy. He thinks men are superior and expects Sue to do everything for him in the house, even though she has a job herself. The children object to this and decide to leave home. They discover that Mac is being bossed by the foreman at work in the same way as he bosses them at home.

The family decide to live and work together as friends, Pete and Christy joining with their mother and stepfather to fend off the representatives of the capitalist system – a money-grabbing landlord, a frustrated petty gossip, a slick salesman, and a bossy foreman.

This description implies a quite dull plodding scenario – but in practice, with actors playing confrontational yet positive children using current slang and popular vernacular expressions, together with a peppering of ingeniously fitting song lyrics, this was a production which worked very well with the audiences of German schoolchildren we played to.

These plays, devised in the 1970s and performed by ACT in the 1980s, were very much of their period and might be less well suited to the contemporary context of the twenty-first century where the young have had to learn to be more knowing of family problems. However, at the time of their creation they were innovative and exciting. I recall them with great pleasure and regard them as some of the most worthwhile work I did at that period.

Stiltman

GULLIVER'S TRAVELS – Jonathan Swift

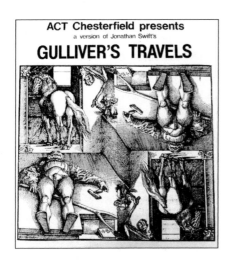

ACT Chesterfield presents
a version of Jonathan Swift's
GULLIVER'S TRAVELS

Writing of my work with ACT, I use a web of references, memories, scripts, encounters, notes, quotations and surprises. I have no overall pre-conceived plan either thematic, chronological or stylistic, but rather wander in a field of rich experiences wondering how many of the eighty two productions I put before the public might be worthy of description, be of interest to a reader. From time to time I am blocked. What to do? I wait waiting, and then, as if from nowhere some small something triggers a contact and I sense a way in.

A week ago I bought a coloured lithograph by the Yorkshire artist Maxwell Doig which I had originally seen in an exhibition at The Hart Gallery twenty years previously.. On that occasion I chose to buy a different example of his work – a small pastel drawing of a figure stitching up a massive bale of raw shoddy, dyed wool, which chimed a childhood memory of lorries delivering these great bundles to the woollen mills on East Ardsley road outside Leeds where my Grandma ('mi gramma' in the dialect) lived. I recall late autumn evenings, walking a couple of bus stops up the road so I could watch the arrival of bale laden lorries then watch them being unloaded by gaslight for the night shift. And I saved a pennysworth of my bus fare home.

Doig's subject matter, and his strongly perceptive representations of the human figure in unlikely postures and situations had immediately intrigued me. Particularly engaging had been the Stiltman series of prints, out of my price bracket at the time.

The Stiltman I now own is stretching awkwardly, teetering unbalanced at the point of a tottering tumble, tensioned, naked, gripping his stilts at arms length angles, attempting the dangerously near possible.

I feel we are kin. The image becomes ever more apposite when I glance at it propped beside my desk as I write. My theatre work was a similarly tricksy balancing act. I would set out on another new path, often feeling naked and in alien dangerous territory, believing I wouldn't fall, but knowing I might.

Once, just the once, I did lose an audience when fifty per centre of those who left at the interval did not return, and the final applause was decidedly muted. This was during the performance that involved stiltwalking.

Every so often a group, a culture, will produce an event so peculiar that you feel it could not possibly happen anywhere else, that it epitomises something weird about the situation even though its causes turn out, on appraisal, to have a logic of their own. These occasions have occurred infrequently – but they did occur and left me STILTS AHOY! Wondering how on earth...

and why...

Stiltman was a trigger.

Scene Two: Brobdingnag – The Land of Giants

Picture this – A square area, fourteen feet by fourteen, has been marked out on the Studio floor. It represents a table top which when completed, will be raised off the ground and painted as if covered with a white lace-trimmed cloth. At its head will sit two twelve feet tall giant painted figures with moving mouths. They are the King and Queen of Brobdingnag, the land of enormous giants visited by Lemuel Gulliver on his second voyage.. To give the set an appropriate sense of scale an enormous (everything has to be enormous!) pair of spectacles with lenses two feet in diameter will be on the table. Gulliver will bend to gaze through these at the frighteningly magnified audience on his first visit to the monarch of Brobdingnag.

But that will be for later.

Whereas now, in rehearsal, two young women on high stilts step forward onto the table top, where their extended height will allow them to look the King and Queen in the eye. They are Julie Nelson(Jooj) to whom my collection of ACT photographs is dedicated, and the beautiful Tamsin Gregory who is playing the Monroesque lead role in our concurrent production of the musical *Little Shop of Horrors*. I know they are word perfect, they understand their space and moves, they are very good friends and work ever so well as a pair. The scene begins. We watch them attempting the dangerously near possible. They can barely stand. They twirl, rush, arrest, helplessly struggling to remain upright and spout gabbled lines, the result of being quite incapacitated by alcohol. Aghast and amazed the cast look on at their stupidly drunken attempts at dexterity. It is frighteningly dangerous.

I love them.

I'm Cruel, I make them finish the scene, then send them home.

Chastening time tomorrow.

All the Brobdingnagians, all who dared, are on stilts, some become adept and confident, others remain cautious and worried. Half masks swell bulging cheeks and foreheads to make fuller faces for the giants. Cath Acons has done a great design job.

We solved the problem of being gigantic and achieving a fitting sense of scale by using a small male doll, Barbie's Ken, bewigged and costumed in blue velvet coat, white britches and black buckled shoes just like the lead actor, to represent Gulliver when picked up and treated as a plaything by the ladies in waiting. Ken enjoyed many real life roles, including plumber to astronaut and everything between, but always claimed to find none more rewarding than his role as Lemuel Gulliver on his second voyage, in spite of the fact that he struggled with fake panache to maintain his usual cool when one of the maids sat him astride her nipple and gently but repeatedly squeezed his legs together.

The rulers of Brobdingnag are benign, their subjects reasonable, gentle, kindly and fair in their treatment of the tiny creature who visits them. However, Gulliver becomes increasingly petty, small minded, bigoted and unforgiving in their company. He finds their pimples grotesque, their hair coarse, their bodies noxious and is utterly appalled by their dollops of excrement (we did consider constructing an enormous steaming turd, but the idea was voted down. Such is the depressing limitation of democracy!) When Gulliver describes English society to the King its every aspect appears self-serving, aggressive, competitive, avaricious and totally irrational. Gulliver's offer to explain how to make gunpowder so that he can destroy his enemies is regarded with disdain as the most appallingly unbelievable inhumanity by the king, who considers Gulliver brutally uncaring, barely a human being.

Scene One : Lilliput – The Land of Tiny People

In total contrast was Gulliver's first voyage which took him to the land of the tiny Lilliputians who were engaged in an endless war between the Bigendians and the Littlendians, all a matter of the correct way to eat boiled eggs, and who happily allowed Lemuel to tow away the entire fleet of their enemies.

The Lilliputians are pompous, puffed up self important bundles of frenetic and pointless energy, giddy, antagonistic and egotistically irrational. Ministers of state are selected on the basis of how many somersaults they can turn, how many hoops they can jump through. The cast were brightly costumed as members of different sectors of society – a footballer, a nun, a policeman, a ballerina, a burglar, a lady, a waitress, a bowler hatted gent etc., and each had mastered a circus skill – juggling, balancing, plate spinning, hula hooping, fancy skipping, tumbling, acts which punctuated every encounter. Their performances were erratic, eccentric and suitably silly. Their voices high pitched, painful.

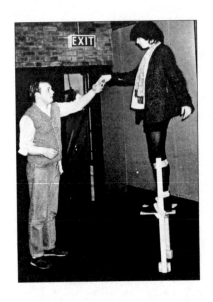

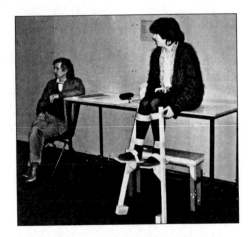

The set consisted of a tall, narrow, raised platform to make big Ian Rochard even taller, with a very long balance bar stretched from it across the stage area. The people of Lilliput had to balance on this bar whenever they spoke to the giant who towered above them. Again physical agility was at a premium. There were a few tumbles, but the sequence played well.

Gulliver feels increasingly superior to the Lilliputians and becomes the lauded hero of the land when he extinguishes the Great Fire that breaks out in the royal palace. A small paper model of the palace (they are very little people) is held aloft on a metal tray and ignited. As flames leap upward the palace becomes a blazing inferno. Gulliver, on high, opens his trousers, takes out his splendidly authentic looking penis and pisses a yellow stream down onto the flames until they are dowsed, thus rousing cries of jubilation and applause from both the cast and the audience. Lemuel himself, flushed with pride is also relieved. Ian, the acting Gulliver, fashioned his uncircumcised penis from a plastic Jif squeezy lemon bottle masterfully remodelled and disguised. Rob Crump, the narrating Gulliver built the flammable palaces and held them aloft with fear and trembling. Probably fear of being splashed, probably trembling because he was aware of the rash illegality of what we were doing. Or perhaps he was acting?

Scene Three : Laputa – The Flying Island

The third voyage, to Laputa, was difficult to realise. Charles Monkhouse built an inspiring large circular floating set based on part of an orrery, with a complicated bit of slatted gadgetry set in off centre. How did it float? On air, like the economy stupid.

The purpose of the voyage to Laputa is to show up the follies of cranky science and dubious intellectual philosophising. Swift wrote always in opposition to the Enlightenment and as an enemy of 'modernism': Science, he believed, gave sanction to the idea of progress, deluding men with the promise of an ever-expanding and improving future which, to Swift, seemed necessarily chimerical, man being limited as he is. He distrusted science because it seemed irrelevant to the moral life of man. It is interesting to consider what would be his response to the things science has given to our contemporary world: daytime television, the common cold, Hiroshima, billions of plastic bags.

Our Laputan performers engaged in lots of affected posturing and nonsensical reasoning and riddling, much of it in nonsense languages. Pale faced loons aimlessly wandering wore gold lamé robes and dunce's hats. Judith Green spent the entire sequence improvising abstruse activity by manipulating whole fresh cucumbers in the absolute belief that she could distil light from them. She experimented with ever increasing elaboration and

determination but light there shone not one jot. She might have tried one manoeuvre which would surely have brought a sparking light to her eyes, but she didn't, and I wouldn't have allowed it anyway.

Janie McPhie comments

I have very strong memories of translating and performing Gulliver. However it was certainly not the version I remember as a child. When Jack suggested we use the original inflatable devices that Morris Dancers once used to 'bop' people over their heads in order to re-awaken both the audience and the philosophers of Laputa from daydreaming and pontificating, we, the cast, agreed unanimously 'No'. We believed that being 'bopped' over the head with a pig's bladder would probably be a little too much for the younger audiences to take... as well as the actors on stage being 'bopped'! Jack sulked. We used balloons instead.

We were aiming for the ludicrous brilliant tenor of a Monty Python sketch but didn't get the bite, and I let the scenes run too long believing that pointless repetition was part of the message of the whole charade. I think our audiences got the idea, but were glad to see the end of it.

Scene Four : The Land of the Houyhnhnms

The one I expected to be the simplest, but proved in practical terms to be the most troublesome and difficult, was the fourth voyage to the Houyhnhnms, a land of beautiful thoroughbred horses who are perfect in every way: perfectly correct, perfectly emotionless, perfectly polite and mindless, the embodiment of pure reason, and therefore perfectly boring. They are the absolute masters of their land and masters of the Yahoos, human like creatures who, dirty, feckless, harsh, grovelling, lustful and ugly, are the slaves and servants of the Houyhnhnms.

The climactic fourth voyage is the great section of the book. It has provoked violent attacks. The most powerful single symbol in the whole of Swift's writing is the Yahoos, which do not simply represent the author's view of mankind, but rather the bestial elements in man – the unenlightened, unregenerate irrational elements in human nature. I offered the cast a free choice of which group they would play and found it fascinating, perhaps predictable, in the approximately 50/50 split, to see which actors chose to be horses and which Yahoos. I now wonder, devilishly, whether I should have made them play the opposite to their personal choice. It can be revealing and exciting to cast against actors' natural instincts. That sense of danger must not disappear.

Martin Wiltshire designed a raised interlocking Greek key pattern walkway for the Houyhnmnms to prance and strut their stuff, with cramped burrow-like spaces below for the Yahoos. He also designed and made eight wonderful horse heads cut out and folded from a flat cardboard pattern (the kind you used to find on the backs of breakfast cereal boxes). These constructions were the very essence of horseness, each differently coloured and quite believable when viewed from whatever angle. One, the loveliest, is the Strawberry Roan with whom Gulliver falls madly in love. His experiences with the superior, eugenics practising, Houyhnhnms cause Gulliver to increasingly and utterly despise the Yahoos. On his return to England the Voyager goes insane, rejecting the whole of humankind in his madness and opting to live with his horses in their stable. He eats only straw.

In performance the Yahoos enjoyed an indulgent whale of a time. I suggested they study animal behaviour, the outcome of which manifested itself very suggestively: there was a lot of bottom flashing, nit picking, mutual grooming, fiddling with their bits and outbreaks of angry squawking confrontation until called to order by the Houyhnhnms. Then they acted scared and sullen, scurrying away to their hovels making farting noises until they collapsed into blatant deep sleep. Judith Green writes

> I spent much of my time worrying about not being too disgusting in the Yahoo scenes, and even now feel a tremor every time the word Yahoo pops up on my computer screen.

The Houyhnhnms had a tough deal. Sight-lines were limited, non-existent some claimed, when wearing the heads with dinner jackets or black cocktail dresses. The walkways were too narrow to make passing easy, high heels were suicidal, when I asked them to herd together they became frightened, their voices were muffled, nuzzling one another made their heads wobble and as they had all been cut to the same pattern, man-sized, they each had to devise a way to wear their head with pride whilst having it wedged stable, and as if that were not sufficient – "YOU" they yelled, "YOU'RE not up here don't keep telling us to nod and shake our heads when talking so the audience knows who is speaking when we don't know who is fucking who ourselves nor where the fuck we are! We are bleeding blind and you don't know, you have NO IDEA how impossible and frightening it is raised up here with that ignorant bunch scrabbling around and farting under our feet and don't you dare laugh YOU BASTARD!!" I did not laugh... the Yahoos did.

I explained calmly that their language was very unseemly for Houyhnhnms, but they HAD made their choices.

It's tough at the top!

With a much extended rehearsal period we would have achieved more, but effectively our whole approach needed to be rethought from square one. Whatsoever, we made it, they came through. The Houyhnhnms looked splendid, elegant and assured. Splendid but rather static. Alluring even. I developed feelings for the Strawberry Roan. "Stay away", Tamsin snarled, "Just don't you even think of it when I have this head on, or I'll trample your balls to a squishy pulp!" I took a backward step.

There's a lesson here. I think. Swift believed that all we human beings are of the H and Y both parts mixed. Our confrontation demonstrated as much. I am generally recognised as being a total Y, but in this context conducted myself with the calming grace of the most assured H, whilst the supposed H's behaved with the demented fervour and venom of the most bestial Y's.

ACT Chesterfield presents

Book and Lyrics by
Howard Ashman
Music by
Alan Menken

in Darmstadt

to celebrate
the 25th anniversary of Twinning

We had been invited to take a major production to Darmstadt to celebrate the 25th anniversary of twinning with Chesterfield. Money was available if we would bring something both classic and very English. Being unsure whether classic and very English meant Noel Coward or Harold Pinter in Germany, I made the grand Napoleonic gesture (c'est magnifique mais ce n'est past la guerre) and chose *Gulliver's Travels*. I agreed to take a second production – something popular, suited to a younger audience. *Little Shop of Horrors* was the choice; we were given the rights for Germany but not to perform in England as a star packed production was touring the United Kingdom. Working on this refreshingly straightforward musical with music director Paul Stone and arranger Phil Wright was a real pleasure. Performed largely by students it proved to be uncomplicated, straightforward and very successful. But it had eaten into time which might have been better spent meeting the particular challenges posed by Swift. After an intense rehearsal period the piece was as ready as we could hope for.

We performed the *Travels* in four distinctly separate spaces, with the audience accompanying Gulliver to each successive country. It worked a treat. However in Darmstadt we performed in the vast wide open space of the Duke of Hessen's Orangerie, and because there had been lots of advanced ticket sales I decided to group the four stages close together in the centre of the room with the audience on banked seating at either end. The consequence of this was that only a quarter of the very large playing area was in use at any one time and three quarters of the audience were too distant to truly appreciate the performances. With such a numerous attendance it would have been impossible to present the promenade performance I had originally intended even in this vast space.

However, we lost a part of only the first audience. I was able to prevent its recurrence by improvising some pointedly explicit narrative links and suggesting to the actors that their scenes should be played at the more distant audience rather than for them. As always the people of Darmstadt were very generous in their support, and we certainly fulfilled their request for something special, worthy of the 25th Anniversary, a European landmark.

It was very special for me. Stilt high, I just about held my point of balance. And the choice? Jonathan Swift is a brilliant brilliant writer, his satire devastating, his subject matter and his strangely perceptive representations of the human figure in unlikely postures and situations has always intrigued me. The book tells of finding oneself in totally bizarre and unexpected situations. We lived that experience. And avoided madness. Sheila Harding comments

Working with ACT you often had to master a new skill – this usually involved pain.

We had managed the dangerously near impossible, we put a Gulliver together.

But!

What it fatally wasn't was angry. All satire must be born from cold anger. All our energies had gone into creating the show, rather than the thing itself. It wasn't ICONOCLASTIC.

Other Realities

MECHANICALS ALIVE, AVATARS EVEN

There is a particular particularity about theatre that imbues it with unique and extraordinary possibilities of expression. The quintessential importance of words, of a space fitted and fitting to the purpose of each production, and of the ways performance in action serves to generate emotion and danger are the basic structures on which theatre are built. If an audience is not engaged, either emotionally or by the sense of danger, one's work has not been worth while. But then there is a fourth magically particular element, strange and potent, lifeless yet living – the possibility of Mechanicals, things that come alive, as Avatars even, a feature of our strange apprehension of the world in which we live; agents of order or disorder, they can become essential and occasionally central to our experience of theatre.

"There is no perfect stability in the human condition, only approximations of it, sometimes fragile because created by culture." That fragility, that approximation may sometimes be represented by extra-animate objects/things which have symbolic, thematic (or even betoken godlike) significance, their presence being essential to the presentation and resolution of a drama. They surprise and entertain and serve to make better sense of the mystery of the plundering of the human condition which theatre undertakes. Though inanimate their function is to animate.

I frequently took advantage of these, things which pass beyond the status of mere props. They garner symbolic, or practical or amusing or disturbing importance from being the chosen best available way to communicate a particular human experience. They offer a counterpoint, an enriching alternative to the flesh-bound human presence of actors.

The nature of their fascination is in the choices made. For example, why choose a boy-sized, fairly realistically articulated, puppet for the role of Arthur in the trio of *Arthur in the West* stories by Alan Coren that we toured to primary

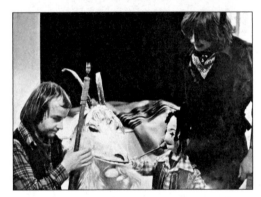

schools, when young adult actors played boys in the Grips plays and *Veronica Dribblethwaite*, and young girls in our adaptation of *John Dollar*?

Arthur is the hero of stories which are rich in period accuracy, true to the Western myth, funny and exciting (The Third Western). If you wanted to know why the Seminole Kid had an iron hook where his left hand used to be, or why Herbert Tiddle was nailed to a table, or what was the terrible secret of the Sheriff's trousers, or who hung Memory Nobbs from the coat-hook and what did he have that brought terror to Dognose Gap, then Arthur was your boy. He was a wonderful and convincing lead player, worked hard in rehearsal, learnt his lines and moves quickly, never lost his concentration and interacted sympathetically and naturally with our young audiences. He was the consummate performer, but outside performance his true character came to the fore. He was lewd minded, sexually provocative, somewhat aggressive, and even worse behaved when being manipulated by Ros and Geraldine, the two actresses who along with Bill, Gary Birtles and myself made up the rest of the cast. It was very strange that the puppet had its own personality, and that must somehow have reflected the interactive chemistry between us five actors. He was anarchic, selfish and dangerously over-sexed, often touching people inappropriately. However, when he played Arthur he was brilliant, giving us a foil and possibilities for interaction that seemed to be much more than any mere human might. It's not simply a question of suspension of disbelief, nor of opting for puppets for children, but rather an intuitive realisation that a certain narrative will be more compelling, more believable even, if information comes out of the mouths of puppets who interact with humans.

There was a second puppet in this production – The Talking Goat, a magnificent life-sized head and neck puppet with proud horns and articulated mouth created by Don Wilkinson. It was a source of reason and good advice, with a calming godlike presence, that of an avatar. The Goat remained distant from the goodies and baddies of the world he occasionally entered with great discretion, but when handled by Bill he took on a remarkable lifelike identity whilst conversing with Arthur, a totally different flawed and human creature. Beyond the performances the Goat had no existence, a mere thing kept, carefully, in a box.

Don Wilkinson also made for me a full set of beautifully detailed Punch and Judy puppets for another primary schools production: *Kite Girl, the Clown and Mr Punch*. This was another production that depended on the interaction between puppets, actors and audience. Mr Punch pops his head through a classroom door, the kids notice him, he asks to come in, and enters to squeals of amazement, asking if any one has seen his sausages or a crocodile. We discuss what to do? The kids talk to me and to Mr Punch on my left hand; he talks to me and the kids. It's the sausages he's most worried about, so we leave together to search and turn up at another class where a Clown is doing sillying. Mr Punch gets into an argument with the Clown, the kids take sides with lots of "oh yes he is!", "OH NO he isn't!", mostly directed against Mr Punch; with forty youngsters milling around things get hectic and chaotic. Mr Punch decides we should all go look further afield. In the school hall or playground, we find Kite Girl with her dozen outsize differently designed and decorated kites, which Charles Monkhouse made for us. If we are outdoors Kite Girl flies a kite while she tells the story of her arrival in this strange place, seeking to know where in the Universe she is – England? Is that in America? Is that on the planet Jupiter? Kite Girl is very nervous, worried, as she points out a strange creature hiding amongst the kites. Mr Punch recaptures his crocodile with help from the kids. As we all turn back to Kite Girl she is now wearing a necklace and explains that on arrival she landed on a long string of soft squishy things that make a very nice necklace – sausages? What are they? Eat them? EAT them? Ugh! As she lifts them to her lips Mr Punch and his class shout – No, No, NO, they're mine, mine, MINE! And they are not cooked. Now at last Punch can perform his show on his stage.

I never mastered the swizzle but my voices were pretty good, the audiences wide eyed. The beatings, the hanging and the incipient cruelty of the show were questioned by some in the increasingly cautious late seventies. But, so it goes. After the run of the T.I.E. programme I enjoyed a good two years of intermittent Punch and Judy shows for a variety of children's groups. I've never been more popular. But this was pure puppet performance; what increasingly fascinated me was the credibility of interaction between living actors and living puppets.

Punch was reborn, incarnate, radiation bleached and frightful, a decade and two thousand years later in our production of *Riddley Walker*. His role was that of an avatar, an all-knowing god-like manifestation who riddles the memories of Way Back Time Back before the Wun Big Wun which destroyed civilisation as we know it. Punch has the nolej of men flying in iron and picters coming thru air. In a confrontational meeting with a large, totally different, clanking two-dimensional and crudely articulated Mr Clevver, Punch debates the nolej, the wikideevil, the fate of mankind. These two, who share no generic similarity whatsoever, apart from their essential puppet being, engage in vivid and increasingly threatening verbal jousting. Ian Rochard recalls it as the most powerful and enjoyable scene he ever played. Mr Clevver is the Devil. The scene was frightening.

Frightening in a different register is the resounding throat-grinding command: FEED ME! of the plant whose reality is created with four increasingly large puppet mechanicals until it becomes the carnivorous giant gulping down its gawping belching gullet real human beings. It is another example of puppet-human interaction in which the alien living creature decides the fate for better or worse of human characters. In our production of *Little Shop of Horrors,* which licence agreements allowed us to perform only in Germany, the plant, as it needs to be, was the star, drawing gasps of amazement in its final giant appearance amongst an overwhelming stage filled with an abundance of plants, blooms, flowers galore.

Other mechanical avatars take on the embodiment of a concept but remain inhuman in form. The dumb waiter in Pinter's short play was effectively the leading character operated with perfect precision by Tim Anger. Its every trundling arrival, anticipated with bewildered, doubting concern, was again defining the fate of the two gangster characters whilst seemingly having played with them as flies to wanton boys. Likewise, in Beckett's play, Krapp's tape recorder functions as a kind of alter ego as it obsessively drives Krapp to explore his fate, his past. I believe it must assert a presence, become one half of a strange relationship, rather than simply functioning as a mere clanking mechanical object.

In other productions the mechanicals become a motif, a reminder; that is their function. They are passive but symbolically significant.

In *Trummi Kaputt* the wireless-operated toy robot serves as an example of capitalist exploitation of children; Trummi was fun, provoked audience laughter and applause, but rapidly trundled to a motionless breakdown with a pathetic squeak and a puff of smoke.

That wooden black head in *Africa* which endures persistent carefully precise torture throughout the duration of the play was emblematic of the fate of the black people of South Africa during the apartheid era. The head's presence, continuously visible on stage, as an inanimate symbol, seemed more fitting and more powerfully engaging in the context of our performance than any live action could have been. The method of torture, a small egg-sized lead weight bound in a leather pouch and repeatedly tapped behind the ear, was reportedly authentic and left the victim unmarked.

With similar impassivity, the vulnerability of the neglected child that Jo Smith played in Jim Cartwright's *Road* was defined by the worn bedraggled teddy bear to which she whispered before dropping it abandoned as she returned upstairs. Jo later played Veronica Dribblethwaite, another child, but this time a comic-book adventurer whose confidence and success in solving a mystery was defined by the soft toy mallard duck which accompanied her everywhere. The duck was always there, a partner, a comfort, who never abandoned Jo.

Ultimate passivity, its very nadir, was achieved by Barbie's Ken in *Gulliver's Travels.* It was a case of casting by size, and he certainly looked the part of Gulliver in Brobdingnag, the land of giants. But his performance remained pure plastic. He failed to enter into the spirit of the work, and never forgave me for the embarrassment of the nipple incident.

Totally static passivity is another feature which can generate a particular potency within a drama. The gaunt, silent, somewhat forbidding figures with which Martin Wiltshire dressed the platforms and odd seats of two carriages of the Berlin Underground's *Line One* are a case in point. They engendered an atmosphere of ominous expectation, their stillness unsettling when set against the self-absorbed bustling busyness of the live passengers; their stilled solitude echoing that of the lead character, the girl seeking her lost lover as she travelled the length of Line One.

There is a similar dramatic instance in Trevor Griffiths' *Comedians*. Two static mannequins, one a dinner-jacketed male, the other a bejewelled evening-gowned female, are taunted and abused by the trainee punk comedian played by John Connolly. The point of their presence in the comedian's set is their total bourgeois impassivity in the face of the young man's angry and abusive attack on their values. It's a very cruel paradigm.

In the same play there is a brilliant counter-intuitive intraversion of the puppet principle. Two brothers are trialling their comedy act in which one of them plays a ventriloquist's dummy seated on his brother's knee. Their relationship is fractious, their comedy pained, a situation heightened in our production by the slow burning real-life animosity that existed between Ian Rochard and Reg Shore. I left them to their own devices when working on the sequence; it was taut and dangerously unpredictable at every performance. Ian comments:

> I was profoundly affected by this play. It made me much more reflective, not just about humour, but about the people I know, the way I related to them and the values we share (or did not share).

Shared values were a natural ingredient of our working process and the subject matter we broached. The Big Ripapart Rag Doll challenged our presumptions when we undertook an adaptation of three Grimm's Folk Tales for primary schools. Each of the stories had a similar trajectory: the characters faced a dilemma and a woman realised its resolution. In each tale the woman is initially portrayed as being weak or silly, altogether inferior to the bombastic male characters, but quickly proves the utter falsity of this clichéd stereotype. Two actresses, Angela Dickinson and Sheila Taplin, worked with Bill and I as we devised and then toured this project. We had considered doing a parallel production of Angela Carter's versions of the Grimm Tales for adult audiences, but other commitments obliged us to opt for the programme for primary schools..

The last story was *The Closed Room*. A man's new wife was forbidden to enter that room by her husband. She is curious, finds the key and foolishly unlocks the door; inside she finds the remains of her lost sister, represented by a life-sized rag doll which had been velcro ripped to pieces. The new wife organises a grisly end for her husband, and reassembles her sister who comes back to life.

This sounds horrendous.

With hindsight it was.

The three traditional tales were performed in a bold lively comic-book style and received positive support with no adverse comments from teachers at the schools we visited. And the children applauded and booed with delight at every possible opportunity.

Towards the end of our run Bill invited some of his friends to see our work. They were appalled. Bill accepted and understood their objections and decided he could no longer perform the show as each story presents women in a negative misogynistic light which is more crucially significant than the eventual triumphant female-engineered outcome of each tale. I honoured the outstanding bookings with a stand-in actor, but did not extend the run. This was the early eighties. Political Correctness ruled.

This puppet, the one we called Ripapart Rag Doll outside performance, the one that came back to life, the one that was the sister but had no name, was, perhaps, a grisly step too far. Its story demonstrated too well that there is no perfect stability in the human condition, only approximations and fragility.

When plundering – don't be over subtle.

Beware.

The How and the Why

UNDERSTANDING

Some ask what was it really all about. Was it important? I give a different answer every time.

Here. On this occasion I think I've found the best explanation – the best so far.

> "Contemporary philosophers of the Self argue that its most important constituents are time, space, a sense of physical embodiment and stories that fire the imagination."

That's a quotation from *The Return of Ulysses* by Edith Hall, a book about the many rich and varied ways the Homeric stories have affected and influenced civilizations through the centuries.

For me the words express the true deep experience, joy and benefit, essential to the nature of theatre, of creating theatre: an enhanced sense of one's Self in the world.

We had time, which we could allocate, structure, control and define in the process of creating a second period of time that of the drama.

We had space, an open space initially, in which to interact and explore, which ultimately became the space of the drama, a meaning filled space.

We had a sense of physical embodiment, ours was explored and expressed in preparation and workshops where bodies and voice were stretched and pulled to new limits in pursuit of that particular, unique to the individual, disciplined physical embodiment of becoming the protagonists of the drama.

And we told stories, stories that fired the imaginations of actors and audience alike.

Here, Sheila Harding describes the how and the why :

Members of Arts Centre Theatre came from ordinary jobs and ordinary lives: that was part of our strength. Probably none of us would have thought of ourselves as theatre professionals, although several went on to be. But neither did we bear any resemblance to the average amateur drama group.

Part of the difference was the level of commitment which ACT required. This was not only a matter of time – but also of focus. Whatever happened that day at work, whatever personal crisis we were in the middle of, had to be put aside, because ACT working methods were demanding and Jack unforgiving towards whingers and slackers. Those not working or with part-time commitments gave of their time freely, rigged and re-rigged schedules. It was both exhausting and exhilarating.

Then, there was a level of challenge which rivalled, perhaps surpassed, anything the average professional actor might meet. Each production was different from the last, sometimes wildly so, yet keeping its ACT identity, its signature. All the material we worked with was at the least interesting, more often controversial, inspiring and stimulating. There were no pot-boilers. We were often expected to play multiple roles and work close to the audience, sometimes even among them. There were rarely elaborate sets or special effects to hide behind. No-one was an understudy or a spear carrier, no-one was type-cast. If Jack decided that a production required circus skills, voice

work, dance or puppetry, then we learnt them bringing in specialists to run workshops. When the material was devised or adapted everyone participated in the process, arguing our way through to a version we could work with.

For most of us, it was the process of development and rehearsal which was the main point. The kick we got was from working as a team, from making something of our own out of a play script, a novel, or sometimes just a basic idea; making something from our own bodies, voices and emotions. Public performance was part of this, sometimes we got high on audience reaction and applause, but there were no extended runs, no bouquets or glossy foyer photos. We always moved on quickly to the next project, often feeling that we had just started to get it right on the last night.

"I don't understand why you people do it" – this from a moderately successful professional actor – "Why put in all that effort when you don't get paid?"

Sometimes I saw his point. It was true that many of us who worked regularly with ACT were also holding down full time jobs and had family responsibilities. More often than not, far from getting paid, we were often considerably out of pocket because of our involvement. We worked evenings and weekends and went on tour in our holidays. Yet I always said yes to the next project and my life fell flat when I wasn't involved.

Why?

Because ACT provided much more interesting experiences and challenges than anything else I was doing; more than I suspected most professional actors would ever be offered.

It was certainly nothing like the amateur theatre I'd been involved in before. For a start, we often devised or adapted material ourselves and when we did use a play script the choice was always interesting. There were at least three or four projects a year and no two projects were remotely alike. We were expected to challenge ourselves physically, emotionally and intellectually. No one was an understudy or a spear carrier.

Why?

Because working with ACT gave me a sense of the closest co-operative relationships.

I learned much more about negotiating skills, group dynamics and stress management than on any course I ever attended. We always worked co-operatively; there were no stars and we all felt responsible for the quality of the work. Those of use who became regular company members grew to know, trust and react to each other intuitively, so that we could work confidently and quickly. But almost every project had someone who was doing it for the first time, someone facing a physical or emotional challenge they had never met before, someone who surprised themselves and the rest of us by what they achieved. We brought with us a range of backgrounds, outside experience and sometimes pressures. I suspect we were a richer mix than most professional companies because of this and the way we worked together reflected that diversity.

In the course of a project we became a community, trusting each other physically and emotionally. For those of us who were involved over several years ACT became the source of some of our best memories and most enduring friendships.

Cryptic Titling

THE POSSIBILITIES, Howard Barker

A TITLE – The Weaver's Ecstasy at the Discovery of a New Colour.

ACTOR'S COMMENT – We are trying to get to grips with Howard Barker's set of short pieces, *The Possibilities*. More than anything else we have done, these intrigue me. Each one is a dangerous little box of ideas in which meaning seems just out of reach. The characters and situations have to be felt and believed in without fully understanding them. For once, the existence of a script doesn't seem like a limitation. I love the visceral images, the sack full of heads, the severed hand and the chance to develop unusual visual symbolism ourselves. I have come up with a long, formless piece of scarlet knitting for one of my characters, a wife waiting for her husband to return from war. I'm particularly pleased with this. We perform in the black studio – an airless little box which seems just right for the material.

A TITLE – The Philosophical Lieutenant and the three Village Women.

THE POSSIBILITIES is a collection of ten short plays, very short plays, the longest seven pages in length. I had been enthralled by performances of Barker's longer plays performed by The Wrestling School, the company dedicated solely to his work, and as I was thinking of using a language-based work for the next tour to Darmstadt I chose *The Possibilities* which allowed me to work with small casts as and when they were available. We prepared seven of the ten plays and were able to take five of them to Germany.

A TITLE – The Dumb Woman's Ecstasy

A QUOTATION – Howard Barker has emerged as the most original and controversial dramatist of the group of theatre writers who made a profound impression on the English stage in the 1970s and 1980s.

A TITLE – Only some can take the strain

A QUOTATION – The Theatre of Catastrophe takes as its first principle the idea that art is not digestible. Rather, it is an irritant in unconsciousness, like the grain of sand in the oyster's gut.

A TITLE – The Necessity of Prostitution in Advanced Societies.

THE CASTS – Dawn Dickenson, Karl Wilson, Jamie McPhie, Margot Bartlett, Hazel Collis, Sandy Hodgson, Sonia Wiser, Kathy Cooke, Heather Boardman, Paul Thtereve, Andrew Cook, Sheila Harding, Anthony Wheeldon, Ian Rochard, Siobhan Taylor, Lisa Benton, Brian Sargent, Rebecca Thompson, Claire Dakin.

A TITLE – Not Him

THE PLAYWRIGHT ARGUES – We grew ashamed of the I in the theatre and learned to talk of the We. Rightly because the art is collective, and because we were doing new things, rapidly making enemies.

I also wanted to belong and found at once the actors were the allies who knew by speaking what struck and what missed better than the managers, who are careerists or idealists, or writers, who follow each other.

I sensed the authority of the spoken word but still did not grasp its range, its arc of effect in a culture frantic with images, fevered with pictures and products, visually sick.

A TITLE – The Unforeseen Consequences of an Act of Patriotism.

DIRECTOR'S COMMENT – Quotations are from a collection of essays *Arguments for a Theatre,* which informed our approach to the plays. This work came late to me. It was a rare privilege to grapple it with a group of experienced actors, supplemented with talented students, who were prepared to tackle the texts with open minds, repeatedly edging towards getting the tone, the balance of interaction and the necessary conviction for each piece. I am not a theoretician.

A TITLE – Kiss My Hands

THE PLAYS are set in varied historical and social contexts, each of which proposes a moral or ethical problem which is pursued or resolved by a possible, but unexpected, means or route. The issues confronted include conformity to social and gender roles, the power of sexuality, censorship and freedom of access to knowledge, totalitarian control and the practice of torture, prostitution, and patriotism.

A TITLE – Reasons for the Fall of Emperors.

ACTOR'S COMMENT – It was the language, the language that held me. I played the Old Bookseller whose handcart of books is officially sealed by a Miss Leighman from the Ministry of Education. A man returns and insists on taking the sole copy of one particular book.

BOOKSELLER.	What is this reckless thirst that masters you?
THE MAN.	It is the only copy.
BOOKSELLER.	How many did you want?
THE MAN.	I am breaking the seals.
BOOKSELLER.	You are going to disseminate it! I knew when I saw you, he is either a policeman or a disseminator! You will copy it on machines and leave the pages in launderettes.
THE MAN.	Yes.
BOOKSELLER.	I knew! What do you think knowledge is Sherbert? (THE MAN is cutting the seals with a knife.) Enticer! What are you trying to do, wreck people's lives? **Only some can take the strain!** (The MAN covers THE BOOKSELLER'S mouth.)
THE MAN.	Speak and you die. (Pause. He frees him, finishes cutting the seals, and removes the book. He conceals it under his coat. THE BOOKSELLER is still. THE MAN turns to go.)
BOOKSELLER.	Zurich. (THE MAN stops.) Down by the river. (THE MAN leaves.) Under the tree.

A TITLE – She Sees the Argument But

A QUOTATION – The audience is divided and goes home disturbed or amazed. It is time we started to take the audience seriously and stopped telling it stories it can understand (Howard Barker).

"a rollicking excursion into impropriety"

LYSISTRATA, Aristophanes

"It is shock that counts, the elemental shock of good sense insisted upon to the point of absurdity. For what could be more sensible, more wildly absurd, than that the women on both sides should call a sexual strike to halt a war that no longer had meaning nor promise of hope."

Linda Lee is painfully thin, a compulsive smoker, an explosive bundle of scatter-gun talk, and a wonderful American folk musician, singer and song-writer. A novelist, she teaches creative writing at Sheffield University. Linda was at Mal Nix's memorial gathering in Sheffield, and it was there that we met up more than twenty years after she had been musical director of *Lysistrata – Lizzie Strata*. Sheila had introduced me to her then, and the week following our current encounter we met at her small terraced town house for a meal.

We sit around her kitchen table catching up on past times. She takes my hands, holds my gaze, and says:

"Jack, honey, when you talk you use your hands with such eloquence, such grace, I can't help but watch them, so expressive." All this at her slower, considered, scatter-gun rate. "But you know, you really should clean the dirt from under your fingernails when you're invited out to dine!"

I grabbed my hands away, and blustered: "I've been gardening, Linda. I'm Yorkshire born and bred, where there's muck there's brass, man of the earth! I need you to know I'm not just an arty, darling, theatre type whose pretensions..."

"Gee, I know that, Jack sweetie, but you really must clean those fingernails. I don't wanna say so but they are pretty disgusting."

She's leaning forward to look again, drowning me in the heavy haze of tobacco smoke that accompanies her everywhere.

I had chosen a script by the American poet Dudley Fitts, a free version of what is one of the great defining comedies of theatre. We'd been doing heavy stuff and were ready for a break, needed a laugh, a dose of roistering, a chance to sing and dance. And this version written in the low comedy burlesque talk of the Deep South with its fabulous hillbilly lyrics fitted the bill.

Linda Lee had agreed to work with us. She was inventive, adaptable and practical, finding solutions for actors who were not trained singers and writing original music for linking scenes, and researching an appropriate tune for the Appalachian dance.

I introduced the cast to the comic world of Li'l Abner, whose adventures I had devoured when visiting my cousins as a boy. The gorgeous blond and busty Sonia Standell was readily persuaded to play Lysistrata.

Everything set. Nothing to lose.

The women were to create their own characters bearing in mind the tone of the world of comics we were entering; they needed strong outlines, well-defined features, rip-cord voices. There was the primly, pretty dizzy doll, the cheeky street kid urchin, the wise-cracking cool Mae West, the stern-faced cowgirl, the corn-bowl pipe-smoking Granny and big bold bosky Lizzie Strata.

The men were uniformed soldiers, "loud and clear, Sir, soldiers of the U.S. Of A. Sir. Yes Sir!" with a penchant for flag waving. Confederate flags. I suggested they played down somewhat, should work on their pathetics.

To stage it we would build a long high platform, from where the women dominated the action, as if on high battlements, and below them the walls were painted with a sequence of graffiti-like images from L'il Abner.

Below, stranded, the men were corralled on the round 'floating island' stage built for the Laputa voyage in *Gulliver's Travels*, which was filled with an overlapping montage of L'il Abner images. A blue hint light wash would trap the men, while the women glowed in warm sun bright light.

The mysterious white-draped figure which set apart the two groups was finally unveiled to reveal the Goddess of Reconciliation, and the play would finish with men and women dancing a lively jig.

With Linda's help we worked to master accent, caricatured walking and gestures, practised the songs and seemed set to succeed. But, of course, we must hit the right note, after all this play was written in 412BC, and "of all Aristophanes comedies this has the sharpest relevance to our times", and all the men should wear erect penises. "Whopping great ones", cheered some, and the show hit the buffers.

I argued that this was the practice in Ancient Greece. Why not here? But certain party's feelings were seriously against penises, even when I demonstrated what ridiculously wonderful knobs could be fashioned from a

length of plumber's spongy pipe-cladding tube and even when I referred to the built-in obvious laughs in the text:

"Oh quick girls, quick! Come! A man.

A man simply bulging with love."

Somebody said, "they can stuff socks down their pants, inside", and I used the word ribaldry, but all to no avail. There was no way we would achieve the level of lewd robust ribaldry I had hoped for, so for one of the few times in my working life I bowed to peer pressure. What the hell, nobody's going to spoil the party, and we worked on.

The eighties were a strange time in England, conservative values reigned, feminist ideas had emasculated men's confidence, including mine, there was a tightness in the culture, perhaps especially so in the provincial culture where we worked.

In performance the production was well received. The music and singing gave it tempo, carried it along, characterisations were strong, and the division between warring males and peace-seeking females was significantly marked in both the acting and the design of the piece. But for me the show, whilst good, was slightly disappointing. It didn't drive home the real hard points. It didn't cohere.

Members of the Arts Centre's administrative staff, all women, attended the opening performance, and the message came back with Margot:

They say they enjoyed it,

but it's not

POLITICALLY CORRECT.

Criticism! That zeitgeist buzz-phrase! And I rejoiced, and when I rejoice I bounce off walls, and sometimes I swear:

"Of course it's not fucking politically correct!! for Christ's sake! Stupid cows! Who in fuck's arseholes name expects Aristophanes to be politically correct? Ridiculous. What the hell do they mean? It's anti-war!! The women win win win. It's celebrated for being 'a rollicking excursion into impropriety' and even with no cocks we barely got there! Why do I bother?!"

And I was angry that they hadn't got the point, but glad to have ruffled them. But if they were right, it could be a miss, and my fault. A slight part of my being was always haunted by The Goalkeeper's Fear of the Penalty. That insecurity thing. Could I afford to miss the save or had they kicked the ball clean over the bar and out of the stadium. Should I adapt to these mean-spirited loads-a-money grabbing times; or, more likely, should I one way or another have been stronger, hit the bastards harder, scalded the stupid bastards with the pain we put into our laughter.

Confusion reigns. In his introduction to the script Dudley Fitts writes:

> Noone could possibly take Lysistrata's proposition seriously; it is a joke, brutally pure; but the absurd has its own tragic depths, and it may be that our simplicities offer more hope at the end than all our complexities and distinctions.

Perhaps we were caught up in the complexities and distinctions of our times, and I had failed to plumb the absurd's tragic depths. There is no perhaps. Our simplicities offering hope didn't turn up, never surfaced. The time was out of joint. This despite the fact that the final production was rich in variety and a joy to watch.

Sheer Good Cheer! (So, does the Devil have all the best songs?)

A MIDSUMMER NIGHT'S DREAM, William Shakespeare
OUR DAY OUT, Willy Russell

A Midsummer
Night's Dream

An A.C.T. Production

So few things can be so just right: the understanding complete, the casting magically perfect, a shared sense of delight in rehearsal realising that we share values and aims in a totally positive working environment. It is so rewarding to put your faith in someone at the same time as they are committing theirs to you. Together we become a buoyant assembly of skills, where each is willingly putting themselves under intense scrutiny – that being the name of the game – and it feels wholesome, validating, right. The effect is thrilling and humbling.

I enjoyed this sense of a very special conjunction of time and people on a number of occasions, most frequently perhaps when the material we were developing had a lighter impulse, a comic tendency. This, the case with these two productions, ranks them high on my sheer good cheer register.

After a number of challenging and difficult productions I decided to embark on *A Midsummer Night's Dream*, being partly inspired by having seen the première performance of Cheek by Jowl's production in Buxton. Their work is exceptionally clear in vision, very neat, precise and uncluttered, very wonderful. That clarity of presentation I found remarkable, an approach in direct contrast to the rich, verging on the anarchic, rampaging of my natural inclinations, and I made it the starting point of my inspiration. The defining decision was to perform in the round, using stage flooring to define our playing area with the audience seated within inches of its edge. We dispensed with any set apart from a couple of rostra at diagonal corners. The playing area had to be small enough to be practicable in village halls and similar small venues. A very tourable production.

As is common practice we doubled parts, the Duke and Hippolyta with Oberon and Titania, the fairies, a rabble of unsettling punks, with the

Mechanicals. The four young lovers were markedly individual, eccentric, and desperately bewildered in their confusions. The cast made a wonderfully close and amicable community; it was real pleasure to work together. One nugget of outstanding brilliance was the playing of Puck by Martin Aistrope under the zapping control of Paul Sansom's Oberon. This pairing, totally memorable and astonishingly effective, triggered a vibrant life into the whole production.

Martin worked with me only four times: as a White South African apartheid torturer in *Africa*, as a drink-soaked Glaswegian in *Line One*, as the zanily accident-prone courtier Count Backwerdz in *Count Backwerdz on the Carpet*, and as Puck the first time he worked with us. It was his introduction to theatre, an opportunity to explore something new whilst his American girlfriend studied pottery at the College of Art. About a year later he followed his girlfriend to her home town of Chicago and within months sent me a review of his performance in an adaptation of a Dostoievsky story staged by the famous Chicago-based Steppenwolf Theatre,t he company of Gary Sinese and John Malkovich.

It is fascinatingly strange that out of the many many outstanding performances actors created for me, the two that are lodged most deeply and distinctly in my innards and my psyche, the two that leave me stunned with admiration, are Shakespearian, Martin as Puck and Pippa as Miranda.

Perhaps a degree of sentimentality comes into this. Part of me hates the notion. It's not what we were about – being best, having favourites. But, that's what they were, and they remain so, in my mind, in my memory. Nothing, nobody, was ever so bad as those people who, on those occasions, were so very very good. However, there were a few weighty blunders which do weigh heavy. They were badly miscast, they were my responsibility. Of course, I take no responsibility for the outstanding natural talent, each quite exclusive of the other, that Martin and Pippa enjoyed, but their casting, based on my instinct, was, in both instances, absolutely serendipitously right for these productions.

My approach to casting was unconventional in that I never auditioned. I had a great reluctance, almost a hubristic fear of that tradition. Mine was another way. I admire the films of the Hungarian director Béla Tarr; they are shot in a very particular style in black and white with long complex revealing takes which give his work a uniquely individual look and feel. But it is his philosophy regarding participation that I particularly share – he wants to make films with those he calls 'my people' rather than with film stars or professionally trained performers. When newcomers joined ACT they would spend time with the company, share activities, talk as and when, usually find the context unsettling and bewildering, gradually begin to know me, and either pitch in for the duration or leave. This was the case with Martin, and likewise with Sharon Burns, who played Hippolyta and Titania. Sharon originally came to operate the lights and still complains of the criticism she received in that role,

but stayed and played important roles in *Africa*, *Riddley Walker*, *Biggles* and *Gulliver's Travels*. Sharon also worked on scripting projects including *Means Test Man*, where her contribution was invaluable.

My instincts were generally good, but not infallible; I learnt a number of lessons after clumsy handling of newcomers. One which still haunts me occurred in the early years when I was preparing *Female Transport*. At the time I was still approaching work in a warily careful, quite formal way. A good-looking working man with a rich presence and strong voice had joined us, who I thought would be ideal as the ship's captain. The cast sat together in the Chapel Studio and began a read-through of the early scenes, a practice I subsequently more or less abandoned to the chagrin of some conventional performers. The newcomer struggled desperately with the reading. It became difficult and embarrassing, we ploughed on. My mistake. In private the cast suggested we could not continue in this vein, we needed to move on quickly. In my inexperience I accepted their argument and asked the man to leave without, I fear, offering an adequate explanation or consolation. It felt dishonest. I was inadequate. What must his feelings have been as he left the Studio? I have regretted it ever since. My practice was hopelessly wrong, I should have prepared him individually, and then offered him a trial, an audition effectively, which would have resolved the situation one way or another. But from that incident I learnt to spend time with people allowing them to become part of the group and accepting their decisions as to when and at what level to share in the work. Most people have an honest, ready awareness of their ability and how far they wish to challenge themselves. There was no competitiveness about who got which roles, in the last analysis my choices had to be final, but as far as I am aware there was no jealousy about who was playing which roles. Perhaps I'm blinkered, but I think not.

Over a decade later I carelessly made a similar blunder. An exceptionally talented young concert pianist, overwrought by nature and struggling with questions regarding his sexuality, joined us. He was very needy, seeking to lose himself in acting, a false assumption. I offered him a role well within his capabilities which might have been a breakthrough of sorts. It was an objective decision with no foundation in instinct, and I decided my decision was wrong and I wanted him to take an alternative, admittedly more isolating role. Not a lesser role, but it was less central to the action and less physically demanding. He left. He was adult. Late that evening his mother phoned to tell me I had unfairly damaged her son's confidence. They were rich. He went to some Acting School, and some months later he returned to explain he was now fulfilled, at last life was wonderful, and he was working with a wonderfully talented woman with whom he shared so much in common, and they were part of an exceptionally creative and adventurous group with plans for this and that. Some things cannot be disclosed. I couldn't believe him. It was the truth told slant. I thought he was talking about my life. Within a year or so he killed himself. I had truly been careless. This was George who had found our trip to *School for Clowns* so difficult.

I have veered off course, perhaps in the cause of balance. But this is the sheer good cheer section.

And *A Midsummer Night's Dream* was pure pleasure, full of giddy delight, pyrotechnic prose, whirlwind openings, bewitching inventions, and yet imbued with a sleight of darkness that confounds all expectations. We toured Derbyshire throughout high summer, and took the production to Darmstadt. It earned bragging rights. The final performance was scheduled for Youlgreave; at the time I was preparing the final rehearsals of *Pommie*. A friend brought her eleven-year-old son to see the play, and as they returned home he told his mum he wanted to do Shakespeare. That was validation enough! But then Bob Eaton, the creator of *John, Paul, George, Ringo and Me*, the musical which had played successfully in the West End and on Broadway, attended this same performance with Jack Longland, a renowned national radio broadcaster, and generously commented that it was the best, most enjoyable Midsummer Night he had spent.

Its ending, and especially its last ending, was enchantment. All confusions and issues resolved, the cast sing "By the light, of the silvery moon, I love to croon, with my honey I'll swoon love's tune" (borrowed, a tribute to Cheek by Jowl) and the actors take their partners in a closing romantic dance – the softly gentle singing, the dancing, a dying fall, magic, aaah! Marcello!

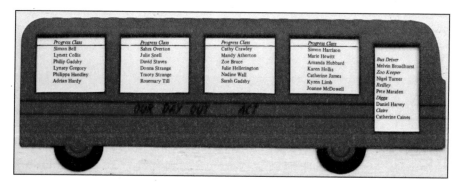

Bob Eaton was the composer of the songs in *Our Day Out*, the play by Willy Russel about a class of unruly 'remove' pupils on a school day trip which I had directed three years earlier. Another sheer good cheer experience which took me back to my days as a secondary modern boys' school teacher in Cambridge when days out with boys of a similar age and character to those in the play were among the highlights of my calendar. The fourteen boys and girls who volunteered to join the ACT production were excellent, seriously positive in application and outlook, but a real fun-loving group and such a refreshing change for me.

Our Day Out is a piece which could be weakened, like all comedies, by playing for laughs and sympathy so we spent time explaining the need to approach the script with heartfelt seriousness. Jackie and Alan Williams, who had performed in *The Widowing of Mrs Holroyd*, were responsible for the music and singing. My heart still lifts when I recall the singing. There is nothing more moving than a group of kids singing with heart and soul.

The script is wonderfully constructed, full of revelation and surprise. One particularly effective scene was the visit to the zoo. As the class return to their coach after spending time at Pet's Corner they are caught in the act of trying to smuggle a few new-found furry friends onto the bus. These friends included a puppy, two guinea-pigs, some stick insects, a lop-eared rabbit, two gerbils, a grass snake, a goldfish, a kid goat, a white mouse hidden in a boy's underpants and a cardboard cut-out of a hippopotamus. The physical management of this scene was amazing. The play was performed in the round and we decided the kids should pass through the audience from several directions. Everyone loved it, and the final moments spent finding the white mouse so ridiculously effective. I felt for that creature. Each of the animals were the cast's own pets.

The way you end a comedy is so important, especially one as serious as this. The scene which made me most proud of the kids was the one when, tired out, they are returning home on the bus and realise that two of their young teachers are falling in love. Quietly a melodic chant begins:

It's all gone quiet at the back,

It's all gone quiet at the back,

It's all gone quiet,

All gone quiet,

It's all gone quiet at the back.

CLAP CLAP.

The tempo quickens and the volume rises until at that moment, that just right moment, the mocking breaks into a beautifully pitched, exquisitely tender solo by one girl. It begins:

I'm in love with sir

But sir doesn't care

'Cos sir's in love with her

Over there

With the hair

It isn't fair.

I loved being with those kids as they practised under the tutelage of Jackie and Alan, although I did ruffle a few feathers and even drew tears on one occasion. But that's pressure. They would take any criticism of their acting, but closed ranks and became resentful when I commented on their singing. In that area their total allegiance was to Jackie and Alan.

The play ends with a parent yelling at the smallest, most deprived child, around whom the whole day out has pivoted.

> Carol! Where the friggin hell have you been?
>
> Just get in this bloody house.

And Carol begins the finale song:

> No one can take this time away
>
> No matter what they cannot take the day
>
> No one can steal
>
> Something you just feel
>
> And although the picture fades
>
> No one can take this time away.

Which is taken up and continued by the rest of the cast to create a wonderfully poignant and tender ending.

The play is more than a romp – it points up the depressing present and empty future for these kids from the back streets. In *The Times* Irving Wardle wrote of the original production:

> The skill and zest of the show derive from its success in following the adult argument through while preserving all the fun of a story for and mainly played by children . . . I have rarely seen a show that combined such warmth and such bleakness.

I feel we were true to this assessment, and the show was prepared and played with sheer good cheer and delight. But there is a strange rider – not one of the kids who joined us had a home or educational background remotely like those of the children whose lives they were enacting.

This leaves a dilemma. About the choices a director makes. A casting issue? The easy option? Accept the best. It gives me some consolation, and a little pride, that I had spent eleven years working at the chalkface of schoolteaching with the less advantaged kids of our society.

My title for this piece asks a bracketed cryptic question: Does the devil . . .? Well he doesn't, literally. I loved all the sheer good cheer experiences and value them enormously. They were wonderfully life enhancing, strangely precious, almost aberrant events, so rewarding, so enriching. However, I would not have wished my work to have been defined by them, nor to have lived my creative life with an endless succession of them. They did not fulfil the deeper, more complex needs that the dangerous, awkward, unsettling projects confronted.

A plausible impossibility is always preferable to an unconvincing possibility: Aristotle (who knew about these things)

OUR ISLAND OF OUTLAWED DREAMS

Adapted from Marianne Wiggins' novel 'John Dollar'

This one took us into the Heart of Darkness, but it is also a Hymn to Love.

The novel is described as being "all but unbearable in its horror, the more so because its beauty leaves us almost without defences....... no better writing is being done." And, by another: "Much of her writing has the feverish mysteriousness of a vivid dream......John Dollar succeeds best at projecting a mood of woman on the move, adventuring into the unknown, stumbling all the while yet constantly seeking to make the world anew." And another: "The writing throughout is masterly......almost any sentence may be shot through with tracer bullets". It is also described as "a vision of hell that is rare in modern literature". It is "mesmerising and quite unlike anything else".

The book has 4 sections

1.   CHARLOTTE
2.   ABOARD THE CHARLOTTE
3.   ON "THE ISLAND OF OUTLAWED DREAMS"
4.   JOHN DOLLAR

Each section is divided into a number of subsections, some of which are but a few pages long. These have wonderfully evocative, allusive titles –

Last Act of the Apostle – The End of Strife – Ek Burra Bill a Da – Charlotte and the Dolphin – What the Snake Said – The King's Birthday – Why the Brown Man Made Blue Gods – (1) One (2) Too (3) Many – Sea Eggs – The Girl Who

God Made Twice – Heads and Tails – Principles of Flight – Recalling the World
– LOVE.

A part of me feels impelled to list them all. There are 42 in total. The last, Number 42, is LOVE. There is no mention of the word LOVE in any of the many blurb comments. There has been little mention of the word in my writing but it is the underpinning, the binding theme, of many of my productions (*Macbeth* and *Mooncusser's Daughter*, The Lawrence plays and *Our Day Out*, *Midsummer Night's Dream* and scenes from *Tira Tells Everything* and *Lysistrata*, *Krapp's Last Tape* and even *Nana*) and also of my life.

We have many loves, but few passions. Passions burn fierce and bright, becoming love for the lucky few and sometimes for the luckless few. *John Dollar* is the story of a passion. Number 42: LOVE begins:

"To love is to accept that one might die another death before one dies one's own."

As time went by, as I matured, aged a little, I was increasingly drawn to challenging, difficult source material, (not the natural stuff of theatre,) narratives with a mythic dimension: subject matter that tended to be controversial, that contributed to a reputation for sex and violence, where in fact I was simply seeking to examine emotion and danger at moments of human crisis.

In his book *Shakespeare is Hard but so is Life*, Fintan O'Toole says of the plays, and particularly the tragedies, that :

they evoke chaos without themselves being chaotic, they journey
into disorder in 2 senses: venturing both beyond the confines of
society and into the disordered regions of the mind.

And then, so important for the audience:

it is not because they teach us lessons that we care about them,
but because they enact something that is dangerous, powerful and
disturbing.

This is what engaged me. *John Dollar* is such a work.

I discussed his position as an artist with Paul Day, the relief sculptor whose work, which hinges on moments of human crisis, is so at odds with the expectations of contemporary sculpture. He asks:

Where is the poetic reflection on the Human Predicament: love and
loss, humour and tragedy? Where is the strength of vision or the
breathtaking ability to express human emotion through subtle and
powerful control of raw materials?

Marianne Wiggins' book, mesmerising and unlike anything else, is a wonderful exemplar of an answer to these questions.

Remembering that the only thing that all forms of theatre have in common is the audience, our purpose was to present it on the stage. Words and actors were my raw materials. Audience the necessary complement.

You'll never see the play we made.

You could read the book.

Picture this – A child walks on stage. She is Portuguese, Gaby (Gabriella) 7 years old Gaby makes and flies kites, the most wonderful kites, with her Grandfather, who refuses to wear clothes. The family have accepted his nakedness as part and parcel of his being though her mother still required that he free his penis from his left hand please, whilst eating. I want to be that Grandfather. Gaby leads me on stage, grizzled, whiskery, bowed, chicken-shanked with drooping sun-hat and shuffling gait. She, neat, sweet, in bright white frock and cute brimmed hat announces herself to the audience. She carries the kite herself to the audience. She carries the kite which her Grandfather tells her he will be able to see as it flies high, higher and higher when she flies it from the island. Grandfather is the friend of Dolàr, el capitão of the boat "Carlotta", on which Gaby and her school friends will sail to the island.

But I didn't dare propose the idea, I chickened out   they, YES, they would have said Yes, Yes, Yes do it doitdoitdoit! DO IT! Such was the cohesive bind of their grouping. They would have dared me,   taunted, giggled, mocked, and there could have been no backing out for me. I was asking so much of them. Claire, small, and the youngest, plays Gaby. Later Gaby flies.

She seeks escape.

She climbs a tree, and believing she can, she flies.

There are 7 girls aged between 7 and 13; the others are English, except for Menaka (Monkey) who is half-Indian. Originally they were 9, but 2 were uncommitted and I dropped them, which helped bind those remaining ever closer. The girls are in Rangoon, Burma, when the British Empire is still all-powerful. The year is 1919.

In succession, each girl in white frock and sun hat, face scrubbed, hair brushed, button-strap shoes highly polished, very proper, walks on stage with aplomb and perfect confidence and in precise prepared speech presents herself to the audience, offering a neat indication of character and background. I feel a helpless amused affection for these girls played by students aged 17 to 23.

But then, there's the But then!

Picture this – The children are stranded on a deserted isle after a terrible storm and tsunami which has wrecked the "Carlotta". They have come across the broken half-paralysed body of John Dollar their captain. He asks the girls to drag him deep into the jungle heart of the island, safety for themselves, and instructs them to collect what few supplies they can. Their governess, Charlotte Lewes, is lost. Their parents had left the girls in her care when they left to hunt and fish on another island. The girls adapt strangely, some with fear and diffidence at their isolation, others with an adventurous searching spirit. John Dollar is barely alive. From their safe retreat they watch their parents brought back to the island to be massacred on the beach and eaten by cannibals. When the natives leave, the children return, confused, disturbed, to the beach and smear their bodies and faces with the shit the cannibals left, which the actors prepare before each performance – very convincing dollops and sausages of squidgy brown clay. Earlier, before the storm, the older girls had spied on their new governess making love to her new love, John Dollar, in the boat. This knowledge begins to define the ways the older girls relate to him, a subtle key to the actors to aid their characterisation and the playing of their parts.

Now, picture this – Later, much later, amid power games, petty jealousies and behaviour presumptive of the consequences of their ages and their upbringing the older girls have deified John Dollar. They dare to touch his penis and see what happens. One is haunted by the red snakes visit, menstruation. They find laudanum with which they drug him, kill his pain. Nolly, daughter of the Very Reverend Norris Petherbridge sits astride the torso of their catatonic near death ship's captain and razor slices strips of flesh from his legs. Amanda, daughter of Sir Edward Sutcliffe, Colonial Governor, assists her. They are accepting, eating the flesh of their god, which the actors prepare in advance. Both are vegetarians. I have no idea what ingredients they used, but they created convincing blood dripping slivers of raw red meat which with backs arched, heads high, throats bared they swallow in ecstasy.

You have to know this.

The book ends with the girls dead, some killed by Charlotte, except for Menaka who has found her wandering another part of the island and brings her to the beach and the mutilated corpse. Charlotte cradles the diminished body of her lover. To love is to accept one might die another death before one dies one's own.

The book begins six decades later when Menaka is taking Charlotte's body down the hill for burial in the cemetery of St. Ives in Cornwall. Whereas the story begins in 1917 when Charlotte, newly married, receives news that her husband has been killed in the Great War. Seeking a new life:

She applied for a posting to Burma.

She grew restless and dreamed she

had lost her acquaintance with conscience.

She lost her old habits of thinking to God.

At the end of the month the letter arrived

which confirmed her worst fears.

It gave her a date of departure.

It gave her a place of asylum.

Rangoon.

The first parts of the book have a lightness, an adventurousness of spirit, a comic touch, as she endures and enjoys the long voyage to Asia, meets her employers and the single ex-patriate bachelors who importune her with suspiciously, ridiculously hurried proposals of marriage. She meets and delights in the company of the children who fascinate her. She enjoys teaching them and the responsibility. But she doesn't settle to the formality and structures of colonial life, preferring the life-affirming bustle of the real Rangoon and its street-based culture. She takes to wearing native dress, visits markets and explores the riverside, and gradually begins to release a true self. Choreographing the bustle of Rangoon was one of the more exciting parts of our adaptation.

One day she swims with the river dolphins and meets John Dollar, a seaman, a man apart, and a great love is born.

Characterisation is sharp, distinguished, colour rich and bold, the whole adventure becoming filled with the darting, laughing joy of the girls as they prepare for a trip in two boats to a special island where they will celebrate the King's Birthday with a great picnic party and camping.

My spine tingled as they sailed away, the girls' raucous singing "On The Road to Mandalay" melding into a calm-inducing elegiac rendering of the "Eton Boating Song", which paused to silence as they sat in their boat wondering, bright eyed yet sleepy. Stilled, comfortable, aware and waiting, we held the audience, held them, held them. As night falls the girls spy on their governess Charlotte making love with John Dollar in their boat, the Carlotta.

With 16 actors we were able to conjure a wholly realised context of narrative and action to create the two cultures, the strange madness of their conjuncture and its awful consequences.

We had no set as such. Just two 'boats' which, on end, became mountains, and overturned became the bier for John Dollar.

The writing, rich and full of wonder, was a pleasure to explore and use. We relied on the words and devised slightly modified styles of acting to represent different groups: formal, stereotypical, slightly caricatured and eccentric characterisation for the colonials; restrained and private, then together/ together! for Charlotte and John Dollar. The girls, I let them run loose, it was all fun and laughter until it became unbearably horrible, bright white frocks transforming to tattered filthy rags, barefoot, a nascent animal savagery, or a despairing descent into lost silence. Theirs was the most utterly wonderful and convincing ensemble playing. I recall a moment, the end of a performance in Germany when we were truly in control of the material. Gaby and Menaka, Claire and Rebecca, clasped in terror, tears streaming, snot trailing, bodies shuddering, bereft.

Picture that.

"No false feeling.........quality in art is inextricably bound up with emotional honesty and truthfulness" (Lucian Freud)

Acting took us only part of the way. The use of narrative, direct address to the audience when pitched with proper delicacy is of especial, crucial importance, its contrast heightening and interweaving with the acted sequences. This work came almost a decade after my troubled stumbling approach to Dickens. I had learnt so much since then. I now knew how to feed narrative into action, how to use it to draw the spectator into identification with the spectacle, how the use of the active present can lead an audience into believing they are there in the actuality, living it with the narrator, how apposite description can produce belief in an action, how time and place shifts are made acceptable. All this is different to the somewhat distancing process of watching action and listening to dialogue. Direct address to the audience allows entrance to the lived in space, invites involvement in the actuality of the drama, compounds and reassures that actuality. The audience is not addressed as an extra scenic element, rather it is integral to the ensemble. Come, come close. Come closer.

Whilst writing I have read a book by Jenny Strauss Clay, *Homer's Trojan Theatre*, which examines the ways that Homer uses such techniques in order to dramatise the battle scenes of *The Iliad*, make them visible, tangible even, to the listener, positioning him in relation to the action, to the Gods, to the geography of the battle arena. (I love *The Iliad*, once hoping to direct Christopher Logue's *War Music*, his brilliantly erratic yet authentic rendering of the essence of the epic poem.)

I have tried to write this book with these ways of telling in mind.

And what of love? Where is love in all this?

That is the binding element, that which makes the book both special and really meaningful.

The love shared between Charlotte Lewes and John Dollar underpins and gives a wholly deeper resonance to every action of the telling.

Without the love the narrative becomes pure schlock, an unconvincing possibility.

I placed it. I knew what I wanted of my production. But I think I may have underplayed its importance with the actors. It explains so much, and somehow that love makes it all worth while. The interpersonal binding of the couple, also binds the disparate elements of the story, making it plausible.

A plausible impossibility perhaps, but profound none the less.

- that which has carved a trace on the mind

NANA – Emile Zola

You need the right Nana. You need to put her through the ringer. She's got to have a life force, appetite. She finishes wrecked and wretched, broken. At the close she clambers up and over the bodies of the men she has known, smeared lipstick thick and grotesque coarsely marking her mouth, face and neck blotched red. She is dying of smallpox, her body deformed and rotted by the disease. She uses everyone and they destroy her. Nana, the slum girl turned demi-mondaine who humiliates the class responsible for her former misery. She is the victim of her own self. I told her every man should leave the audience wanting to have her, and every woman wanting/not wanting to be her. On his card files describing her Zola writes,

> "She is nothing but flesh, but flesh in all its beauty. A bird brain, very merry, very gay, never does harm for harms sake but ends up regarding man as material to exploit and becomes a force of Nature, a ferment of destruction. She eats gold and swallows up wealth. She makes a rush for pleasure and possessions and leaves nothing but ashes. But, above all else, a good natured girl."

This was the production with the chicken wire bra, and the foot I fucked.

You need the right actress. Claire Dakin was petite, slight but stocky, very strong, she had been at the Royal Ballet School since the age of eight, but in her later teens abandoned ballet, a world of precision, control, imposed discipline, and joined our rough house. She chose to play the part in a White Swan ballet dress with bovver boots, her blond hair cropped short, her eyes blackened, her self created image conducive to the emotion she must evoke, the encounters she must experience. Nana had to hold a distance, apart yet engaged, sceptically exploitative of the world she joined. She was wilful, I gave her her head, loved the challenge of working with her, encouraging her into tricky territory. Claire was never easy, remembers herself as "a bit of a loose cannon", she had a very individual presence and sense of style, was not yet really mature, but nor was Nana when she began.

After watching her performance at the Buxton Festival Fringe, the director of the Opera House told me that I had "asked so much of that girl". He was wanting. On one occasion she coasted and I was very annoyed; she said I scolded her like a schoolgirl; I thought I was straight-talking and firm and, of course, right, she had been lazy. The following day I got her to gallop through the part, words, moves, no other actors. She was word and move perfect, even pitched her playing just so at the mad hyper express speed, then looked me in the eyes. Without Claire I would not have attempted Nana.

Nana, is one of the better known of the twenty naturalistic novels written by Emile Zola to reflect the society and manners of France's Second Empire, which, under the rule of Napoleon III, lasted from 1848 to 1870. The novel covers a period of three years between 1867 and 1870. Nana's story parallels that of Paris during this period. In 1867 Paris held an Exposition Universelle to celebrate the city's reputation as the most civilised capital of the western world; in 1970 the Prussians under Bismarck invaded France, besieged Paris and left its population starving and in political chaos. The fate of the one young woman reflects the fate, emphasises the cheapened values, of the society she inhabits. The defeat of Napoleon III in the bloody welter of the Franco Prussian War and the collapse of the Second Empire vividly parallels Nana's fall. Zola points to moral corruption and the frantic greed for luxury as causes of the destruction of this society. He crudely described his book as:

> "A whole society hurling itself at the cunt. A pack of hounds after a bitch who is not even on heat. The poem of male desires."

In this there seem to be some echoes of our own compulsively consumerist society, our devoted pursuit of pleasures and possessions. The play presents a society with selfish values, obsessively collapsing with its shallow false pretensions.

I was aiming for a particular intensity of performance, a physical attitude. We worked on bird movements, a stance, neck stretching, head postures, perched, shuffles, squawking flight reactions, preening, squabbles, stillness, eyes alert or blinked close. The birds were vulture, crow, parrot, hawk, flamingo, seagull, cockerel, penguin, crane. The ridiculous. Nothing pretty.

Meeting, pre-mating display was especially important, highly caricatured but then toned down to create this sexually fluid society. Many men meet Nana, each with his individual display gesture, the women likewise vied for attention.

Claire was not part of this, she had to be different, strong, straight, confident, a natural animal, before tipping into the abyss, before descending in pained, broken disillusion, all loss.

Once our bodies have confidence we work on the voice, again each one aiming for distinct individuality. The women might be cooing, sibilant, the men all cock. We played encounters, then scenes, using nonsense language derived from but not using bird sounds, and practised this way to generate the fulminating overlap effect I was seeking out. It was a cinematic jump cut effect, whereby the audience suddenly finds itself elsewhere, at another time, picking up on action and conversation mid-term. The activities worked well, they were both valuable and enjoyable – not only did they help locate the temper of the society I wanted, they also made learning lines come more easily, speech naturally slotting into key moments already encountered.

A production must not be depressing. Mine was challenging, it was quick, energised, full of bewilderment, each speech overlapping the previous one, an ensemble playing technique stolen from Robert Altman's movie technique, it was restless, it was a reminder, with moments of silence shared between actors and audience.

This is important. The sharing. It could be that this will be the most important paragraph I write. In my work my commitment was to explore human nature, consider human values and share these with an audience in a context of entertainment. However dangerous the material (the book was banned in England, savaged as obscene, its publisher jailed) that connection, that shared experience, must be. I am so pleased and fulfilled that those who worked with me, and audience members, have confirmed this. So many plays are watched, simply watched, I know this from twelve years working as an assessor for the Arts Council. It's the privilege of those occasions when one experiences genuine, felt, engagement that is special. ! never accepted or wanted a fourth wall; but rather we were all, actors and audience, in the thick of it together.

Steve Cox has written :

It wasn't just the plays themselves that were fun, it was the whole process of forming a company with everyone having a common purpose and together creating a story from the page and sharing it with an audience. It was probably obvious to other people but I hadn't realised that the audience was part of the process, or at least, how much the audience contributed to the performance. I suppose the whole thing, as experience, is greater than the sum of its parts.

For Alan Clarke

Larkrise smelt of poverty and simplicity... and this was the key to the production's credibility; it managed to achieve a fine balance between sympathy and sentimentality... at no time did the production lose its sense of reality. We felt the ordinariness of the people, the unenviable hardship of their existence, the sadness of their neglect." (my emphases)

Charlie Watson recognised the effect :

The troupe were astonishing... forming a bond with the audience that it was impossible to break away from until the end. An end I did not want to come.

He is writing of *Riddley Walker*.

Judith Green pursues the idea. When playing a Yahoo in *Gulliver* she recalls worrying about not really allowing herself to be truly disgusting.

From my time with ACT I picked up a real dislike of 'Acting'. Not quite sure how, but I think it is something to do with actually being in the part, that quality which makes the watchers forget that they are watching and feel they are in the thing. When I saw ACT perform Nana I thought they were exceptionally good. I had seen a performance in London and the ACT show was streets better. Partly it was the Yahoo thing again, being able to show things that are horrible and the ACT performance did.

She then throws me a bouquet, in parentheses (*Jack took on the really awful role, and did it so well!*), a bouquet of sorts – perhaps?

After seeing a powerfully convincing version of Zola's *Germinal* at Derby Playhouse, a group of us travelled to see a production of *Nana*. Attempting to evoke a Belle Epoque period look it was awkwardly ineffectual with performances and a sensibility that hovered in a kind of mannerly hinterland, a quite tasteful place which no one would wish to inhabit. The novel is about sex, it is unforgiving in its portrayal of both Nana, the young woman who uses her bodily allure to advance in society, and of the men, young and old, who became variously besotted with her. The touchstones for my production would be the drawings, raw and sexualised, of Egon Schiele. The performances by fourteen actors playing thirty-two characters would be totally concentrated, verging on but not tipping into caricature. The ACT production is derived from a stage version of the novel which has been cut and adapted to create a piece suited to ensemble-playing on a restricted staging area. The production takes pointers from the period of the original but has eschewed historical accuracy in favour of creating the sense of a tightly organised, decadent society besotted by material and sexual delusions, and denying any sense of community or of the ominous problems looming in the future. I added narrative from the novel which was addressed directly to the audience. This was to engage the audience, make them complicit, I always

wanted audiences to wish to inhabit the worlds we created, especially the most challenging. When not performing the actors sat with the audience. Before touring, the show would be performed in the claustrophobically fitting space of the Black Studio. The set would be simple, a movable floor painted by a talented young artist, a raised platform at one side, two screens, and a large wheeled costume box.

The play begins with the hubbub of a theatre audience, filled with expectation, the cast perform a rousing rhyming vaudeville song, in which the Greek gods assert their powers, Neptune, Mars, Vulcan, Cupid, Jupiter, are going to have a party now everyone is here. They've told their wives its a conference so now they're in the clear. The goddesses, Juno, Diana, Minerva, Ceres take the stage, they know that Venus is the issue. Their lines are witty and pertinent. In the final verse they call their men to account :

> We know you're there!
>
> You can't call this a conference
>
> Out with you now
>
> We will not have this nonsense!
>
> Venus must be told;
>
> She'll bring the world to ruin;
>
> We all know what she's doing
>
> And it makes our blood run cold.

Nana appears from the costume box and dances a provocative, coldly erotic burlesque dance – you have to watch – you see her body – you are hooked, and caught in the impressionistic account of this beautiful young woman's life. Triumphant here, the tone is joyous, she is flattered, flaunted and enriched, but then... we moved miles from the naturalistic tenor of Zola's writing, pushing the imagery to more dangerous limits – in one sequence all the women slowly and voluptuously put on lipstick and fix their hair, the men become dogs, are kicked, lie back panting, howl as the women grind their heels into the men's groins; in another Nana holds the head of a kneeling aristocratic boy to her bosom, she believes she loves this boy, his mother, played by Margot, is standing behind Nana and offers the matronly succour of her bared breast to her son, who shortly after kills himself. Nana forms a relationship with Satin, another young prostitute, and they kiss passionately and touch. She bears a child, which dies, without its mother noticing. There was so much emotion in the production generated by Claire, it was difficult to bear. Difficult to get away at the end.

I have two photographs that I value, perhaps too sentimentally: they record such contrasting emotion that they leave me tremoring still.

One is of Pippa, Muse 1, as Miranda filled with wonder and puzzled dawning as her father describes how they came to the tempest tossed island they inhabit. The other is of Claire, Muse 2, as Nana so desperately pained, so wretchedly defeated. The one marking a life beginning, the other an ending.

- there must have been a moment when we reached what perfection was left to our lives.

WELCOME TO HARD TIMES, DERIVED FROM THE NOVEL BY E. L. DOCTOROW

The Fourth Western (Learning about acting – part 4)

Read this.

Read the opening, I say to Beverley

> The Man from Bodie drank down a half bottle of the Silver Sun's best; that cleared the dust from his throat and then when Florence, who was a redhead, moved along the bar to him, he turned and grinned down at her. I guess Florence had never seen a man so big. Before she could say a word, he reached out and stuck his hand in the collar of her dress and ripped it down to her waist so that her breasts bounded out bare under the yellow light. We all scraped our chairs and stood up – none of us had looked at Florence that way before, for all she was. The saloon was full because we watched the man coming for a long time before he pulled in, but there was no sound now.

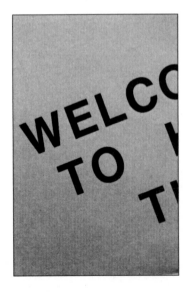

Can you face doing this, Bev? I think so, she replies. He takes you off stage. There is screaming and fear and smashing and begging, and then a single gunshot. I can get authentic Colt six-guns. I can get them from the American Adventure Theme Park at Heanor. Later you will return, bare, broken, bloodied, dead, to sing that hauntingly beautiful song that Vivienne says is too difficult for you. That's in my version, not the book. Can you do it? I will try, she says.

This could be the End – the book is about community what community means, its fragility. Its ending has shocking negativity, suggesting that only growing wealth grows community. Destructive impulses more that counter good intentions. I think this will be the best production I ever undertake.

Little Jimmy Fee, whose father, the builder Big Jimmy Fee, was killed by the Man from Bodie, finds a book. He is unable to read. That will be you I say to Little Karl. There's a lovely scene where Blue takes a stick and scratches letters in the sandy surface of the street with you beside him laboriously attempting to copy the letters which spell out your name and Molly and Blue.

Then, I explain to Little Karl, Molly counterpoints Blue's efforts. She buys you a Colt revolver and a shotgun. She is preparing you for the Bad Man's return.

How do you fillet a 154 page novel which spans a period of 18 months into 2 hours of continuous action? There cannot possibly be an interval – it has to be unremitting.

I contrive a part for Claire. We sit on a wall in the car park. She is shivering, hunches up, looks doubtful. You will play Jenks, a shootist, a kind of autistic strangeling. He dies in the book, but you won't. Between us we kill the Bad Man at the end. Earlier, when the town has begun to grow, you will dance a strange dance, solo. She looks at me. Why? Why what? Why me? Because you came balletically clattering into my life 3 years ago, a fascinating erratic bundle of charisma and complex naivety. And now you're Muse 2. So shut up and do it. She thumps me hard and strides off. Away. She will do it.

This is the piece of work in which I learnt the 4th lesson about acting – that it can be a burden because you can be strong and weak, cowardly and determined, loving and inadequate, and live the whole thing alone, knowing so much and so many depend on you.

The Big Man from Bodie demands a second woman after killing Florence. The townsfolk are intimidated, weak, evasive, simply wanting to survive. It will be Molly, the Irish girl, the 2nd bar-girl, who is close to Blue.....

> Oh, God, Molly said, so this is what it's come to, how did I ever end up in this godforsaken town, oh Christ this is the end. I'll tell you something you didn't know, Blue, I left New York ten years ago because I couldn't bear bein' a maid, I was too proud to say "Yes Mum." Doesn't that tickle you?
>
> We do what we can Molly.

Her face was twisted up and tears were streaming down her cheeks
as she walked by me saying: I hope he gets you, Mayor, I swear I do,
you and the rest of the crawling bastards in this miserable town.

This is the piece of work in which my insensitivity to personal feelings will
threaten to break ACT and my lover's heart.

I gather ACT together and tell them we are about to do the 4th Western. This
group have no knowledge of the first 3. I tell them it's set in a frontier territory,
in a town called Hard Times. A woman is horribly raped, left damaged for life,
receives inadequate support. The times are hard.

One actress walks out cursing me for my obsession with sex and violence.
They are homesteaders I explain. Good people at heart. There is one Bad Man.
The Bad Things happen in minutes. She never returns.

This is too close to the real / too real Beastly Bestial Violation by one man,
failure to amend by the Other.

I stand accused

This is theatre

Too close / too close to the bone.

But I can't / won't change now.

So many problems, so many issues, lack of courage, some exaggeration, so
much compromise, little self-knowledge, a 4th western, the 4th learning, failing
friends, family, loved ones, colleagues, living in crisis, trying to make my next
move but can't move. They've got my lollipops!

The Bad Man destroys the town before leaving.

As it is rebuilt, as confidence begins to grow, so does the population. Gold
miners in the hills. A regular weekly stagecoach, a store, a saloon. There is
hope for the future. Molly curdles with hatred, fearing the return of her rapist.
Blue cannot reach her, "his wife".

And this was too personal for Margot. There were long and tearful arguments.
Pain and difficulty. Despairing thoughts of suicide.

I suggest to ACT that I play Blue, the self-styled "Mayor", the main man, the
writer recording these events in ledgers. A man who keeps letters and papers
and listings and ledgers to order and define his role, a comfort zone in the

unstable anarchic land he inhabits. He is a weak man who tries to do better. It is both complex and ordinary, a challenge I would like to meet. They accept, surprising me, they know I should play the part of Blue. Perhaps it's my eyes. I realise they are warming to the prospect. Just a little.

Such inadequacy – so difficult to express, to explain. Betrayals – No – Not betrayals. Let's move on.

To Casting

Derek – the mute Red Indian, John Bear
Big Karl – the store keeper, Isaac Maples, a twin
Rochard – Zar, the Russian pimp and entrepreneur
Sarah – Adah, the fat motherly whore
Beverley – Florence who dies
Claire – Jenks who doesn't
Margot – Rebecca, the whore
Little Karl – Jimmy Fee, 12 yrs old
James – Bert, the besotted young miner
Ben – the stagecoach driver, Alf
And others as townsfolk, immigrants, victims.
We need a tall blond Swede.
I know the perfect Chinagirl.
Someone to play the Agent.
And then the mine directors, small parts.
Sandy and Isabel – Molly (not a decision, not a compromise, but a weakness, a gesture to diplomacy.)
And THE BAD MAN, HARGREAVES! – but John H is dead already.
Mike Haigh will play The Bad Man from Bodie.

Cath Acons takes on design and costumes. Does she share my vision? Will her work be late? Cath's work always arrives late.
Roger will build the set and stage manage, then he ups and leaves for better things.
We will need a lighting operator.
Charles Monkhouse will make the stagecoach, a conceptual stagecoach!

Was it sensitivity? Sensitivity/Insensitivity! – sounds like a Jewish joke. The desire to pull through. The attempt to assert positive values. In the last analysis: Belief in community.

Or was it practicalities? A theatre burning to cinders! Myself bleeding to death! Impossible to do.

And Molly? Molly is more important than Blue. I soften her, save her, some would say sanitise her, in our drama. I would not face the horrifically pessimistic ending. The rebuilt town burning. The Bad Man and Molly locked in a terrifying despairingly cruel embrace and she repeatedly repeatedly cutting and stabbing the already fatally wounded man. And young Jimmy Fee blankly, coldly blasting the pair of them to death with the gun she gave him. And Blue with his left hand shot away bleeding to death; he had grasped the end of the barrel to deflect the shot just as Jimmy pulled the trigger. And Jimmy immediately leaving Hard Times, and Blue knowing the boy has a harder centre, and could well be a next Bad Man.

Time healed our mutual wounds. We worked well together after negotiating so many faultlines.
Or even because of the faultlines.

I promised naturalism but can't deliver. We have no winter snow, nor coyotes howling in the foothills. The bullets in our guns are not live. Florence, dead, does return, and sings beautifully at Chinagirl's wedding to Bert the young gold miner who adores her.

After the Bad Man's first visit, when he destroys the town, many of its occupants move on. The few remaining survive a bitter winter with neither food, nor fuel, nor substantial shelter. They kill the weakest horse to feed themselves. They drift together on Christmas evening. Huddled, they light candles, talking shapeless figures wrapped in animal pelts. They sing, in the bleak midwinter. It is a shared enriching tremor in their bleak lives. They sing "Stille Nacht". Stillness – and the space – the candles extinguished, they return slowly to their hovels. Adah's warm contralto sears me still.

Plumbing memory to recall these times in writing is causing similar anxieties as did creating the original production. No script exists.

In spring the stagecoach returns. A wagon brings supplies. A woman arrives with three chickens and begins to sell their eggs. Blue sells water from his well. Miners arrive on Saturday nights seeking booze and entertainment. A federal agent arrives with papers for Blue to file – Territorial status may become Statehood. Young Bert woos and wins the heart of Chinagirl but has to buy her from Zar before they can marry. Everyone tidies and cleans themselves up for a great and wondrous wedding ceremony and procession. The bride, an exotic oriental beauty, carried shoulder high. Her groom a blushing boy. Blue feels the beginnings of reconciliation with Molly. The air is freshening. They dance an Appalachian clog dance. Blue watches. Molly dances. We are charmed and relax, the mood elegiac.

Have I mentioned pride?

Not the most, nor the best memories, but we did come through, we made it together, and eventually we all believed in it, a very special, greatly satisfying sense of theatre, known.

The townsfolk, feeling they are on the edge of flourish, erect a banner:

I had promised them naturalism, a work of deeply felt, honest naturalism. But you can take the bitch out of her bucket, but not the boy out of his bag.

I had a few GREAT IDEAS! (and will describe 3 of them)

1) Zar the Russian arrives in town with his team of 4 prostitutes. They are bridled like horses, he holds them with reins, a whip to hand, and pulls them to a halt.

2) The stagecoach arrives with Alf its driver, and Isaac, Ezra Maples' twin brother. The stagecoach is a single, 7 feet in diameter, open wheel that slowly rumbles into the settlement with passengers walking alongside, and later it leaves Hard Times. It is a Charles Monkhouse piece, a sculpture.

Don't ask! I can't explain. These two were decisions based on instinct. The third is a compromise, and a compromise might work, but in all honesty, it can not be a great idea.

3) The rape of Molly was played out as a forced, slow motion, schematic tableau. It was strong and graphic, but did neither me nor the two actors involved little credit.

That was the necessary and the only compromise in the whole production. I regret it. One bit player who had lived through our early differences complimented me by saying it got the idea across, being powerful, and tasteful. He was young and inexperienced.

I wanted to smash him to pulp.

Re-reading the novel, I pause over a paragraph two-thirds through, and read it a second time, and then notice that the page corner is turned down. The only one in the book. The paragraph had chimed with me over 20 years earlier. Here Blue writes about Molly, his reconciliation with Molly.

> Sometime between that heady evening she relented and that day we danced – there must have been a moment when we reached what perfection was left to our lives. "We've both suffered," she said, but words don't turn as the earth turns, they only have their season. When was the moment, I don't know when, with all my remembrances I can't find it; maybe it was during our dance, or it was some morning as a breeze of air shook the sun's light; maybe it was one of those nights of hugging when we reached our ripeness and the earth turned past it; maybe we were asleep. Really how life gets on is a secret, you only know your memory, and it makes its own time. The real time leads you along and you never know when it happens the best that can be is come and gone.

This is the piece of work in which my heart, my nature, will not allow me to follow the trajectory of the novel to its appallingly despairing negative end. I chose not to face up to the novel's last pages.

So

As they knew he would.

The Bad Man from Bodie returns to Hard Times.

I can name him – Clay Turner.

Blue and Jenks had prepared a trap, a rope, stretched to entangle and trip him in his drunkenness. As he leaves the saloon Jenks jerks the rope. Clay Turner is pulled off balance, stumbles. My shot wounds him. He staggers on and drops his gun which Jenks grabs, and aims, and hesitates.

> In his balls!
>
> I yell.
>
> And then his head.

Two shots, and Claire finishes him.

An end to Sex and Violence.

The townsfolk are stilled, still frightened. Slowly their bodies relax, at peace, all issues resolved. Calmly now, they move slowly through that same pattern of movement that was a hectically erratic and busy repeated hurry at the opening of the performance of this life, their lives. They repeat the pattern calmly now, once, twice, as the sun is setting. Then they stop one by one and turn towards the healing sun.

Blue stares across the wide bleak landscape into the distant darkening evening. Claire stands beside me, dropping Clay Turner's gun to the ground where I had dropped mine. As the sun's setting glow fades, so ever so very very slowly, the strange dancing man she had played gently touches me. The light darkens, darkens to black, a hint of a glimmer on Turner's corpse.

We all leave Hard Times.

No bows

No applause

None needed

This had been the piece of work that had presaged some kind of ending. A last stand. There is one photograph of its ending that conjures something of its essence. It had been a slow gestation, and remains in my mind as a half memory, loved but half lost somewhere. At the end we felt fulfilled, rested, and, I'm sure, a little saddened to lose it, yet settled.

ACT didn't do end of show partying. We cleared the set, held our breaths, and parted, ones, twos, alone or together.

My writing will perhaps not communicate what or how it was, but we knew we had made something special.

My original thought for a title for this piece was:

ELEGY ———————————→ RESTING

True, but inadequate.

When, in later years, I mentioned *Hard Times* to Sheila Harding she explained that while watching the play it simply made her want to be part of it. After the performance he attended, Cath Acons' husband, who ran the Theatre Studio at Sheffield University, remained in his seat for a full five minutes. Then he came to me and said it was one of the most thrilling things he had ever seen. Such nuggets nourish me now, reassuring the pride I feel for it. A profound experience.

We are driving up and out of Chesterfield. Both quiet, tired, needing to relax. Drive slowly she insists, then; You are passionate. I glance at Claire, amused and wondering. About the work, she continues with a sly grin. We are nearing The Red Lion at Kelstedge. I want to say let's stop at the pub and drink ourselves silly, but drive on across Beeley Moor. The sun has set, the moon is rising. It is full and brightening the landscape with a strange dreamworthy magic. So why are you going? she asks. I shrug. Cuts. We live in hard times. They don't want me any more. She thumps my arm, hard, it's a way we have of communicating. I taught her to find her strength and now she uses it to remind me she is close and life is real. Welcome to Hard Times, she says. What will you do? Another shrug. We do what we can Claire. We are in the Peak now, moonlight casting shadows across the rocks at Curbar Edge. And then, slowing as we approach the panoramic view of the Derwent Valley, I glance at her again. She is lovely. Gritstone and Moonlight. Got you on my mind.

Might I? Would she?

I wonder.

Could we? Perhaps?

Now.

Here.

She must know that I ………….If………..…I wonder

Together. By moonlight. On Gritstone.

Another glance but I dare not ask her. We coast slowly down the steep winding hill road and ride along the valley in silence.

She speaks softly, as if to herself:

No more ACT

the tiniest most hesitant gossamer thread spider's web

of a pause:

What will people do?

In my heart I smile. That's the very naivety that makes me love her so. I begin to feel older.

No more ACT   What will people do?

I dropped her off. Claire Dakin, Muse 2, at her parents' house in Wensley, took the quiet back road by Gratton Dale to Youlgreave, walked the footpath down Bankside, and stood on my terrace.

Every night I spend some moments here. In all seasons, all weathers, I <u>stand</u> for a while, just <u>stand</u>, calming. A ritual which helps keep me whole.

Far above an airliner's light flickers heading south from Manchester. The rock-strewn profile of Robin Hood's Stride stands stark, moonlit, bold against the horizon. The bat is fluttering by and back. I hear the river's flow in the Dale below. The angry squawk of a disturbed moorhen.

The air is cool, refreshing on my face.

I stand.   I stand.   Bankside   Home

Fin de Partie
"Ce n'est rien donner
que de ne pas se donner soi-même."

POSTLUDE

When I think back to my first memory of –
it doesn't matter that I have probably
got some of the details wrong. It might
be a fiction but it is my fiction and
I treasure it. Memory is like that. It
makes story tellers of us all.

CHARLES FERNYHOUGH

Phrases came. Visions came. Beautiful
pictures. Beautiful phrases. But what
she wished to get hold of was that very
jar on the nerves, the thing itself
before it has been made anything.
Get that and start afresh; get that
and start afresh.

VIRGINIA WOOLF

The sense of danger must not disappear.
The way is certainly both short and steep,
However gradual it looks from here;
Look if you like, but you will have to leap.

W. H. AUDEN

Losing it

THE HOW AND THE WHY OF ITS ENDING

I had a little over a month to make up my mind. A meeting with the powers was very dismissive of a development plan I proposed. The position of Director of the Arts Centre had already become redundant. They made me an offer I decided I couldn't refuse.

During the later years of ACT pressures were put on me to formalise my work on an educational basis. Initially an Advanced Level General Certificate of Education in Theatre Studies was proposed, and I was able to suggest that Ian and Margot were better placed and better suited to teach that than myself. After more pressure I instituted a one-year full-time Theatre Foundation Course with Ian and Margot contributing about half of its input. Two years later a National Diploma in Theatre Arts was created. This course was a two-year full-time course which attracted more able students. I suggested Ian should be Course Leader in order to allow me to continue with my ACT and Community work. I helped design the course, and taught part time on it for three years. Those three years were exciting, offering me the opportunity to work directly with young people again. It was fifteen years since I had worked with the Youth Theatre. The pool of students was highly motivated and some were very talented. We were able to integrate them into ACT productions which enriched their experience in ways that other educational institutions could not offer, including work experience in Germany, at the Buxton Festival of Musical Theatre and with local small-scale touring.

When I began this writing I contacted a number of the students. It was a pleasure. Phil Coggins, who runs *Babbling Vagabonds*, a successful, and very ambitious environment-based theatre company, said, when his girlfriend asked what I taught him, "Everything!" This, coming from the new generation, meant a great deal to me. Jamie McPhie, who is now a Degree Course Lecturer on Cultural Landscapes and Aesthetics in the Outdoors at the University of Cumbria, wrote reminding me of the four years he spent with us. As he was very young at the time I found his contribution both touching and reassuring, astute and generous, emblematic of all I would have hoped to achieve:

"My time with ACT afforded me the most wonderful opportunity in my life, one that I have never forgotten for the most positive of reasons. The engaging, collaborative and hardworking nature of ACT helped develop a highly original, creative, social and literate performance group. The various socio-demographics of the group helped produce an interesting mix of ideas, contributing to one of the many reasons why ACT was so successful. Jack actively encouraged this diversity, especially concerning those members

who were finding it difficult to find employment at the time. This added to an underlying ethos of social commentary and narrative that seemed to link much of the work the company undertook.

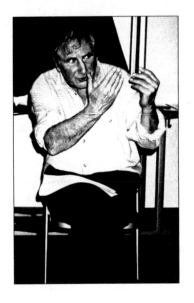

For more personal reasons I hold a very important place in my memories for ACT, especially for Jack and Margot as they were my role models, guides and friends during a crucial phase in my development as a free-thinking person. In these years from 16 to 20 years old, I learned more about people, and, I suppose, more about many aspects of life than I did over the next 10 years of my life and career, including undertaking a first degree in Performance Arts and having a full-time professional career as actor, director and writer. I think most of this came out of the atmosphere that Jack moulded out of the social and literary materials available to him rather than merely gathering together a group of thespians, he encouraged input from a diverse range of people from the community including artists, musicians, teachers, designers, dance instructors, students, circus trainers and those with any number of practical skills."

Jamie then goes on to describe a number of "incidents", mostly "risky" and "physical" which he recalls, culminating with the day a cue was missed in *Slab Boys* and things went very awry.

"………Damien, being professional, simply stood silently letting the pie dribble in large blobs from his unamused face. The other cast members stood silently. The audience sat silently. Jack…..wide eyed, as ruddy as a beetroot, began his descent into fury. A reaction that I don't think I've ever sparked off in anyone else in my life. As I took my newly improvised cue to leave the set and walk down the shameful steps backstage, Jack followed, with only a thin sliding wooden door separating us from the Studio, where the other actors were desperately trying to rescue the rest of the performance for the sake of the open-mouthed audience left wondering what on earth they had come to see, and why! As the door slid to a close Jack launched into what can only be described as a tirade of – "What the EXPLETIVE do you think you are doing? That was the most" – "Jack, the audience can still hear you!" – "I don't give a EXPLETIVE! that was the worst conduct I've ever……EXPLETIVE!" and so on "EXPLETIVE", and on and on. This is my memory of how I perceived it at the time, 23 years ago, and remember

it now in all its bastardised glory! A fond memory all the same! I don't suppose Jack sees it quite that way, although I've never been brave enough to ask him or even mention it until now.

So it goes. Nobody's perfect.

The Greek who sat beside me

THE HOW AND THE WHY OF IT STARTING

You could tell it as pulp fiction

The day was mid 60s bright and hot. The city was beginning its rest, there was an ease, a bright lightness on the streets. It was June, it was always one June or the other, summer bright, vivacious, May Balls. Cambridge. He had cycled back.

Slumped, languid in a corner chair, none of that preoccupied him. The staff were chatting, term closing, they were friends, but he scarcely joined their conversations, either too shy, too closed, or too tired; today he was wrangling personal issues, the kind that nag to the bones. The Inspectors had near demolished him, all to do with the standard of marking and a broad Yorkshire accent. They were threatening his career, taking issues to The Ministry, until, on the very last morning, Frank told them he had made a movie with the kids, and they asked to see it, and then they flipped. He would never be the golden boy but the heavies backed off; a small act of creative artistry was saving him from The Ministry and was setting his course. In the film *A Manor of Madness* – a class of schoolboys kill their various teachers in deviously cunning ways. In the final scene the entire school population charges across the playing fields to invade the school. The film, a kind of concoction of Ionesco's *La Leçon* and Lindsay Anderson's *If*, was silent, with a taped jazz accompaniment, shot on Standard 8 format. He kept his accent. He was learning a healthy scepticism of authority figures.

The English Tripos just completed, he was still adjusting to his disappointment. He had worked as a schoolteacher whilst studying in order to support his wife and family and meet the fees, generously reduced, that Fitzwilliam College charged him. The rationale was that whilst the rest were rowing on the Cam or Footlighting he was teaching. It worked, just. The school, its headmaster, Paul Lewin, and staff had supported him wholeheartedly; now it was payback time, but he was still wrestling to settle his life. His grey cells rattled their bars, snarling: Cuckold! He had just learned that his wife had seduced her best friend's husband a year ago. His wife was now 7 months pregnant with their second child. The best friend had seduced him a couple of weeks ago. He shifted blame shamelessly, finding himself in unfathomable territory, hardly comprehending, barely believing its black joke ridiculous complexity. But then, it was the mid-sixties, sexual intercourse had been discovered in 1963! It was filtering down.

He sat, churning, and then the Greek sat beside him. He had been aware of her in the last few weeks on her occasional appearances. He looked twice. He was everyman. But they had never spoken, his brooding introversion tending to maintain invisibility.

The Greek (the Broad?) was small, she radiated vivacity, a kind of beauty he supposed. She was a vibrant looker, nudging fifty he guessed, with darkly intelligent eyes and a lush lower lip. Hitching her skirt she reveals man-strangling legs, the toned legs of a professional dancer, tipped with the highest, harsh pointed high heels. He was a short man, she was shorter, even in the heels. In weeks to come she would regularly challenge him to race, throw off the shoes, and – to the next lamppost, or to the school's goalpost, or as far as that flowerbed, or down to The Plough, or through the edge of the wood – fly swift striding ahead until he pipped her at the post. He got the impression she didn't mind being beaten. Pipping them at the post remained an abiding strategy. Her décolleté is unsettling, provocative, what the hell inappropriate in this all-male context of the Manor Secondary Modern School for Boys.

The Greek who sat beside him has come to talk. From that moment they were inseparable and very, very close.

Vita Despina Papareeta's father was an admiral in the Greek Navy and a distant cousin of the King. She was brought up in the aristocratic luxury of their Athens home with nannies, houseboys, maids, servants, even servants of the servants. Until hard times hit the family, a combination of gambling and politics, when a swift exit to England was deemed necessary, and they lived in poverty in a small remote cottage without amenities on the Sussex Downs. The Greek always maintained that he and she had that experience in common, but the Sussex Downs is not the Yorkshire Moors and hers was the kind of poverty that allowed her to be privately educated. She boarded at a girls public school which had expansive playing fields where her cousin would land his two-seater light aircraft on weekend summer morns and fly her off to Jersey for breakfast, champagne breakfast.

She trained as a dancer, his instinct had been right: she danced the lead role in the original production of *The Green Table*, by Ballet Jooss, which was hailed as a major breakthrough in European Contemporary Dance, When the piece was revived 60 years later he suggested to the Greek that they should see it, but she declined, too old, the wrong kind of memory.

She lived through the Blitz in London. He was born that same year, 1940, that she married a ranking Canadian airman and bore him a child, her elder daughter, Andrea. When her boat was leaving for Canada at the end of the war she chose not to be on board. She campaigned for the Labour Party in 1945, and trained as a teacher, to guarantee she could support the child, more or less rejecting her past (but not her heritage, her Greek nature), and hoping to make the world a better place. Years later, out of caring rather than real love, she remarried, a Scot, and bore a second daughter, Sara. This child was a year older than his own first-born. The Greek's husband got a job as education advisor in Cambridge. She had come to the Manor School to do a few part-time hours' special coaching with the lads with special needs. He taught those lads.

She was High Culture; he was His Culture, working class in origin but as deeply felt and strong as hers. So they met and matched. They were an outrageous conjunction.

He had established a team to develop the Arts and Humanities programme for the older non-academic pupils. The basis of the work was activity, less formal grouping, combining art, music, drama and English, with block timetabling and team teaching. Vita joined the team; prior to arriving in Cambridge she had been head of a boarding establishment for emotionally disturbed children. Earlier in her career she had been a demonstrator for Peter Slade, the man who effectively invented Educational Drama as a tool to aid the personal and emotional development of adolescents. He wrote the first book, *An Introduction to Child Drama*, on this subject. Another colleague had been Brian Way, the man who subsequently researched and created the Theatre in Education movement.

So the Greek sat beside him. Their good fortune was to meet and work in positive times. There was freedom, adventurous new initiatives and much encouragement. They converted a derelict building into a Drama Studio with the support of the Drama Advisor, and worked with University students to devise Theatre in Education projects. They attended courses and felt they were ahead of the game. They organised major inter-school events which the "? less able" pupils presented. It was education for all. Drama was at the heart of the process. They learnt with and from one another.

He introduced the Greek to French New Wave Cinema, rough sex, contemporary poetry and suggested she practise with Tony Harrison's 'School of Eloquence'. She tried to make him less obdurate, more giving, and patient. It was a great passion; they knew it could not last.

After five years he needed to move; personal, family, professional pressures and an urge to creativity and new challenges. She felt they had more to discover. It pained her when he left. The Greek took over his role at the Manor School. When she retired she worked at the University Institute of Education and Hills Road College. She taught both Nicholas Hytner (Director of the National Theatre) and Simon McBurney (of Complicité Theatre), choreographed musicals and became Chair of Cambridge Arts Theatre Board. She offered courses on Greek Tragedy, learning more and more.

They met in Cambridge regularly, and she loved the Peak District, travelling north to stay several times each year. She often chose to walk alone down to the River Bradford, along to the Lathkill. In the evening the Greek would drink whisky and relax. The Greek tells him stories, some of which he cannot speak of here. But this I can relate and will relate. It's short.

Her husband was a pillar of society and a mason, his pride was boundless and she respected that – but thought perhaps he had a contract on my life………..He died, and she lived alone, but I was sworn to secrecy and denial.

He tells another story she tells him. A younger woman meets her at a party and says you don't know me. I can never forget, the woman says, it's years ago now, and I taught in the Manor Girls next door to you. I would be standing at the staffroom window at lunch time, and you are walking over to Jack Blackburn's motor bike and sitting up behind him and riding off skirt flaring, high heels, no helmet. It seemed so liberating – we had our sandwich boxes. – It was liberating, says the Greek.

More pulp fiction

The day was – 2009 a new century – bright and hot, a hint autumnal. He leaves at 6 am driving south, careful not to push the limits. He is tired, tired as a dog, tense. Today he is wrangling personal issues, the kind that nag the bones. Margot's leaving had demolished him, their adventure was done, gone, vanished into thin air. Like the quick spirit. Driving is distracting not consoling.

The Greek is in a home. He had sent letters, but not visited for nearly 3 years. In writing he told her of Margot's illness and death – a short note. She replied with a card – Very sorry. With love – scrawled, barely legible – Vita.

The city is at rest, there is an ease, a bright lightness in the streets. He parks the car, head bowed thinking, slaps the dashboard, it's obdurate, not giving. He walks to the door, finds it locked, rings the bell, a carer opens, smiling, and

? ? ……… I'm here to see the Greek he says. Yes, down the corridor, in the alcove, on the right, you'll hear her.

There he finds this tiny creature, tiny, so much shrunken, fragile, tiny beyond belief and fragile, button bright, holding court, telling something, telling something high falutin' and persistent to a group of six as old as her. She grips a copy of a book, an Introduction to Marxism as it seems and the subject of her compelling talk.

He is watching her, wondering. He doesn't move and when she notices him – This is my good friend, Jack, we go back a long way. And she flashes a cheeky grin. We had a grand passion – and then continues her spiel. An oration.

He interrupts – Could we go somewhere? Speak a little?

There is nowhere, she replies abrupt and sure. The group in unison tell her but there is. Where? She asks. You're in room six. Am I? Where's that? Six, room six, down the corridor with your number on the door.

They go to room six. She sits on the bed.

He asks how she finds her new home.

I don't know. I only came yesterday – there are moments of silence. He wants her to know that Margot is dead. Her daughter had read her the card he sent and she says it made her cry, remembers and cries again. She recalls their times together; he knows it's always the same stories now. Vita is so very tiny he finds it difficult to hold her.

Vita Papareeta, the Greek who sat beside me and set me on my way, died in January 2011. At the funeral I spoke with Sara, her younger daughter, who I had not met since she was a child of 11. She hugged me with genuine warmth. I was very very close to your mum, I whisper. I know, she replies, Vita told me everything when I was 26, but I knew anyway, mum's voice changed whenever you phoned. The Vita became Vita.

So close. No one knew the Greek as I had.

With one bound!............

THE HOW AND THE WHY OF LIFE GOING ON

I fell into a spin. I drove aimlessly around the Peak. My relating to Margot was unsettled; she had issues which overwhelmed mine. I worried about money, but didn't seek out paid work. I developed a paunch and jowly jaws, neglected my house, my garden, my self. Friends suggested alternatives which I found no incentive to follow. We'll work with you. Maybe, was my reply. I half-heartedly applied for theatre work, but got no interviews. I was young (?) fit and unemployed. I made excuses. After 32 years of hard demanding work I needed a pause, and decided to take, perhaps, a year off.

Rainer insisted I keep the Darmstadt contact live. He proposed a series of Director's Workshops to demonstrate how I brought texts to life. I would work with teachers of English, trainee teachers, and students to help them appreciate the living fibre of the English language, its rhythms, its subtlety and wonders when spoken aloud. I have now returned to Germany each year for two decades with an ever-expanding series of workshops which introduce participants to active ways of making a script come alive in performance when body, voice and soul express the sentiments, experience the essence, of the human condition dramatised.

My personal learning in this arena has been immense and invaluable. I know so much more of Shakespeare after regular evolving workshops including *Macbeth, Othello, Hamlet, Lear, Richard III, The Merchant of Venice, Julius Caesar* and *The Tempest.* These have been complemented with modern classics, *Death of a Salesman, The Crucible, The Glass Menagerie, Equus, Our Country's Good, Gizmo* and others. A fascinating side dish was a number of workshops in French, with trainee teachers of French at the University of Mainz. We used Sartre's *Huis Clos* and Emmanuel Roblès' *Montserrat* as the base texts. Last year, 2011, which was scheduled to be my last visit, a woman in her late thirties contacted us from Darmstadt University, explaining that 18 years previously, she had done the *Macbeth* workshop when she was still a student. Would I do the same workshop, exactly the same, for her group of 14 post-graduate engineering students? And of course I did, making no compromise with either language or activity. They were thrilled, so was I, regarding it as a fitting way to end my visits. But then the younger generation, the new teachers, have invited me to continue visiting.

I have one more story to tell you. It caught me by surprise last year, making butterflies flutter and my heart beat faster, but if you've followed me through this book you'll...................you'll readily recognise the sentiments, the signature, of an old man mad about theatre.

- such stuff as dreams are

MUSE 3

In rehearsal she is inquisitive, gentle, polite, with expressive eyes that work too hard when she is acting. With hearty will she thumps his upper arm, but tentative, not understanding, stands close when needing protection from Rainer's threatening Caliban, prepares an attack, then softens into Miranda's speech, still struggling to master Shakespeare's verse. Then RUNS!! as Hannah yells the crudely vicious compound *Tempest* words.

Because his book is about words and making them live, he values the opportunity to test the work in progress before a public audience in Germany.

In rehearsal he gives her the poignant *Hard Times* paragraph........"a moment when we reached what perfection was left to our lives", and initially she handles it less well, until instinct overrides nerves; she will impress our small audience in the Literaturhaus because her face is so expressive, her eyes welcoming yet wary, her presence eye-catching, her body balanced. She thinks about character, pitches responses just so. Then, just do it – stop acting he reminds her; how many times over the years has he said be there, just be there – with me, in the car, crossing the moor: "No more ACT. What will people do?"

At the evening's performance she explains to Bernd Schafer: "I play Miranda and Claire." With pride, "I play Muse 1 and Muse 2." After the reading, as they prepare to leave, "Jack", she calls and hugs him quick steps back, catches herself surprised, emotion welling in her eyes. He feels older again. Older and older again, recalling the day he had needed to touch Pippa.

Helena Bodem is 16 years old, they are working together for the first time. She approached him during a break in the *Lord of the Flies* workshop with the Drama Group of Edith-Stein-Schule, asking: "Excuse me Mr Blackburn but how old are you?" and he suggested she guess. She looks at him some moments – "I would say....70?" He admits to 71. And you? – Her English is near perfect: "my mother has taken me to my first English class when I was 4 years old."

He had already planned to invite Hannah Nagel, his favourite, an older student who had worked with this group for two previous years, to join him for the public reading. He admires her forthright assured confidence and knows it will enrich the occasion: she will match his energy with light and shade, playing the nurse in the Prostate conversation, and Florence in *Hard Times*.

Helena has a different being, a nature that will complement his. And so he decides to invite her to join them after watching her work through the workshop, and, "Yes please if you think I can it will be nice, so nice," she says.

Originally he had intended to read alone, a final goodbye. Now he can change the plan – make theatre – the three of them plus Rainer as Caliban. He arranges rehearsal times. He chooses dramatic rather than descriptive passages from the 6 sections he decides to use. They meet to practise. They appreciate the dynamic, the real-time immediacy he is asking for. They make a team. And it's then that he realises he is asking Helena to play the 2 Muses. The roles fitted.

They each have to sing, unaccompanied. Helena finds her own melody for the finale song from "Our Day Out": "They will never take this day away" – sings with a tender delicacy, sharing, quietly repeating the plangent final line, and more and sweetly quiet fading to a nothing, a stillness. "I want to do it like that ", she says.

To finish he had wanted to get a gun, a replica, anything loud so that 2 shots would echo through the Literaturhaus and finish Clay Turner as Jenks/Claire/Helena finished The Bad Man, then stood beside him and dropped the gun to the ground and gently touched my arm rather than thumping. An END – to sex and violence! And we pause in the tremor. And then they drive across the moor, and that was to be the end of our readings – No more ACT . . . What will people do?

Helena was troubled by the thumpings – "But you liked her," she said to him. Yes, it was a love/hate relationship, but more much more love than hate; strange, I know; true but slant; I'm like that; it was important at the time over twenty years ago.

There was a strangely honest intimacy about this, finding myself working with a girl who engenders my past experience with such sensitive touch. I think I know enough of dramatic re-creation to recognise genuine felt involvement in, and real shared engagement with that complex web of memories, romanticised, sentimentalised and perhaps even falsified, that were being awakened. This girl I barely know makes a compelling synthesis of my original experience, rendering it intense, surreal, re-lived in a sequence of extracts from a work in progress. It becomes, anew, a live rich seam of past life – 40 years past, 20 years past.

The evening was a success. Bernd served Chesterfield Tea and English Biscuits in the interval, and a shot of a good Single Malt Whisky at the end. "You've done it again, Jack", says Rainer as he shakes my hand, nods, smiles.

Muse 3 – Yes, it won't leave me alone. Strange threads. He purposefully misses the opportunity of returning to the Drama Group with thanks and a small gift for Hannah and Helena. He avoided the meeting. Cowardly. Introvert. Inappropriate. Strange theads stitching a life. A fickle old fool, wary of an old fool's feelings.

I sit with a coffee in Buch Habel, Darmstadt's large bookshop. I recall the character she came up with for the lost boy in the *Lord of the Flies* workshop. A bolshie lad, awkwardly rugged though slight, hands deep in trouser pockets, a scowl, brow furrowed, pacing relentlessly, building a single line of repeated dialogue – Shut up! carn't yer, repeatedly, again and again – Shut up! carn't yer – Shut up! carn't yer.

Can you modulate that?

SHUT UP! CARN'T YER!

Come close.

Here, by Carl Sandburg, is one last quotation.

Come. Come closer.

> You can go now yes go now. Go east or west, go north or south, you can go now. Or you can go up or go down now. And after these there is no place to go. If you say no to all of them you stay here. You don't go. You are fixed and put. And from here if you choose you send up rockets, you let down buckets Here then for you is the center of things.

And finally

SO MANY THANKS!

First – John Connolly, Stephen Cox, Judith Green, Sheila Harding, Jamie McPhie, Ian Rochard, Brian Sargent, Alistair and Barbara Scrivener, John Henry Simpson and Charlie Watson who accepted my invitation to recall their experiences with ACT and so vividly enriched the book.

Their complete texts are available in the Archive section of www.strangethreads.co.uk.

Second – Val Cornish, my neighbour, who noticing me writing on my terrace at Bankside, showed interest and was very positively encouraging after reading a few early drafts. And, Charlie Watson who, as soon as he learnt I was writing, monitored my progress, insisting that I keep it real, rough textured and honest. In Darmstadt, Helena Bodem, Rainer Lohnes and Hannah Nagel worked with me to present a lively dramatised public reading from the work in progress whose success helped determine me to complete the book.

Third – for Help, Advice and Support, both pleasing and provocative: Doug Aston, Maggie Ford, Nadia Groom, Sophie Hunter, Sue McGoun, Simon Seligman, Sharon Waller, Billy Watson and Leslie Wheeler.

Fourth – Jeni Edwards who typed my repeatedly modified hand-written manuscript with Val Cornish. Joyce Weddell who generously and scrupulously copy-read the final very imperfect version. Duncan Beal and Clare Brayshaw of York Publishing Services who worked with me to design and create the actual book.

Fifth – My work was the product of an ensemble approach, likewise this book. It is created from available resources. Strange Threads. I have borrowed many words, phrases and quotations from varied sources most of which are acknowledged, but some of which I can neither trace nor recall. The design, graphic and photo skills of many people are evident, and the majority are included in the ACT listing, but, again, a few are the work of people I can no longer recall. In all these cases I have endeavoured to follow the principle of fair use.

Sixth – Some friends have generously sponsored a coloured photograph page each.

DARLINGS!!
I Love You All.

Our Work

THE PRODUCTIONS

MACBETH FOR BEGINNERS, from W. Shakespeare (company adaptation)

WIND IN THE BRANCHES OF THE SASSAFRAS TREES, René de Obaldia

THE MAGICIAN WHO LOST HIS MAGIC, (T.I.E.) (adapted)

TIRA TELLS EVERYTHING THERE IS TO KNOW ABOUT HERSELF, Michael Weller

THE DUMB WAITER, Harold Pinter

MR. NOAH AND THE SECOND FLOOD, (T.I.E.) (adapted)

THE DAUGHTER-IN-LAW, D. H. Lawrence

AS IT WAS, (T.I.E.) (adapted)

THE TEMPEST, W. Shakespeare

MOONCUSSER'S DAUGHTER, Joan Aiken

THEATRE LIVE, THE MERCHANT OF VENICE, (T.I.E.) (created)

INDIANS, Arthur Kopit

CITY SUGAR, Stephen Poliakoff

FEMALE TRANSPORT, Steve Gooch

THE TOOTH OF CRIME, Sam Shepard

THE HARD WAY UP, Hannah Mitchell (scripted from autobiography)

THE KITE GIRL, THE CLOWN AND MR PUNCH, (T.I.E.) (created)

IMAGINATION DEAD IMAGINE, Samuel Beckett

NOT I, Samuel Beckett

KRAPP'S LAST TAPE, Samuel Beckett

OLD KING COLE, Ken Campbell

THE SURANGINI TALES, (T.I.E.)

A MAD WORLD, MY MASTERS, Barrie Keeffe

KING LEAR, W. Shakespeare

THE RESISTIBLE RISE OF ARTURO UI, Bertolt Brecht

DUSA, FISH, STAS AND VI, Pam Gems

SCHOOL FOR CLOWNS, Ken Campbell

LARK RISE, Keith Dewhurst

CANDLEFORD, Keith Dewhurst

MACBETH REHEARSED, (T.I.E.)

COMEDIANS, Trevor Griffiths

THREE GRIMM TALES, adapted from originals (T.I.E.)

THE WIDOWING OF MRS HOLROYD, D. H. Lawrence

THE STONE BOOK QUARTET, Alan Garner (T.I.E.) (adaptation)

OLIVER TWIST, Charles Dickens (company adaptation)

ARTHUR IN THE WEST, Alan Coren (T.I.E.) (adaptation)

OUR DAY OUT, Willy Russell

RIDDLEY WALKER, Russell Hoban (company adaptation)

FARNDALE AVENUE TOWNSWOMEN'S GUILD DRAMA SOCIETY PRODUCTION OF THE SCOTTISH PLAY

BIGGLES, (company creation)

POMMIE, (Youlgrave community play)

GULLIVERS TRAVELS, Jonathan Swift (company adaptation)

LITTLE SHOP OF HORRORS, Ashman and Menken

ROAD, Jim Cartright

LINE ONE, Volker Ludwig (Grips Theatre)

MEANS TEST MAN, Walter Brierley (scripted from novel)

AFRICA, (company creation)

A MIDSUMMER NIGHT'S DREAM, W. Shakespeare

SLAB BOYS, John Byrne

COUNT BACKWERDZ ON THE CARPET, (T.I.E.)

LYSISTRATA, Aristophanes

ACAB ARET, (company creation)

TOUCHED, Stephen Lowe

JOHN DOLLAR, Marianne Wiggins (adapted from novel)

TRUMMI KAPUTT, (Grips Theatre)

RED DEVILS, Debbie Horsefield

THE POSSIBILITIES, Howard Barker

WARNINGS TO CHILDREN, (T.I.E.) (created)

THE TEMPEST REHEARSED, (T.I.E.)

FALLEN, Polly Teale

MAN OH MAN, (Grips Theatre)

THE THREEPENNY OPERA, Brecht (student production)

KING LEAR REHEARSED, (T.I.E.)

WELCOME TO HARD TIMES, E. L. Doctorow (adapted from novel)

NANA, Emil Zola (adapted from novel)

VERONICA DRIBBLETHWAITE AND HER LOST LOLLIPOP, (company creation)

NINE ANNUAL PANTOMIMES, (originals – Shadows)

3 Plays, (created with Shadows)

4 T.I.E. projects at Cambridge Drama Centre

THE SURANGINI TALES, THE STONE BOOK QUARTET, THE HARD WAY UP and A MIDSUMMER NIGHT'S DREAM were revived with new casts.